A TATTERDEMALION'S TESTIMONY

a memoir

SARAH VIGUE

tatterdemalion

tat·ter·de·ma·lion
\ˌta-tər-di-ˈmāl-yən, -ˈmal-, -ˈma-lē-ən\

Noun
DEFINITION
: a person dressed in ragged clothing : **RAGAMUFFIN**

(merriam-webster.com/
 dictionary/tatterdemalion)

A Tatterdemalion's Testimony
by Sarah Vigue
ISBN: 979-8-9998802-0-8 (hardcover)
ISBN: 979-8-9998802-1-5 (softcover)
ISBN: 979-8-9998802-2-2 (e-book)
ISBN: 979-8-9998802-3-9 (audiobook)
Copyright © 2025 by Sarah Vigue

All rights reserved. Printed in the United States of America. No part of this book may be used or reproduced in any manner whatsoever without written permission except in the case of brief quotations embodied in critical articles or reviews.

Published by: Meredibly LLC

4 Oak Street Apt 2

Beverly, MA, USA

sarahvigue.com

Categories/Genres: Biography & Autobiography / Personal Memoirs / Christian Memoir / Christian Narrative Non-Fiction / Christian Inspirational / Inspirational Memoir / Coming of Age Memoir / Trauma & Healing

Keywords: memoir, family history, personal growth

Description: In this raw and courageous memoir, Sarah chronicles her reluctant journey into faith. Both gritty and grace-filled, this is the story of a person unraveling—and being remade.

Library of Congress Control Number: 2025917800

Scripture taken from:

CEV; ERV Easy-to-Read Version (ERV) Copyright © 2006 by Bible League International; ESV The Holy Bible, English Standard Version. ESV® Permanent Text Edition® (2016). Copyright © 2001 by Crossway Bibles, a publishing ministry of Good News Publishers; HCSB; KJV; MSG; NASB 1995; NCB; NET; NIV; NKJV; NLT; TLB; VOICE

Disclaimer: This memoir is a true account of the author's personal experiences, thoughts, and memories. It includes descriptions of traumatic events, which may be distressing to some readers. These experiences are presented from the author's subjective point of view and reflect their honest recollections, although memory is inherently fallible and may differ from the recollections of others.

This book is not intended to accuse, blame, or defame any individual or institution. It is a personal story and is not meant as a definitive account of any events or relationships mentioned. The author does not assume responsibility for how the content is interpreted or used by readers.

The material in this book may be triggering for individuals who have experienced trauma. Reader discretion is advised. The author and publisher disclaim all liability for any loss, damage, or distress caused by the content of this book or by decisions made based on it. This memoir is not intended as a substitute for professional legal, medical, or psychological advice.

Contents

Before We Get Started vii
Chapter 0: Your Story Is Unique, like Everyone Else's. 1
Chapter 1: The Foundation 13
Chapter 2: Pangs 22
Chapter 3: A Life on Layaway 35
Chapter 4: People Are a Lesson or a Blessin'. 46
Chapter 5: Puberty POW. 65
Chapter 6: Hidden in Plain Sight. 73
Chapter 7: Clouds Without Rain 81
Chapter 8: A Sheep Tangled in Death 96
Chapter 9: Drive-Through of a Glass Darkly 117
Chapter 10: Wrangling Demons. 132
Chapter 11: Growing Discernment 143
Chapter 12: Finding Thorns and Thistles 153
Chapter 13: Church Fright and Embarrassment. 158
Chapter 14: The Cleanup After the Storm 165
Chapter 15: Recycling Foolishness 170
Chapter 16: Accountability: A Call of Duty. 175
Chapter 17: Choosing True North 185
Chapter 18: So Now What? 189
Chapter 19: Bible Covers with Clichés. 195
Chapter 20: Miracle Call 203
Chapter 21: DVDs and Celebrities, Not Scrolls and Camels?. 209
Chapter 22: Goodness 217
Chapter 23: Letting Hope Change Me. 223
Chapter 24: Growing Thicker Skin. 230
Chapter 25: Hosea and Gomer. 237
Chapter 26: Two Unexpected Revelations 241

Chapter 27: Playing Christian Dress-Up 246
Chapter 28: The Word Small Redefined as "Un-Friggin'-Believable" . 252
Chapter 29: "You Have to Go to Him Because He Won't Come to You". 260
Chapter 30: Too Much Love for Gomer. 267
Chapter 31: Temptation. 272
Chapter 32: The Warrior Is a Child 294
Chapter 33: Planting Seeds and Growing Fruit 307
Chapter 34: The Finish Line. 312
Works Cited. 322
About the Author. 323
I HAVE A FREE EBOOK FOR YOU! 324
Thank you so much for reading :-) 325

Before We Get Started

Looking into the sky, resting after chasing cousins playing in my stepfamily's yard, I filled my lungs with the same air that traveled up to the kingdom that God made. As a skin-and-bones, ash-blonde girl, I wanted to make clouds and taste them to see if they were sweet like the sugarcane that grew around me in Georgia. I would cast the clouds into shapes, lying in the grass or sitting under the "creepy trees" (Spanish moss) that canopied every dirt and clay road for miles.

At four years old, I understood from Sunday school and AWANA Club that that's where God lived—in the clouds. I loved AWANA and felt that Jesus loved me. My siblings and I would sing a made-up song in front of the small Pentecostal congregation:

> I wish I had a little red box
> to put my mother in.
> I'd take her out and kiss, kiss, kiss,
> and put her back again.
> I wish I had a little red box
> to put my father in.
> I'd take him out and hug, hug, hug,
> and put him back again.
> I wish I had a little black box
> to put the devil in.
> I'd take him out and punch, punch, punch,
> and put him back again.

We were empowered to feel bravado against the devil, even while wearing slippery tights and stuffy church clothes. The best defense: Be a good girl so Satan couldn't send me to the lake of fire.

The lessons of Jesus and the activities of building houses on rocks, not sand, made sense. It was so inborn and natural at that age to hear, "There is a loving man named Jesus, and He cares about you." I believed. I was also told, "When you're born again, you don't have to burn for all eternity. Ask him into your heart to save you from hell." I did, was baptized, and was given a certificate. The sincerity of a four-year-old is so precious, but I wonder if that's too young to be considered a permanent Christian conversion, at least for most.

I liked how Jesus treated people. Walking in his city with gold streets and opening his pearly gates sounded nice. I envisioned going there after playing in the forest and making raindrop flowers from freshly squeezed clouds. It's like God calling you in as moms do when it's dinnertime. After all, what could I do in the kingdom? Nothing at that age—because Heaven was like the inside of a church. And I had to die first to get up there beyond the clouds. So I thought, *Someday I'll be ready. When I get there, I'll make fat clouds and build them all around the towers and buildings so Heaven won't fall out. It'll be safe.* I knew Heaven was all clouds—where angels lived, perfect and beautiful. For many years, I wanted to be an angel, and I wanted to play in Heaven, the *Wizard of Oz*–like city in the sky, just beyond where I could see.

When rain drummed on my granny's tin roof, I waited for the thunder to rage and crack, smiling and feeling secure and protected when it beat deep and shook the shanty-like trailer that, to me, was a spacious ranch in the woods. Sometimes there was a little fear. Where the thunder and lightning lived, something else made me feel safe. As I said, this Jesus, who was both God and man, was so easy to let into my entire being; the Lord's Holy Spirit was in me and every living thing, like carbon. How innate it was to know him. My young mind was free to imagine, one day, being a part of God's glorious sun bursting from the clouds throughout the sky kingdom until these dreams, like the clouds in the summer sky, slowly drifted away and other things moved in.

I read what I just wrote, and it hurts. In adulthood, I don't dream like this anymore. The '80s were so long ago and I was so young, like any other child—wondering about being a part of something instead of being apart from people, from life, all the time. I wasn't dreaming of slowly bleeding out on spongy, deep green grass—my craving since age twelve, if only I could shake the childhood adage often explained to me by my churches: "People who kill themselves go to hell. If a Christian does it, you're murdering God himself and you're turning to evil." Not knowing that there are different schools of thought on whether you can still get into Heaven after suicide did at least stave off direct suicide attempts on my part. What the Enemy intended for evil, God used for good (Genesis 50:20). This was just how my life played out. As a child, I would look into the sky, resting from my play, as an adult, I played at striving and it cost me everything.

Chapter 0

Your Story Is Unique, like Everyone Else's

Now whenever the cloud lifted from the Tabernacle, the people of Israel would set out on their journey, following it.

—Exodus 40:36 NLT

There are things I need to tell you—or rather, things I'm not supposed to tell you. Literary experts have warned me that what I write will scare you, that you'll put me in a box because we're "not supposed to talk about certain things." It's not the first time in my life I've been told this. But I haven't survived this far in life by being silent. Being told not to share the truth—and feeling shame—is soul crushing. I'm tired of that. So this honest to goodness, ragtag voice of mine is trying to use my weird story to interrupt the silence. We have stories to tell, and being vulnerable is how we share them with others.

It all started, around age thirty three, on a beautiful day I refused to let myself enjoy. The clouds were beautiful: evolving forms that shaped themselves into stories like the ones I would not tell. I'd been fighting the urge to share my Christian testimony because it involved telling too much of my past, too much of being unwanted and worthless. Ruminating on where the clouds originated, what they meant to those gazing at them, and where they were so quickly headed—pointless, I thought. It accomplished nothing in the end, much like telling stories and having a voice. Having a voice makes you a target, and sharing stories doesn't pay the bills. But the full-figured clouds were so pristine white—my favorite. It's hard to be a serious, focused grown-up when plump globes are floating around you. "Gorgeous," I admitted.

Years ago, I gave up cloud gazing, a time-wasting activity meant for babies and weirdos. "But I'm weird," I said aloud to my thoughts. This disillusioned old dog had very little fight in her, despite only being in her thirties. I slipped off my sensible shoes and filled my spirit with the energy that comes from lush grass and sunshine. I shifted my work folders, heard my car keys fall, and watched my empty lunch container bounce onto the ground. Sighing, I piled everything together and looked around at the day. Normal people outside walking, suburban sounds, sun and vitamin D happening. I rolled up my pant legs for the coveted sunshine to deliver the vitamin that doctors tell me my pale skin and depression-prone brain need. I fingered the large thigh scar glaring at me, red and angry.

Images floated through my mind like clouds—images of waking up in the operating room finding that, while my left knee might be fixed, a patch of skin the size of my palm was missing just inches above the surgery site. It had looked—and felt—as if most of my left thigh had been badly burned. The images of the months it had taken to "heal" the wound darkened like storm clouds. They darted like debris in a whirlwind when I recalled the various procedures where the doctors scraped at the burn site until the team smiled at the muscle beneath the growing thin layer of skin. They had seen success as the pick pulled at my scabs and tender flesh; I had felt the cost of vulnerability. A routine knee arthroscopy shouldn't involve neglect and electrocution, but *shouldn't* isn't a definitive word. Sigh. "Heal me. Make it go away," I said into the vibrant sky. A breeze greeted me—nothing else. Just another person with an unwanted scar, just another unanswered prayer.

I rolled my eyes at the clouds and my earlier, childlike wonderings about all that the clouds saw and the lands they passed. Then I adjusted my glasses and picked up my things. Allowing one last guilty pleasure, I shuffled my bare feet in the spongy grass, then slipped on my shoes, leaving the clouds in the sky where they belonged. The tug inside me to share my story—the whole story—stamped down. My life bore the wrinkled scars of one well trained to move on; so I did.

The next Saturday, my inner adult felt more agreeable. The sun was shining over Gloucester Harbor, and the Massachusetts weather was glorious. With plenty of free time, I followed the walking path that connected my apartment to Stacy Boulevard. There was only a tiny barbeque stain on my fitted Walmart shirt—yep, on my substantial chest as always—as the inklings of this manuscript drifted into my mind. If I was going to catch my second wind of Christianity, some deep pain needed healing.

Starting the solitary walk, I asked God for direction—out loud and with feeling. "I can't write this. Yes, I want to feel like a new zealous Christian again, but I can't get my big, heavy body over this hurdle. I know revisiting my Christian life and the two-year mission will give me insight on what you had me do and why, but writing stuff about my childhood and vulnerable moments . . . I'm thirty pounds overweight and a Christian. Don't you want to convict me about that? I haven't even bent over my gut to count if my toes are all still there. There's no excuse; no painful low back flare-up in months!" Silence.

I switched the drink in my hand from left to right and dug my feet into the ground, taking a stand. "You cannot write a testimony without explaining why it was so impactful. That's way too personal! I can't write this!" I needed to work around the invisible obstacle before me, and God was watching, so I tried to figure out what I could do and what I was willing to do.

I could work with myself on remembering why I recorded any of this story—my testimony of faith—in the first place. Then I could maybe relight the burner connecting me to God that just would not stay lit. The only way to connect my pilot light to the burner was to picture people alone, unprotected, and in need of spiritual answers. If someone somewhere was saying, "That's it. I can't live like this. I'm desperate. Someone point me in the right direction," then I should help them. Well, I was qualified to do something. I could do desperate and give basic information, share some experiences to help others. Shoot, that's not so bad.

Talking to God like this, as if He were around me, I still felt less than a Christian should feel from God. The year 2012, when I become a passionate Christian, was an incredible, unpredictable time. I missed being a yahoo for the Lord and not caring how unpolished my tangled hair and even more tangled personality were, because this Jesus stuff turned out to be real and perceptible. However, I was searching for his tangible presence now and intensely imploring the Lord to give me answers. Walking into the territory of pokeberries—deep purple in the late afternoon sun—I felt a gentle urge to pull the berries off the vines and squish them.

As I degloved the fat little berries, they filled my right hand where my fingers waited to crush the thick juice out of the skins. I had nowhere to be, no place I was needed, and so I squeezed a few more pokeberry vines and watched the blood of the fruit slowly drip through my fingers.

The blood at Christ's crucifixion came to mind. "This is my blood, shed for thee," I repeated aloud while drawing a crimson fingertip along the center of my forehead in the shape of a cross. There's power in his blood. Even when we feel disconnected from God, there are ways to reconnect. We must never give up on him because God never gives up on us, and his blood is a reminder.

I continued telling God what was on my mind.

"There's something beneath my surface, God. Something that I just can't reach on my own."

I balled up my blood-red fist and covered it with my clean hand.

"How do I get to that anger or pride—whatever it is that makes me resistant to back pain healing and antidepressant medication? The doctors and I can't figure this out. Extract the poison from my system and heal me. Take my will and pride. I'm your slave. I'm in your hands."

Quickly, I wiped away the forehead cross to prevent staining as bright as my now-red-and-purple hand. I still had the rest of the walk to finish if I was going to complete forty minutes, and chores needed my attention.

My God moment was over.

I felt good, despite not getting a direct answer from him, so I went about my day, assuming the night would be normal. It is not often that I talk to God like that—it seems sloppy and unrefined to vent to such a powerful deity. That's okay, though, because God is also a person and understands exactly what the full human experience is like.

As night drifted into Sunday morning, I slept poorly. I dreamed I was in a circle of people in a cozy shack, centered in a sparse, New England–style cemetery on a drab day, discussing our writing projects. When it was my turn, I told someone I wasn't quite sure what to do with my manuscript—that maybe it was to serve as a confessional only, something to get out of my system. Never for public consumption.

A woman to my left commented, "Maybe you should call Comcast and ask them. Flip through the Yellow Pages and pick someone." Turning from the rude voice, I faced someone else only to hear her say excitedly to another, "Let's have a séance. That'll scare her." Her companion giggled at the suggestion and made her own snarky comments.

Outside the shack window, thin white tombstones streaked with dark gray accessorized the crunchy grass and the pallid sky. Before I knew it, a vapor-like form rose from the ground in front of one of the stones. Swiftly unfurling into an oblong, upright shape, it darted from my window view on the left, around to the windowed front door on my right.

My view shifted into a melting feeling as my seat slid into a corner, the rude voices and a few others now behind me. My eyes stayed fixed on the ghoul outside the door as it floated and formed before me.

The ghost was a disgusting, horrifying female with stringy, sparse white hair flowing down a long white gown, exposing a decrepit skull and haunting features. My heart beat faster with her formation. She floated through the closed door and hovered in the air, her eyes fixed on me.

My heart was pounding, but I knew what to do! My confidence in the Lord—my faith—was as strong as my racing, kettledrum heart.

With complete surety, I opened my mouth to rebuke the ghoul in Jesus's name—but my breath was stolen. That feeling you get when you roll down a car window and stick your head out, that breathless panic overwhelmed my body, generating so much dry heat.

Nothing. I had nothing.

The nightmarish image oppressed me as it moved closer to me, then I felt something like air expand my entire chest cavity. Someone, or something, was about to speak through me the way a spirit speaks through a medium. As my lungs filled, the words came through me, starting with a guttural croak and ending in my own voice, but all spoken with authority: "Jesus is the Messiah! Leave and don't come back! Shame on all of you!"

That last sentence was mine—finishing off what my Father in Heaven started. Only these words weren't mine; they were given to me. I was a powerless child, protected by my Father's authority. It's stupefying to have a relationship with Jesus like this. Nevertheless, whoever spoke through me (I assume it was the Holy Spirit) will always have my gratitude! Though I was asleep, God came to me and glorified his reign.

I awoke, not from my booming heart but by someone divine stepping in for me when I was most vulnerable. God was answering my earlier plea—allowing me to reconnect with him by letting the Enemy oppress me. I knew I was on the right track; evil doesn't like to see good succeed. The attack made me cling to Christ. God is so powerful, so in control. He answered me and stirred my spirit with the juice of pokeberries.

When the Holy Spirit spoke through me, the words were not "I rebuke you in Jesus's name," something I would have said. Instead, the words were a proclamation of Jesus and his position, something I hadn't understood until that night. "Jesus is the Messiah" overpowered the malevolence whispering in my ear that night. When I needed it most, this truth set me free and radiated God's authority, as it did when demons encountered Christ in the Bible. Mark 5 describes Legion and the demons' response to Jesus—instantly knowing his name and all the authority it carried. What happened in the Bible is still happening today.

When my pulse reset and I cautiously left my bed, I knew I had some thinking to do. *It's time to squeeze some personal direction out of a pragmatic but Spirit-led Christian leader. I don't need to do this alone.* Waking up and fighting back wasn't enough, though it was a vast improvement over how I reacted when I fell into new ageism. It's solid biblical practice to go beyond rallying your family and friends. A trusted Christian authority, someone unafraid to challenge the status quo, offers surety when it comes to protection and sound decision-making. Despite all the mistakes I made when first exploring Christianity as an adult—and because I stuck with it and with the church—I now had spiritual siblings and leaders. I was blessed to be able to choose the right one for guidance.

If you are sleeping in some way and you need to wake up—fighting or not—you study the Word of God, follow the Lord, and rally the Christian troops. The head of my troop for this mission—writing my testimony—would be Darrell, a house painter and New Testament scholar.

∽

I pulled my used Corolla into the expansive, vacant Anglican church parking lot. Darrell's and Marty's empty cars sat side by side, clean and waxed in the light of the setting sun. Doug's clunker straddled the parking lines, somehow angled behind both vehicles. Doug—a modern-day John the Baptist who spends all his time pointing people to the Lord—parks like he has ADHD because he does. That's part of why we're dear friends. Doug, who is the strongest Christian I've ever encountered and the person who introduced me to my Tuesday night theology group, was clearly onto something. I parked right smack in front of Darrell's and Marty's cars, blocking them in. Laughing too hard to appear sane, I watched Joe maneuver his long-bed truck in next to Marty's Audi. Despite over an acre of parking space, we all chose to be sandwiched together—Doug and I no exception—parked like the divergent minds we are. Joe slapped his thighs and yell laughed at my parking job as I stepped out of my car.

"What are you doing? They're boxed in. Darrell's gonna think you've been eating dairy again."

"No, this is all Sarah right now. We're safe. So far," I replied. "Look, Doug's onto another car." We shook our heads in concern—probably another car accident—and entered the octagonal cathedral while I inquired about Joe's brood of kids, all of whom I adore. From inside the sacristy, we heard, ". . . because modern feminism is ruining America. That's why Trump's going to get reelected!"

I approached my place next to Darrell—as the unabashed apple polisher of the class—and asked, "Did we walk in on Christian feminism or politics?"

"Both," exclaimed Marty. "Ware havin' a serious talk about all this political gahbidge. Nothin' but trash on the news. This is why I yousta drink!" Marty's a longtime Massachusetts native, and his South Boston accent and mannerisms punctuate his endless comedy like nothing else.

The guys pretended not to notice my awkward, sciatic sitting and grimacing. Darrell calls it "preserving one's dignity"—a Christian way of giving public privacy to an injured or disabled person.

"Where's Lori?" I asked. "No one's suggested I take up pot or CBD oil to ease back pain in a while. That must mean she's out of commission or in that healing group thing."

Joe interjected over Darrell's mumbling: "You missed it. Darrell told her to stop focusing on blood moons and the end being near. She hasn't been back since." He struggled to breathe through his belly laughter, while Darrell rolled his eyes, saying something in his upper-crust Rhode Island accent. He only breaks it out when he's mocking us for mocking him.

"She's right, though, Joe. Ware all goin' t'hell in a hand basket!" Marty gestured expansively, sloshing condensation from his enormous, icy Dunkin' Donuts cup onto one of the church's Bibles. I shook my head. Can't take these guys anywhere.

Richard, the octogenarian with skin cancer so advanced that pieces of his scalp routinely fall off, used his extrastrength magnifying glass as a gavel to settle down our jocularity. "Are we ready to begin?" And so we were.

One hour into the class, I heard an opportunity to steal some direction for what to do with my testimony-turned-memoir. "We have to grow in a mature way and minister to the people God has placed in our lives," said Darrell. "Eighty percent of the time, prayer changes me because—just like in any other relationship—I have to get myself out of the way."

"A testimony functions in the same way, then?" I asked. "It's for one's own self a little, isn't it? It's deeply personal and unique. That's part of why non-Christians find our conversion stories confusing or interesting—but not that relatable."

Darrell reacted to my uncertain tone. "God is present, and the kingdom is active. We have to meet people with like faith instead of relying on churches divided by denomination, and we also have to speak to nonbelievers."

"Testimonies put feet to our relationships with others," Joe said. "Sometimes people who know nothing about Christianity will say, 'Tell me about your story,' because there's something about you that's interesting. My daughter's friend had never heard of Jesus not being a religion but a savior. He had no background in anything Christlike."

"Verbally sharing my testimony became hard after maybe three years," I said. "It's not so bad if an individual or small group pulls it out of me, but actually giving the full account nowadays . . . Being an authentic Christian is powerfully intimate because it's not unusual to feel the presence of God. Even when there isn't a clear presence, but you feel connected and charged, the atmosphere is different from normal. Trying to capture that for others is like chasing butterflies. People should experience the Lord for themselves. It's way better."

Sigh. "And digging up awful past moments to explain why the Lord's actions are so meaningful—because He let you 'walk with him' . . . I'd rather forget," I admitted.

"We shouldn't forget our first love," Darrell said sympathetically. "We have to grow in the faith. It's not that you can't return to when you were a nonbeliever or a child in the faith, but you can't stay there."

"That's right," Doug said with passion. "We move from mother's milk to meat."

"Darrell's telling me to act my Christian age and to get to work," I declared in my nasal, monotone voice.

Darrell smiled.

I conceded, "I'm in a state of reconciling with my past, so maybe now I can effectively express my faith. But shouldn't Christians focus on being yahoos for the Lord again? One gets so excited when joining the faith—and that's everything."

"But that's not our normal relationship with God," Darrell said, imploring. "Looking for that ecstatic experience all the time isn't healthy. Christians are in union with the risen God. We need to put away the first times. Nothing will be like those first years when you just met Christ, and it shouldn't be."

"Yeah, you haven't had any trials at that point yet," said Joe. "Then suddenly—boom!"

We chuckled knowingly and all started talking at once, saying things like, "Yeah, before you know it, you're religious! You're involved in too many ministries, and people gripe with each other. Be careful—religiosity will get you!" There is nothing worse, for these heart-led men, than to stop caring about something because passionless works get in the way.

Over the din, Darrell announced, "We should open in prayer." We're a little backward sometimes. Still, these blue-collar men—none of them under fifty—with their rough New England accents, show up every Tuesday night to grow in the Lord.

In the summer months, I see paint stains Darrell can't quite scrub from his twice-baked skin, while Marty unconsciously squeezes sections of Bible pages until they're dog eared—completely forgetting the stone dust on his hands, face, and shirt because he's telling jokes, exhausted, and stoked for Jesus all at once. Joe wears his green landscaping sweatshirt, full of holes, and I have no idea why one of his twelve children hasn't told him it's time for a new one. Half the time, the seminary-level class is too intellectual for the kids—some of whom aren't even in high school—but they're the most loving kids (like my niece and nephew), especially the one with chubby, puppy cheeks. Lanky Doug has holes in his shoes and is hopped up on artificial colors and dairy (he's got ADHD, giving him the same food sensitivities as I have), making it hard for me not to laugh at his inappropriate jokes and tangents while Darrell tries to manage him. These are my people now, these fellow Christians.

I reflect on this throughout the rest of the study. Leaving friends behind because you don't like who you are around them is just as awkward as trading friends who don't understand—or support—your new lifestyle or the people now entering your life. I seldom see my avuncular guys outside of Tuesday night classes, but I am so at ease with this family. I made the right trade: from secular to faith.

As we walked out of the church and into the night, Doug pointed to my ridiculous parking. "You're getting worse than I am. We're both on the spectrum! It's like one brain communicating with another. Wow!"

Marty motioned to the others. "Hey, look. Sarah blahked us in. Look at that—she's in the aisle of the pahkin' lot!"

"Yeah, now you can't leave." I giggled.

Darrell's mouth dropped open. "Geez, were you sipping the communion wine again?"

"No," I said. "I only did that once. I'm so much more mature. It's been, like, eight months. And I needed something to go with the communion wafers I pilfered."

Darrell eye rolled.

"You know you guys are spending the night anyway. You'll do contractor talk until midnight—or whenever your wives call."

"I think she's catchin' ohn!" Marty mock whispered.

꿍

The night sky is extra sapphire after many of these Bible studies, and tonight did not disappoint. Back home in the harbor, the weather still cooperated, and the yard bugs were few. When I closed the car door behind me, the sound echoed loudly in the quiet air. When it's still like this, it's as if a vacuum has sucked all the sound in the night. I let myself enjoy it, then plopped down my shoes, purse, and glasses. Lying against the sloped, bowl-shaped yard leading to my apartment door, I itched against the grass until I got comfortable and blinked with the stars—or jets, or marina lights. They all look the same with blurred vision, but they are pretty and peaceful, nonetheless.

Stillness—floating on a cloud of peace—is often what I feel moments after choosing to trust God. When you release the sadness and rest against the hurt, you can't help but accept the truth. It hurts to hurt, but there is honor and integrity in knowing who you are and how far you've come. I sighed. My resolve to follow the Holy Spirit pulled me to my feet—well, that and the shrill whine of a mosquito.

Once inside, I took the final step in making my decision official with the Lord and I set expectations. "God, I have absolutely no idea how I'm supposed to write about Peggy, the Mommy Dearest step-grandmother, or how nine months of living with her affected us kids." I paced back and forth on the living room carpet. "Without you, I can't pull off interesting descriptions of life history: The same one I've had to repeat to doctor after every friggin' doctor or write on some intake form because childhood trauma affects everything. But I guess if my dentist needs to know my life story, then why not every-friggin'-body else?" I got sad. My eyes watered. I kept going. That's what I do.

Hanging my head, I admitted, "I like having a choice—to hold private matters that really don't need to be shared." Sigh. "This is sad."

It's always after this complaining that the Lord gives me insight. I heard my heart yearning for freedom, rights, and safety. I know there's no tenderness or security like the Lord's. He's my everything, and He will be with me, full of love meant just for me, until the very end.

"Crap." I sighed. "Here we go." And I started to write. We need to remember love—and all the pains that make love so excruciatingly beautiful and necessary. That's what telling your story is: It's a way to redevelop your voice, the one that never should have been taken from you. One person's story can change everything. And one person's already has; his example is worth following.

Chapter 1
The Foundation

Point your kids in the right direction—
when they're old they won't be lost.

—Proverbs 22:6 MSG

If I were sent on another mission—like the one at the center of this story or even a normal one without eight-foot-tall angels and a celebrity—I'd still screw something up. Unrefined, I'd ask the Holy Spirit for more direction than he'd give. I'd ask my therapist for a better antidepressant than what is available. On a nonworkday, I'd load my grocery cart with dairy products because my willpower is useless without someone to say, "Sarah, you can't eat this stuff. You'll stay chubby, your ADD will act up, and people will think you're tipsy. Put it back!"

But here's what I wouldn't do: I wouldn't even think of backing down. That mission would be mine and God's in a holy heartbeat. I'd know that perverse and dangerous men would cross my path, as they still occasionally do. But unlike the tagline often used in my childhood to predatory people—"Far greater men have come against me . . . and I'm still here"—I would handle them without great fear and fanfare because nowadays, a thousand will fall at my right-hand side but nothing will come near me (Psalm 91:7).

I'm a bit banged up—mentally and physically—but not too bad anymore. When you are free and cared for, physical scars and chronic pain don't depress you as much and hurt doesn't reach your spirit as often. But here's the thing: It's not quite enough to be free. You have to unequivocally know you are free —and live it.

Of course, this is not how things were in the beginning. Looking back, who could have predicted a life surviving evil that infiltrated the church, a life that confronts the unseen? We are not allowed to forget our stories, the tangled journeys littered with scarred mile markers, even when too often they pointed in the wrong direction. However, we are allowed to accept help and, if we're lucky, to get found and stay found. Luck had nothing to do with my journey.

Forty-something years ago, I was born in a military hospital in Fort Lewis, where my father was stationed in Washington. When Mom describes my birth, it's bloody and bizarre. Before I came along, she became pregnant though she was on birth control. After having the stillborn baby—my would-be older brother and her second child—the doctor tied my mother's cervix. For some reason, it remained tied until she went into labor with me. There we all were: The doctor unsuccessfully trying to cut the binding that would free me, Mom in agony, and Dad threatening to "punch the doctor out."

After a last-minute C-section, I was born and immediately whisked away for three days. Dad returned to work. Mom remained in the hospital, where she was told to make her own bed during her stay. Because Dad was only a private—a low rank in the Army—there would be no special treatment. Assuming I had been removed because I had died, Mom lay in her room deeply upset.

On the third day, a nurse asked, "Lady, when are you going to feed your baby?" My mother collected me. At home, we received care from a Mexican immigrant who took pity on a mother now with two children and a military husband off doing duty. I've wondered about those three days alone in the hospital. Were they a sign indicating my future?

My mother and father were childhood sweethearts in the '70s—she was thirteen and he was nineteen. One would think by the time of my birth (they'd been together for seven years then) that they would have had more of a true partnership, rather than one that resulted in Dad leaving for long enough periods that a foreigner had to be our caregiver. Thank God for this woman. But that wouldn't be the last time someone else had to step in to help.

Mom and Dad never had much money. Joining the military was necessary after the shoe mill and poultry factory in central Maine—their home—closed. Unfortunately, Dad and the Army did not mix nor did he and living outside his insular town.

My start as a small blonde baby splashing mud puddles in Tacoma, Washington, turned into toddlerhood in rural Maine, awaiting the birth of my brother Jeremiah. While Mom was busy settling after the recent transfer back to Maine, a moment with my big sister, Becky, created a shared imprint on our lives.

One day, when I was two and Becky was six, I sat in my high chair playing with a glass feeding bottle. Mom asked Becky to watch me while she used the rotary phone. When I dropped the slippery bottle, the thick glass shattered against the floor, its pieces ricocheting against my baby-soft skin. A shard of glass instantly marred my peach-colored face.

The result was profuse bleeding, a crying big sister, and nurses holding me down in the ER while a doctor sewed my upper lip and cheek back into place.

It would be hard to call this problematic for me—having never been picked on for my semi-mustached facial scar. However, our lives are not our own, are they? The connection between my scar and Becky's guilt over not preventing the accident had deep roots. She housed the guilt in her petite body until her thirties, when she had kids of her own. Only then could she let go of the burden and understand the answer to my rhetorical question: Who charges a six-year-old with watching a toddler playing with glass?

Around the time of my lip surgery, my little brother, Miah, had his own emergency. He weighed only four pounds at birth.

To the world, *1984* is the title of a book, but for me, it's the year of my brother's birth. Only a year and a half younger than me, he was extra special. I loved his high and tight military-style haircuts and would rub his little head, feeling the soft grains of his hair. I cannot remember a time when I did not find him the most adorable, glowing baby or, later, boy.

Miah was small and weak. He has a dent of a scar on his upper left rib cage where the tube was placed into his preemie lungs—a signal to his mom and sisters to encourage him from a young age so he would really be a scrapper (a name our family pronounced "scrappa" and "scruffa").

I compared him to Mighty Mouse: the superhero who was tiny but strong. We told him that he was small but a fighter while we carried him around, even when he grew big enough that we had to waddle-drag him—or when he got tired of his suffocating older sisters.

*

With the changing season, my childhood journey moved along—and so did we—transferring with the Army to a new state: Georgia. Once Dad left the Army, he was free to move back to Maine and find a job there. He left without us after my parents divorced.

Mom believed she found her soulmate when Dad's Army friend John moved beyond flirting with her and they started dating. He had no problems marrying a single mom with three kids, none of whom were receiving any support from her ex-husband. She was so beguiled that she never stopped to think why.

We spent time regularly with John's family in their trailer, located in a remote Georgia town where the majority of them remain to this day. What was a trailer or shanty to others was, to me, so much more. This place—and our off-base housing—was what I loved and considered home, my culture. I loved boiled peanuts and pecan log rolls, and I remember them distinctly, though we only had them a couple of times.

Because Mom and John were bad with money, John bought a brand-new truck and detailed it instead of buying necessities. I spent a great deal of time scavenging for food. I ate many peanut butter and butter sandwiches; I felt so fancy. My uncles, John's brothers, caught animals for eating and told survivalist stories, warning about how to avoid being tricked by a panther's cry: *It sounds like a woman screaming or a baby crying. Don't be fooled.*

Puppy piles with cousins and hugs from my mom were my ecstasies. She was my everything. I soaked up every detail about her, even the colors and patterns of the capillaries under her nose. I took in the contours of her face. I listened to her bodily creaks and groans when resting my head on her stomach and lap.

Just one moment—sitting beside her as a five-year-old, eating Peter Pan peanut butter out of the jar while my siblings played outside—felt like winning the lottery or Christmas. She was in college or working far too often.

With three kids, a full-time job, and nursing school, Mom had her hands full. She was trying to do it all the way she thought her mother did.

My grandmother, Mom's mother, has only ever been described to me as a saint, even by her husband's mistress, who later became my step-grandmother. The mistress, Peggy, and my grandfather even lived with my grandmother until the newly married (and pregnant) couple found their own place. After my grandmother died in a car accident on June 30, 1984, her sainthood in the family's memory only grew.

I'm not sure if she was a saint or simply a great woman who enabled dysfunction, but my mother wanted to be a nurse and do everything else her mother did. What Mom didn't realize until many years later was that my grandmother hadn't raised all her kids while also going to school and working as a nurse all at once.

Mom herself wouldn't be diagnosed with bipolar disorder until I forced her, in her fifties, to see a clinician. Then we learned that short or long stages of mania can involve romanticizing someone—like a new husband coming to rescue you—or idealizing a beloved mother's capabilities. I like to think that it wasn't my mom who made such mistakes in life but her undiagnosed mental illness.

With no loving father, no support from Mom's family, and little help from John's side, she still would have had to make poor choices. For me, this meant learning deprivation on too many levels, too young. It's hard to get the love and attention you need when strangers babysit you, a parent is too busy for you, teachers (I started Head Start at three years old) only have a few hours to spare, and your dads don't care.

When Miah was just a few years old, he and I went to a neighbor's yard to swing on their clothesline. He fell and hit the back of his head. I'll never forget that scene—him crying, pumping his little legs in place, holding the huge goose egg that formed. My heart didn't just hurt, my soul did. I ached so deeply for my tiny, precious brother that my chest swelled with pain. I held him in my arms and walked him home, whispering words of comfort. I couldn't provide the care he needed, but I could give and express love and attention. I brought him to Mom.

A deep empathic scar formed in me that day. It still itches when I think about it. Maybe that's a good thing; maybe it's like what God feels when his children are hurting. That makes sense to me. Any goodness I have is because of love.

Not having decent earthly fathers means having to rely more on the Lord, but if you don't understand or know what that means, fear saddles up next to you and does not leave. My impressionable years were with Daddy John, whose true focus was not love or empathy but drilling manners into us. This dad taught—and my mother allowed—desperate fear and hypersensitivity under the guise of compassion. John delighted in eliciting panic. We all distinctly remember him relentlessly playing "For Annie" and twisting its meaning until it lost the band's intended message.

We routinely drove to be with John's family. "Hear that? He's talking about your cousin Annie," John said. "The song is warning you to help Annie."

"It is?" one of us asked.

"Yes, I heard it before," replied Becky. "Annie can die. She's dying in the song."

Mom nodded, scrunched between John and us while he drove down the dirt road. I loved that trip to John's mom's because each time we passed a forest where the trees formed perfect rows. My attention was slapped back to the truck when John barked at me to pay attention and listen to the song.

His pointed ears and glare rooted me to my seat. He was sharp and angry, like a blonde Doberman. He moved like one too. Ever since a neighbor's pit bull tore open my leg, aggressive animals scared me. John was no exception.

"Hey." He slapped my torso. He wanted my attention, which was hard to sustain as a youngster in a hot, sticky truck playing mellow music. "Annie will die before she's eight if she overdoses on those pills. Listen."

The lyrics painted a haunting and vivid story that stuck to me.

"What's *oba dose*?" Miah asked with his little-boy speech impediment. Someone must have answered him, but I don't remember. My imagination took over, painting a mental picture of Annie's little brown-haired body in our bathroom. She climbed up onto our sink like I did, opened the medicine cabinet. John kept narrating with the lyrics that it would be too late for Annie and that we better tell her Jesus loves her before she dies.

Mom smiled at us, agreeing with John. After she consented, I felt oppressive pain in my chest. I trusted Mom's guidance. She knew about this kind of thing.

Recently, Mom had discovered that I had fallen asleep on the bus ride home, missed my stop, and walked the two blocks home. When she had scolded me, I had explained, "It's not far," and pointed down the housing complex road. "I fell asleep on the bus and then I was there. It was a strange place, so I came home."

"You are four years old—that's too young to be walking alone," she said, frazzled.

"I'm almost five. I looked both ways across the street."

"A stranger could have kidnapped you in his car, and I'd never see you again. Don't ever do that. I'm telling John."

This was not good. My shoulders froze. I grabbed onto Mom as she walked across the wooden floor into the hallway.

"I only saw a white car—Keisha's dad."

Mom turned to me and pointed to the closet. "An older boy killed his little Black five-year-old sister, cut her body into little pieces, and put them in a bag and hid it in the closet. No one found her for two weeks. People were looking everywhere."

I have no recollection of what she said after that—only her tone and finishing whatever errands we were doing, like putting away towels. I looked into the dark closet at a clear dry-cleaning bag, picturing square pieces of one of my little Black friends inside, cut up the way Mom cut my pork chops. Frozen and numb, I was in those thoughts with a painful buzzing in my brain, like the chopped-up body pieces were in the big clear bag.

A vivid image arose of a murderous "big kid" leaving the closet after stuffing the dead little girl into it. The scene shocked my system, and I walked around thinking so many blurred thoughts: *Why? Did she bleed? Did her pieces wonder if anyone was looking for her?* I had been in a haze for several days, my brain stuck, short-circuiting.

In John's black truck, fear swollen in my chest, I trusted my mother's surety in this important lesson. Mom was perfect to me, and I had learned my lesson about listening to her. I gave full focus to the song and the golden wisdom Petra was singing.

"That's cousin Annie?" I asked.

"She has the same name," Mom explained. "Tell people you love them so nothing bad happens and they don't feel bad."

John was tickled pink when our sobs spilled onto our laps. It was dark inside John.

"We're almost there. Don't cry," Mom coaxed, telling John to stop.

He kept goading us.

"Here we are," she said when the long, clay driveway appeared.

"When you see Annie," said John, "go tell her Jesus loves her and that he cares."

He could not stop laughing, even after us kids tumbled out of the shiny truck like a puppy pile. "Find Annie, hurry," he hollered.

"Hush," Mom replied.

Miah spotted her first and pointed. "She's oba dare, oba dare."

Becky shot over to her, beating us. What a relief—mostly.

John's family didn't understand our behavior, and some waved him off when he explained his "joke." We got hugs from the family and played with Annie and her brother. I heard John getting scolded some. He took a seat on the porch. I regarded the man, his thighs looking fat and doughy the way he relaxed in the chair.

He called us to him to inquire what we thought of the situation. He did stuff like this all the time, so why would this moment be special? Becky described how scared she'd been for Annie. John told her Becky liked the song though and that's why he played it. She agreed and smiled. I forget what Miah said, but John turned to me next.

"Are you upset?"

"You're mean," I said with quiet conviction.

His sneering scoff didn't matter. What mattered was my defiance—the strongest I'd ever felt or shown. Though John terrified me, I was never angry with him. That emotion must've lived in me, but I never felt it. I only felt hurt.

Learning to conform to John's manipulation wasn't enough.

John had his own scars—and his seemed to itch worse than mine. There was no mercy or relief. His priority as a soldier was to put the mission first. John's abusive mission was to hurt us without getting caught which was a growing wall cloud, separating my little family from who God intended us to be.

Chapter 2
Pangs

*It were better for him that a millstone were
hanged about his neck, and he cast into the sea,
than that he should offend one of these little ones.*

—Luke 17:2 KJV

THE FAMILY OF my childhood simply existed. When people merely exist, they are not living, achieving, reasoning, being, loving, or protecting. This was the world where my mother, brother, sister, and I became fluent. Whether we were alone in the suburban off-base housing or with my stepdad's family at the uncultivated homestead didn't matter. We considered that season of life our beginning. Until we lived in Maine again for a decade, we still answered "Georgia" whenever asked, "Where are you from?"

Granny Herrin—my stepdad's mother—lived in a southeastern Georgia town so unpopulated and limited it was "smaller than all get out." The area offered few jobs, and opportunities for full-time work were sparse. The drinking water was iced-tea brown, and if you left your home unattended for too long, your belongings, even children's toys, were fair game. It's not as if people took two-week vacations or anything fancy like that. Neighbors and family were always down the road, in a lot carved out of tangled woods, and you knew where to find them even though road signs didn't exist. Imagine the peacefulness and the sounds of nature, like the whippoorwill calling to its mate. The brambles and thickets offered places to conceal yourself—for hide-and-seek or something else entirely.

I'm sure John's mom appreciated peace and privacy when recovering from her alcoholic husband's abuse years before. I'm sure young John appreciated a place to hide when his uncle wasn't sodomizing him. But I wonder: Did John wish that instead of his mother walking in on him being sodomized by his own uncle, she would have known what to do so that John never had to hide in the first place? Silence is pervasive in cultures like this. You remain quiet because you don't talk about that kind of thing.

After Granny Herrin's husband and her brother-in-law (John's uncle) died, she remained in the trailer wearing the same threadbare clothes and somehow surviving. After I grew into a teenager, my mom and I had a conversation about John's family.

"Granny Herrin didn't know John still did things as an adult," Mom said. "She said he had a demon in him—ever since he was a baby. She heard a strangled cry in his crib, and he was different after that."

The backstory was surprising.

I said, "I know John had an affair with his brother's wife, but no one told me anything else. What else was there, Mom?"

"Granny Herrin said, 'I walked in on my brother-in-law sodomizing John. Then John started killing animals, but his dad was a mean alcoholic so . . . I figured the Army would straighten him out.'"

My granny thought military service taught men discipline, which she believed would cure men who killed animals and molested anyone weaker than themselves. My teenage brain was perplexed. The occasional military men I came across were rarely kind and genuine; they varied on the behavioral spectrum. Some were hooligans, others were normal, and a few trained dogs with disciplined comportment.

"She really thought that? What did she do to John's uncle?"

"They didn't talk about it. Granny Herrin didn't finish school. She married too young, and her husband beat her. The boys talked about it. He was mean as a snake."

So back in the late '80s, this culture spilled into my life.

Why would anyone remain in situations or areas like this? It wasn't the 1800s. But in Granny Herrin's mind, there wasn't anywhere else to go. Home is home and that is where you stay. When I've seen "limited" people encouraged to take advantage of their lives and various opportunities, the common reply is: "I couldn't do that. That's not for me," or worse, "We don't do that kind of thing. That's for fancy people." Limited thinking and limited resources couple nicely, and it's a sad shame. I have had both, far too often. This rarely leads anywhere.

Ignorance and pride can slip in too easily. For my mother, her goals mattered more than properly providing for her kids. School, work, marriage, and mothering had to work in tandem. For my stepdad, he wanted control—for example, what we ate, when, and how much. When he wasn't around and it was just Mom and us kids, we had choices. The black-and-white box of USDA government cheese perfected a bowl of grits, and crunchy peanut butter was divine. Food like this could have come from food pantries, John's job in the Army, or churches. Mom doesn't remember because she didn't pay any mind. She never realized how hungry her kids were and still cannot search her memory and see the signs. She remembers comments from people on her "skinny minny" kids, but the comments never took root. She thought Miah was small because he had been a preemie.

Mom didn't experience hunger until she was an adult and needed to provide for us. She assumed that when she went without, it was enough to stave off hunger for us. It wasn't. Because she was too preoccupied with her life, her mental powers of deduction didn't reveal our struggles to her. Without her cognizance and with an unknown mental illness that annihilated her ability to rationalize, we didn't stand a chance. Therefore, we did our best to learn independence. For example, Becky was so much better at doling out butter than I was. I put too much on rice. When Becky saw me mouthing rice like a dog chewing peanut butter, she fixed my food. I was good at situating Miah at the table and playing lookout when we discovered fancy grown-up food that we weren't supposed to get into, like cream cheese—sticky cream so heavenly I asked the name of it while being scolded. Miah was good at eating. Unfortunately, he was too good at it and often ate chunks of my sister's fruit flavored lip balm. When I discovered him doing this with mine, I corrected him—but when I thought about it, I ate it myself. The waxy strawberry stick was sweet.

Granny Herrin's backyard had real fruit: wild berries and black grapes. They were for Granny Herrin, but we had no willpower. We rummaged through bushes, though pickings were slim. There were so many mouths to feed: cousins, aunts, uncles, parents, Granny Herrin, and her sisters. Head Start and kindergarten came with free meals that still make me salivate to this day. It was ordinary food, but I dreamed of the yeast bread rolls and the buttery, crispy grilled cheese. The cafeteria ladies were surprised when I asked how they made such food. It might have been weird to see a little kid just standing at the steel-railed counter where cafeteria trays were meant to slide to keep the assembly line of hungry youths moving, but when your focus is on food, the silliness of the scene doesn't occur to you. It was day school, leaving time for playing in Georgia clay roads or looking for anything edible. Hunger, to me, would beat down the fear of poisonous plants like my angry new stepdad's belt across my bare behind. School was a place to have food and a break from John's corporal punishment.

My siblings and I spent as much time away from John as we could, especially when Mom wasn't around. It was better to be together if he was around, but if we were not together, we hightailed it away. It wasn't just John's meanness but his arrogance and relentless teasing. If someone were to pull out a handful of your hair, you would feel deep throbbing pain. If someone tweezed out those hairs one by one by one, the pain would be different—but both hurt bad. Getting lickins' on our exposed bottoms left burn marks, and switches whipped against our little bodies too often.

Something complicated and scary was manifesting in John, but we didn't understand what. We just knew we wanted to get away from him, and we kept trying to tell grown-ups that we didn't want to be alone with

John. But he was sneaky. He always seemed to find out what we said. He even knew when I tried to approach a couple at an amusement park. I know—why go there when more pressing financial needs existed? The military probably gave us free passes allowing park entrance but not rides. Anyway, the man finished his fries, and the woman gently positioned a little child at the top of the slide. She seemed caring. I wanted to be around the couple, but they walked away, and the man left his almost-empty paper cup on the railing. I started to drink the sugary water with ice chunks, cool and almost relieving, not realizing that John was watching me. His angry voice carried up to me.

There is a unique fear that shoots through you like a fallen power line when you think you are safe (and that there is hope for relief), only to be returned to the reality that you were being watched and were never safe at all. The shock painfully roots you to the ground. I walked backward from the paper cup of water. Miah and Becky heard the bellowing and came over to the wood railing. *Jackpot*, they thought. *Free water!* Nope, John and Mom scolded us for trying to drink something that had a stranger's germs.

Is it cynical to not believe John really demanded excellent hygiene given that he found urine entertaining? In the last Georgia home we would inhabit before moving to New England, we were settling into the seclusion on Lenore Street. The three of us kids played on the floor and couch while Mom and John were doing things around the house. John came out of the bathroom and went to each of us, sticking his finger in our faces.

"Smell it. What's it smell like?"

Miah and I said that we didn't know, but we were young enough to know what that ammonia scent was.

"Yes, you do," he said. "That's pee."

I pulled into myself to get away from him, trying to force my focus onto my dollies. Miah went back to driving his Hot Wheels around the thick coils on the braided wool rug. The truck drove over a race car stuck in the rug groove that was a ditch. "Bigfoot running over cars. Duh nuh nuhn," he sang—his favorite made-up song.

Becky knew the smell, and that made John laugh. Next, he went to Mom.

"What—I'm trying to get supper ready," she said, annoyed.

"Smell my finger."

"I don't want to. I'm busy." She did something to a pot on the stove. He persisted, "No, smell it. It's funny."

She jerked her head back after sniffing. "Is that urine?"

"Yes." John snickered like a boy.

"Oh, that's gross. Go wash your hand," she commanded.

John walked to the bathroom, which was just a wall and maybe thirteen feet away from where Mom was busy cooking and dishwashing. Minutes passed while Miah and I played, and Becky scribble scrabbled on her notebook with a barely used pencil far too big for her little nine-year-old hands. She made using a pencil look so easy—like the conductors at Mom's college symphony with their long, white batons.

"I'm finished," Becky said excitedly.

Mom told her to put her schoolwork away, so she tucked her notebook in her little backpack—stiff and looking oversized next to her small frame and knobby knees. She was a pretty little thing, and photos barely captured her blonde luminosity. She bounced off in the direction of her room—in the same direction as John, still in the bathroom after being tasked to wash his hands. I wondered what he was doing and what he was planning. Becky's little voice mixed with John's, and my attention returned to play.

To understand the rest of the story, it's important to know that for years, Becky had thought everyone adored John because he looked like Indiana Jones, and family praised his beauty. But the new Indiana Jones movie posters showed a stranger—far safer than the man in the other room, playing with bodily fluids and in an adventurous mood. My sister trusted Daddy John not just because she was innocent but also because she was taught to follow what everyone else did: That is what good girls did.

As an adult, she said, "I thought everyone liked John, and I needed to fall in line like when he was training us to be soldiers. I thought I was supposed to follow everyone else even when he did those things. I knew the things he did hurt, but I thought, 'If he is doing these things to me, he isn't doing this to the younger kids—and it hurts.' "

In contrast, I did not trust John. Just because Mom was home didn't mean we were safe. In the previous home on Arrowhead Road, I had once summoned the courage to urgently whisper to Mom, "Don't go. Stay home. John's mean."

Mere minutes passed, and it was too late. The dining room, kitchen, entryway, and living room were small, separated by a large pillar. It took one walk around the donut-shaped path—and a trash bag pulled from the kitchen closet—for John to know what I said. Mom informed him when she asked him to remove the trash. I didn't want Mom to leave, so I adjusted my pigtails and walked into the kitchen to soak up what little time I had with her. He was there. He looked at me knowingly and walked away while talking. I remember his tone was normal, not snarky.

But I do remember being so nervous I peed on the kitchen floor, trying to sweep it up before Mom saw, but I was too young to know about mopping and too small to use a grown-up broom. Mom stumbled upon me trying to sweep urine into a dustpan. She was not happy, even when I showed her that I had gotten a lot of it in the pan. John saw and laughed while Mom cleaned up and went to work or school.

My indiscretion had led to a fresh-off-the-stove pan on all us kids' hands and John's hunting knife bouncing between our splayed fingers on the table and off our shoed feet. We weren't badly hurt, but if "games" like this happened when I reached out to Mom for help, I knew there would be no rest—regardless of location.

The muscle memory of this significant moment returned to me in the house on Lenore Street. I don't think my siblings quite had this same reaction yet, so Becky innocently crossed the path of the man who beguiled her and claimed her trust—by visiting John in the bathroom.

Kids are little sponges, their brains soaking up the world around them. Brain specialists say that trauma kicks our brains into alert mode and some people just have strong memories. Maybe I simply could not squeeze enough love out of Mom to soak up, so I visually absorbed the life around me. Whatever the case for me, my brain was recording everything—though I didn't completely understand the repercussions until decades later.

In my twenties, I replayed the rest of this finger-smelling scene to my mother, warning her that this would be hard for her to hear. "But it's important," I said over the phone. "Becky and the kids are still sleeping in my apartment, so I want to talk with you about this now before they wake up. Can you handle talking about John?"

"Yes, was the weekend good? Did something happen?" she asked.

"No, it was great. The kids saw a nurse shark or something big. It was an okay whale watch. They met some of the people at my church—it was nice."

"Well, that's good. What about John?" she asked.

"Do you remember when John was going around making us smell the urine on his fingers? It was in the yellow house on Lenore, just before he went AWOL."

"Oh yes, that was so gross. What a stupid thing to do," she replied.

"Yeah, well, you know that I can remember these things really well, and when I say something happened, we know from my track record that it happened, so we can rely on my brain, right?"

"Yes, that's helped me a lot. I have to ask you things because I'm just out there sometimes," she said with a self-deprecating laugh.

"Ok, well, this is going to be a lot for you to ingest, so be prepared. Are you ready?"

"Yes," she said hesitantly.

I brought her through the scene until Becky left the room. "So, you are with me thus far? You remember this event or at least most of it? This all sounds solid?"

"Uh-huh," Mom agreed.

"When John made his rounds again, he held his finger under our noses—Miah, you, and me. The smell on his finger was not urine this time. Do you remember that?"

"Yes," she said point-blank.

"You don't remember Becky being in the room, probably—but you might?" I asked.

"She wasn't in the room, but I'm not sure."

"She wasn't in the room," I said. I could hear the wheels in her head turning.

"Okay, I believe it. Yes, I agree. That's my answer."

"It's fine if you don't. I can still walk you through this."

"No need. You can continue."

"Daddy John came up to me and put his finger up to my nose," I continued through my embarrassment. "I stopped breathing, my eyes focusing on John's large finger. The salty smell was feminine. It was not urine, Mom."

"John walked over to you, Mom. You were washing dishes and cooking dinner."

"Yes, and he smelled bad, and it was gross. He was my soulmate, but he did some dumb things."

"So, Mom, what happened next?"

"What did I do?" she asked me. My awesome Mom will easily submit when she knows she needs help. She was a sweetie really trying to figure this out. She trusted my memory and me completely. She is sweet and tender. She tries hard.

"You said, 'I said to stop doing that! Go wash,' " I answered.

"Good! I'm glad, that's good," she said with enthusiasm.

"And you remember John teasing you about washing his hands in the soapy dishwater near you—and you shooing him out of the kitchen?"

She said yes.

"This is a lot, Mom—okay?"

"I'm okay."

"So, you're there in the kitchen, and you know that you were more grossed out by the other smell and more dismissive, right?"

"Yes."

I continued leading Mom, hoping it would trigger realization. "What was that other smell?"

She was mentally stuck, so I explained, "I know you say I'm 'a lot' and 'too much,' but with stuff like this, we are exceptionally unique in being able to have these talks. You are solid, and you understand that we can talk about important things. I have to fight shame, and I'm taking you with me. It's good . . . but I have to tell you more so you understand."

"I understand, sweetie. Yes, I'm okay. We can keep going," she said.

I was scrunching my face like Popeye—a habit I can't kick, especially when uncomfortable and talking about heartrending things. "Well, you know that women's bodies have unique smells, and our vaginal areas don't smell like urine. Would it be safe to say that was the smell on John? Can I say that?"

"Yeah. Yeah. Uh-huh. I agree. That's right." I knew she was nodding her head with her tongue tucked between her side teeth—her factual, ponderous, almost corporate gesture.

"We're gonna go on. You're ready?" I took her pulse again.

"Mm-hmm."

"Where did the smell come from?" I asked.

"I don't know."

"Where was Becky?"

"I don't know. Was she playing with you?"

"No. Remember, you just corroborated that she left the room. So Becky was not with Miah or me in the living room and she wasn't with you."

"Oh drat, that's right," she remembered.

"So, Mom, Becky left. She wasn't with us. John left you after two rounds of us smelling pee and vagina on his hands. He went back into the bathroom area, doing something. Got it?"

"My mistake."

"That's okay. We are getting there. In that house on Lenore Street, there was the side we were on, which was open. Then there was a wall with an open doorway that led to the bathroom and bedrooms. Miah, you, and I were on the kitchen side, and John was on the bathroom side doing whatever."

"That means Becky was on the other side. I got it now," she said, relieved.

"Yes—but there's more, Mom," I spoke slowly and less quietly because I needed her to understand. "John had a vaginal smell on his finger, and it wasn't from you—his wife."

Silence.

"Where did it come from, Mom?" I asked directly.

This silence felt different than the last pause. The truth was dawning on her.

"Where was Becky, Mom?"

She breathed in my patient but potent question.

"Have you got it now?"

After a pregnant pause, she replied, "Yes."

I got through to her—completely. Her bipolar disorder had still not been discovered, but it didn't matter. I had all Mom right then. Praise the Lord, my mom got it and felt the gravity of knowing her little girl's experience. It was one thing to hear evidence at the trial and for Mom's deep denial to wear off a few years after and another thing entirely to have someone point out a specific example of where her blindness allowed evil to work.

"She needs you," I continued. "When you help her, that will trickle down to her kids—your grandkids. She hasn't brushed her teeth in years, and you, as a former nurse, know mouthwash isn't enough. My doctor told me that my sore throat is a *Staphylococcus staph* infection thing. She was staring at the throat culture results, perplexed. I told her sometimes this happens when I return from my sister's. She was still stumped, so I just explained that my sister's apartment is really dirty. I had lice the size of my pinkie nail once. I scraped black mold off the bathroom ceiling. There's rust in the tub like an abandoned Russian warehouse, and the toilet sprays sewage from under the seat and leaks near your feet. I know that's bad, but the doctor still didn't understand that I contracted the sickness from my sister because the doctor was a non–blue collar, suburban kind of person, you know."

"Yep," Mom said knowingly.

"Well, it dawned on me that this whole thing is beyond extreme, it's unacceptable to, like, an American. Becky's still living like those Afghan refugees who lived next to us in Augusta. That has to change."

"Did the doctor prescribe you something?" Mom asked.

"Yeah, the stuff from last time, so I'm all set. Thanks. I'm harping on this because you can say things to Becky with your mom voice and she'll listen to you. If you back up what I tell her, then there are two voices directing and corralling her. When you're with her, she'll take a bath. I haven't seen her use her towel in almost two months. You can tell her that's gross. She needs accountability now."

"I agree things are pretty bad, honey. Becky hasn't shaved her legs in months, and it's like a tarantula," Mom said.

I felt exasperated. "Mom, I don't care about that."

"You're right. I know I wasn't there for you kids. I didn't know Becky went through that," Mom conceded with a softer, less disgusted tone.

I backed down. "We're safe now, don't worry. We just need help. I've got her kids covered. If you help me pull along Becky, the kids will only grow up in poverty and not the nasty stuff. You're hurt by the truth, but we'll make it. We need truth and to soldier on. Becky is the same baby girl she was then—she's just grown up."

"Sweetie, I have to go, but yes to everything," Mom replied, slipping into the usual pattern of concluding the call when I got too passionate and pushy. But this time, Mom wasn't distracted or saying to anyone, "Sarah is too much." She was dry heaving.

While Mom came to terms with her past, I wrapped my arms around my present and future. My little man—my nephew—had startled me when I hung up the phone and turned to cross the yard. I rubbed his little blonde fuzz head and squeezed him almost right out of his little-boy long johns. Becky and Zoe were still sleeping, so Aaron and I plunked down on a fluffy-as-a-cloud comforter and read *The Stinky Cheese Man*. With sound effects and extreme character voices, we passed the time until Zoe, his sister, awoke.

I grabbed my little biscuit babies and fixed Zoe's overnight diaper. "I got extra raspberries and blackberries for your yogurt, but I need you to drink the green smoothies I got especially for you. You like it, but I want you to remember that you can negotiate." They were not in a negotiating mood. They loved fancy food. I loved teaching them they had choices and could create freedom in even the smallest opportunities.

"Auntie," Zoe said, pausing for a response from me, as always. Nobody else does that. I still melt when she does it.

"Yeah, Biscuit?"

"Do these have the special juice?" She pointed to the raspberries.

"You betcha! All the dark berries have it. See these purple raspberries?"

"Uh-huh."

"That's where all the handsome juice is. It'll make you extra beautiful. They're extra sweet—that's how you know. But you're going to pick up each berry and ask me if it's the right one, aren't you?"

Not taking my hint, both kids agreed and did. While the kids ate their breakfast and daydreamed of spending hours at the playground, my sister slept like a log, and I thought about a future where—even if my niece and nephew just had okay lives—their kids could have a fighting chance instead of merely getting through life. I'd try to change the generations. Would my voice be enough to lift the fog that weighed down my family?

Chapter 3
A Life on Layaway

A Modern Prayer:
My father who art far away, Dad is your name.
Your kingdom undone, your will none,
a father missing on earth is a
father missing in heaven.
The government provides our
canned goods and bread,
and we grow in debt to others.
Chained to temptation and abandoned to evil
for Mom has no kingdom or power
to give her fatherless child.
Amen.

Around 1986, John started sexually abusing Becky, who was about eight. Dad lived in Maine, and Mom worked full time and attended school. That meant us kids were on our own. Did anyone notice my sister's abuse—did they see the signs? Did traces of blood ever appear on her little clothes, making teachers, babysitters, church members, neighbor kids, doctors, or anyone think, *Something is off?*

I think about this now because if we examine problems, we can learn to notice signs and establish preventive measures. I've thought about sodomized adults needing stitches. When Becky's painful abuse started, wouldn't she have needed the same—if not more—care? For many years in my adult life, it felt like I was the only one willing to go back in time and face this reality. Where was everyone?

In the years that my first stepdad was in our family, how could no adults notice major trauma? Did they just ignore it? We kids must have been too minor to matter to them. Something in me, for years, regarded my sister and said, *See her. Think about her pain. Someone has to, and someone needs to love her.*

When my sister became a troubled teen, diagnosed with bipolar disorder—then called manic depression—I wondered, *Is she bipolar, or is she traumatized? We don't get to live like other people; there's never enough of anything to go around: food, heat, Mom, family. There's too much pain all around. How can we know if Becky's actions are from what she endured or a brain disorder?*

I was too young to understand that medical professionals can diagnose someone who has both been through trauma and has a severe mental illness. But I couldn't rely on the adults around me. I had to wrestle with a yearning that made me want to fill in the gaps, to be the empathetic seer of my sister. *I see you. I understand. I remember. I know. I was there.* I guess that yearning was the love of a little sister.

Love is more than flowers and good times. It's a responsibility and an honor. Love is a duty, and it felt like I was the only one willing to perform this duty toward my sister. When she messed up, I did my best to correct and to offer understanding. This went into overdrive when no one else would help her. Love compels you to try, even if you're simply trying to fill in the gaps where there's no one else waiting to love you.

Unlike Becky's, my sexual trauma wasn't reoccurring. I was five years old. On a dewy southern afternoon on Lenore Street, wind from the swaying backyard tire swing breezed my way. The neighborhood kids meandered around the swing. Some clung to the large tree, trying to climb it. Some used the tree to trace the grooves of bark. Some of us used its roots as stepping stones while we waited for our turns on the swing.

A few days prior, Daddy John had heard me whistling at a bird and explained, "That's a whippoorwill. It makes a sound like its name and will sing back to you."

So on this afternoon, I hooted out in falsetto, "Whi-ppoor-will, whi-ppoor-will . . ." I showed a friend how to warble like a whippoorwill. We were a couple of little girls with plastic bunny barrettes and mismatched outfits, whooping at unseen birds—quite the sight.

A whippoorwill isn't a pretty little thing and looks a little odd itself. But it has an interesting voice. When it calls out and you speak back, connection sprouts. That relationship makes an unpleasant-looking bird tender and precious. To be noticed by the whippoorwill—and to engage it with a song—was special.

John called to me from inside the quiet, empty house and told me to remove my shorts and underwear so he could touch my half-naked body. His snake's tongue came out as my flesh was moved back and love was awoken "before its time," which the Bible warns against in Song of Songs 8:4 (NCB). There are innate life rules: Men are not supposed to perform sex acts on children. A weird situation of embarrassment and pleasure imprinted itself upon my early childhood mind as a result of an adult disobeying this rule.

As I lay on the couch during the abuse, I noticed the couch's pineapple print.

John asked a few times, "Does that tickle?"

My only response was "No. It's weird."

When I was released to the backyard, I was commanded to send my then–nine-year-old sister into the house after me. I told Becky outside, "It's okay. John isn't angry." Funny, I didn't understand what just happened or the implications that would reach far into my future. I was going about my normal day, wishing Mom would come home and glad I hadn't been called in to get whooped (whipped).

Becky wasn't allowed to bring her little Black friend inside. The friend stayed with us in the backyard as the door closed behind Becky. I watched Becky walk into the house, and my mind recorded the moment and the seemingly random details. My brain often did that, capturing the fullness of moments not because of a hyperactive mind but I think because my feelings and ability to express them were simply blank. God might spare us pain by blocking it temporarily, but a developing mind sometimes just can't feel; it comes back to haunt us at a later time. Being abused without physical pain is extremely awkward and outright bewildering. My mind wrestled with that bewilderment for years. When we got whoopings, belts slapped across our bare skin were sometimes easier to understand than sexual abuse.

My sexual experience as a child did affect me in the short term. It also seemed to put a larger deposit down on the long term so that entering puberty meant feeling drunk with confusion and mental frenzy, though my sexual assault had ended years prior. Sexuality is a door to a hidden world, and when you walk through it, you are aware of two things: the stillness around you and that whether or not you chose the sexual encounter, you are inducted into the world, even if you choose not to speak this discovery to others. You can walk past rows and rows of people without a single one of them knowing your secret. This is no place for children—it's simply too adult, far-reaching, and too sacred to embody in such a delicate creature. The desires of the flesh are a nightmare for little kids to master, especially in puberty when your hormones have more control over your body than you feel you do. But this was my place.

One time, Daddy John derattled two live snakes with a jump from his truck and the flip of a blade. When he shook one of the rattles, Mom had no clue this was a symbolic moment. John was a far bigger snake than the live ones he tossed back into the ditch after maiming them. He clawed his hand, forming fangs with his pointer and middle finger, and undulated his arm mimicking a serpentine rhythm. It was so easy for me to see that Daddy John was the ultimate snake. The bumpy rattles were both startling to touch and grotesquely amazing. Mom didn't want us playing with such dirty things, but John got his way and us kids jiggled the rattles, careful not to touch the severed end.

Was this fun of John's sick? We knew him and his antics. He had his own definition of fun. For example, we had races to see who could untie John's combat boots the fastest when he got home. The winner was supposed to get a quarter, but Daddy John never kept his word, and we eventually grew smart to his "joke." Some jokes and games were not optional. Around the world was one of them.

When I look at Army-issued rucksacks now, I think of how they are full of clothes and supplies. It's hard for me to imagine stuffing children in one and swinging it around until they're disoriented. Of course, Mom was gone and John wanted to play with us kids. His standard-issue Army-green duffle bag held sleeping bags and clothes. Without all that, it held a few kids, tangled elbows and a cramped space. John made us each crawl into the dark sack—all the way.

When one of us kids got in, Daddy John drew the opening shut, tossed the sack over his back like Santa Claus, and walked around the living room in circles singing, "Around the world." I noticed two things: He seemed like Santa with a big bag of toys under the sparkling living room lights decorated for Christmas, and I didn't want to be in the sack hollering, "It's too dark in here. I'm dizzy." Yet I knew from the dread in my chest that my time was approaching.

When Becky emerged from the sack, she was all legs and arms like a fawn being born and trying to stand. This scene made no sense. My sister looked as absurd as the kittens Daddy John tossed up into tree limbs (forcing them to fall-crawl down a tree) or like the kitten he stuck in an empty tire and spun around until it couldn't walk right. My consternation didn't leave when John barked, "You're next."

I obeyed, crawling in headfirst. The bag pulling shut at my feet wasn't as shocking as the unexpected weight of my body suddenly on my head. Upside down, my face and neck crammed against the bottom of the rucksack, I felt myself swinging and spinning. I didn't feel like someone's little girl but like an animal stuffed in a bag. Maneuvering was harder than moving in a hammock, and I couldn't seem to make my eyes open or find any light. I heard loud chaos roaring, and a frenzy of scenarios seized me with panic. It was only when the duffel bag dropped that my thundering thoughts lowered and I heard the other kids calling to me. But hopeless dread was in me and it was so dark.

John told me to find my way out of the duffel bag, but I knew I couldn't. Though I was just a small five-year-old, the bag felt both closed in around me and like a black tunnel so large that I had lost myself in it. My siblings' voices distracted my dreadful imaginings. Their muffled sounds reached me as Daddy John opened the bag and shocking light confused my senses. I turned to the light behind me, but it was too far away. My crumpled body was so clumsy and hard to move in my jarred state. Realizing how far away the light was brought more panic and whimpering. "I'm here. I'm here," I foolishly cried. I wanted to be found.

The kids shouted to me, "Crawl out, Sarah. Come on!"

But I whimpered my response, "I can't. I'm stuck."

Becky responded to the shaky voice from within the duffel bag, "Turn around like I did. Crawl out."

I turned to my left and could not bend as I should. I looked like a school bus trying to pull a U-turn. I simply couldn't maneuver around the sack.

Becky tried to help, but John scolded her, "Back away. She can do it."

Trapped and dizzy, I could no longer escape the terror. "I'm stuck. I'll never get out!" My body had a mind of its own as my brain embodied this buried alive sensation that suffocated my little lungs.

I heard John and the kids direct me, "Turn your body around."

"I can't bend that far!"

"Yes, you can," replied John. "I've seen you wrap your legs around your head, and you can bend back with your feet touching your hair."

"I can't. It hurts my bones!"

He kicked the bag to spur me on. "Don't be Miss Prissy. How are you going to be like those girls in the circus if you can't bend?"

I felt so humiliated cramming my face against what felt like a hard wall. It didn't matter that it was dark, I knew how absurd I looked scraping my skin against the side of the sack, but this little soldier had to do what was required. "Just back out. Crawl out backward," so I did. On my elbows, I shimmied and waddled out of the darkness and into the light. I don't know what John said next because this was a normal type of occurrence and not a defining moment. This was how things were.

Playing around the world was no more monumental than the time I ate rose petals, wondering if they were edible. I expected to taste burning or stomach cramps when I swallowed the petals, but nothing happened. So I bit into an entire white rose, plucked fresh off the bush growing in Granny Herrin's yard. The hunger pains rushed at me the moment the petals hit my stomach. I grabbed another rose, then another, and another, losing myself to the fury until I saw a large grasshopper right on top of the rose I was about to grab. Gross. I left for the time being.

Running across cousins Wayne-Wayne and Kenneth, I shared my find, completely satisfied by the good news and still repulsed by the grasshopper—it wasn't precious like the lightning bugs in the night fields. I thought nothing of what I had done. Just a short while later, my stomach rumbled again. Returning to the bush, I saw that it was picked completely clean. An entire hedge of roses, eaten by the two small boys. I should've kept my mouth shut.

What I do know is the times hunger stalked us kids, and it's still hard not to bring up food when it stands tall in my memory. Not all of my childhood was tragic. Yeast bread rolls brushed with butter and a touch of salt were so good it made eyes roll. Grilled cheese sandwiches saturated in butter-flavored oil with soft centers and crispy crusts still warm my heart and make me smile. These are my warm childhood memories. One of my favorites: In each school throughout my life (maybe nine), I noted that the grilled cheese sandwiches were always baked, no doubt the quickest way to create the appropriate volume for all the students. But I was elated when I connected the dots. *That's the secret! That's how to make them at home.* For me, most of my meals were at school, so there was a big chunk of time where school-cooked meals were my goal instead of the typical home-cooked ones. I'd like to think of this not as a problem but as a passion for something greatly appreciated and just a little different than the norm.

A family of five will have struggles. But my parents' and caregivers' lives did not center around us kids. Normal things like appropriate food and clothes were not always a priority, but things couldn't been worse. Daddy John and Mom brought home powdered milk, government cheese, and canned food, so we were fortunate. This might seem pathetic, but it's true. When Miah ate sand, as he did throughout our Georgia days, he hopped into ditches and scooped dirt and sand into his mouth because he said he liked the way it tasted. Mom did scold him for eating sand and dog food. She was visible in our lives, just not enough. We lacked a lot and moved a few times (even within Georgia), so that meant more instability and change.

What our family needed was an attentive mother and a father who knew how to be a man and provide for his family. Someone should have told us that our mom was mentally ill. Because her illness was undiagnosed, she made damaging choices with husbands and money, which snowballed into many other awful things. I've now come to recognize that I lived with a mentally damaged mother, but I always thought her behavior was normal. You can imagine how that influenced my behavior.

I'd like to go back in time with a solution to heal my younger self. When my mother set the expectation that little girls can get butchered and stuffed in plastic bags, I envision a voice of reason saying, "That was so wrong for her to say. You will be safe. That crime is not normal and won't happen. Your mother's brain isn't normal. That's why she does and says inappropriate things. This might not even be real news." I would have still been in shock and felt like I was wandering in a mirage for the following days, just like the *Looney Tunes* characters wandering in the desert. Without intervention, I was overwhelmed. However, with it, I would have been less entangled in the harsh reality that big kids could butcher and cut up neighbor girls into meat. To be pulled out of the constant and devastating teasing, as I call this behavior, I could have seen my Mom messing up.

John teased like this much more often than Mom, and at least she didn't abandon us kids or knowingly take part in our abuse. I focus on Mom because she wasn't evil like John and we were hers, not his. She was supposed to play a normal mother's role. The problem is that she actually could not be the voice of reason. Without an adult to help me, a deep understanding grew that I was weak, vulnerable, and cheap. I think many can relate to this, at least in some part. When we suffer, the life around us hurts too. Some people make awful choices and have sad lives. If we want to stop people from just dreaming of food and safe shelters, we can start programs and support people in many ways. This becomes more doable when we share our embarrassing stories and when we have more control and freedom, which we get through reconciling with our past.

My story starts by focusing on trauma in my impressionable years. Why? The same reason the medical community focuses on our origins. Medical professionals see childhood trauma as a negative investment in our health. Trauma grows in interest and the sooner it starts, the more compounded the trauma becomes. Doctors probe our stories to see where abuse has borrowed against our health. It's amazing how far-reaching abuse is and what can happen when healthy parents aren't an option.

It's surprising how even "lesser" abuses affect us. For example, we sometimes chose to get whipped with a switch instead of getting spanked on our bare behinds with a hand. There were times we couldn't face the humiliation of getting spanked bare bottomed, especially after the sexual abuse started. Interestingly, we kids won't refer to the spankings as abuse, only the sexual trauma or watching an animal being tormented. It's like the lesser abuse of being stuffed in a sack and being spanked the way we were just doesn't cut it.

Previous generations and many blue-collar families have tales about their whippings. Comedians of many kinds have entire routines on how they prepped for parental discipline with belt spankings. There are variations of punishment that are acceptable and some unfortunate stories that occur. However, I'm belaboring the point of abuse because I'm finding that when I am willing to be vulnerable in sharing my story (with God's guidance), I can use my inward sight to face deeply personal events, like lesser moments of humiliation such as bare spankings, to start pinpointing the roots of bitterness in my life. One grandiose moment of trauma doesn't have to be what created a bitter weed in my life but many little traumas instead. And getting belted by Daddy John because there was less shame still meant that I was getting marked with shame.

While I was in the storm of abuse, my shame felt like lava pouring down thick. Taunting words used to knock my little spirit down, and the objects like hot pans and sharp knives used to "teach" us kids lessons pelted me from everywhere. But when given the choice, my little body tried to preserve a modicum of dignity because shame is unnatural and doesn't mesh with who God created us to be. When an adult has already started sexually exploiting your body or when the charged atmosphere around you is foreboding, you have to choose a sharp whip over a hand navigating your private parts. Humiliation scorches our body the moment it gets touched, and the physical effects even look like burn marks against our skin. The types of trauma—like overt trauma of sexual or verbal abuse—seem like a demonic legion because abusive people find ways to make teasing a systemic problem.

When you are shown that you don't matter, whether through being forgotten for days or beaten, you learn that your life and actions don't matter. It's this and not the loud overt trauma that causes deep-seated hurt, bitterness, or anger to grow. Suffering at each type rewired my brain to an anxious, compulsive, or obsessive state as I played thoughts and feelings, past events, and possible future events on a loop for years. This haunting of the mind was an elephantine weight to carry. The irony is that because I was powerless in this god-awful planting of trauma and its growing side effects, I must also be powerless in its life-giving removal, trusting safe, loving people who will help me on my healing journey. When pain is too deeply planted, special people must reach the places we can't, and I've found that those with the most intimate relationships with the Lord have helped me greatly. Intimacy, not fearful isolation, brings me back to that sacred childhood place where no one ungodly could walk.

Fortunately for me, God read the story written on my heart and saw that I needed something good. I needed salve for my chapped spirit as I was without a loving, active father. I got this and more one afternoon visiting Mom's school a few months later around age five.

My mother's college auditorium was empty and dim except for the musicians. Without a babysitter, Mom needed us near but also away from her class. Too noisy for an empty classroom, Mom planted us in the auditorium, the place where warm spotlights and musical reverberations set the stage for the most mystical moment in my young life. The dark, secluded room absorbed us. With nothing around me but rows of chairs and mood lighting, clean, smooth notes molded mysterious dreams into my brain, and I was transformed like the Play-Doh that I often pressed into with my hands. I was enraptured.

The acoustics were brilliant with musical strings, melodies clear in the night-filled room. My face moved involuntarily, contorting on those rich notes. The conductor introduced the instruments when he turned and saw his tiny audience: woodwinds, the timpani, a bassoon, and a xylophone-like instrument that sounded like tinkling glass. That music was a substance virtually impossible to ingest all at once.

What I remember most is passion bursting from my body. Becky and Miah played in the aisles and hopped on the movie-style chairs, bouncing up and down. I sat absorbing and anticipating the next wave of intimate beauty, completely transfixed. This new, intense feeling and ability was something I craved—even just a part of—and likely will for eternity. I have drawn on this passion since the time it bloomed forth. Too soon, Mom took us home. But perfect, full love birthed a powerful, intimate passion that only the Creator himself could have made.

Chapter 4

People Are a Lesson or a Blessin'

*When I kept silent,
my bones wasted away
through my groaning all day long.*

—Psalm 32:3 NIV

AT SIX YEARS old, the summer of '89 was a time for severed family ties, shocking new relationships, and spilling your intimacies to strangers. Mom's parents were coming for a visit, then bringing us kids to Maine for a month. We'd see our dad and his family too. Miah was a blank slate, too young to remember Dad. We explained to Miah what Dad looked like and how he would dress. Dad had left the military when he left us, so he would wear civilian clothes and would wrestle around with us. "You'll like him." Dad wrote to us that his wife had older kids and we could play with them. With that, Miah was ready to meet the dad he couldn't remember.

We packed our things with Mom's help. We thought the long, cramped drive from Georgia to Maine with Grampa; his second wife, Peggy; and their daughter, Rona, was just the start of a vacation with no understanding that Daddy John had gone AWOL from the Army and that Mom needed us somewhere else during this time. But then, we were too young to know a lot of things. We didn't really know what several weeks away from home meant, we didn't understand that our abuse would naturally unfurl in that time like an overripe fiddlehead fern, and we didn't expect a summer vacation to become an extended stay with a severely mentally unstable step-grandmother. In fact, my brother, sister, and I ended up living with my grampa and step-gramma for nine long months so filled with her likely schizophrenic turmoil, we swore up and down that we lived with them for at least two years.

News of our abuse in Georgia leaked over a bowl of spilled cereal. I immediately tried to rub the milk into the carpet and cover it with the bowl. This small event triggered a reaction and a comment from my sister about how mad Daddy John would get if he knew I was making a mess. That caught the attention of adults.

"What does that mean?" they asked.

So I told them about getting a lickin' when we acted up, sometimes with a switch. I told them a story about Daddy John threatening to get a myrtle bush switch if we were bad. I shared the ominous story and explained that a myrtle switch would be extra painful especially on a bare bottom.

Peggy loved gossip and attention—she craved them more than her basket of prescription pills. But what the enemy intends for evil, God uses for good. Peggy made a big stink about what she heard regarding John putting hot pans on our skin and the knife games. Word spread like wildfire, causing police and social workers to materialize. Peggy had her own ideas on what other abuses could have happened, and our skinny frames and cheap hand-me-downs helped corroborate these ideas, so more tests than necessary were performed. She wasn't worried about us kids feeling further violated from all the physical and mental exams, photographs of our genitals, and visits with numerous social workers. Peggy was on a mission to expose Daddy John and my mother, who Peggy insisted was involved and probably encouraged the abuse. My little girl objections and corrections were too small to carry weight, and our new world was too confusing with all the commotion and the strangers.

Gramma Peggy was an alien force that made us laugh with her overt sexual references. She loved Miah's "sexy bedroom eyes," her way of complimenting Miah on those long-curled lashes. Those dark tendrils brought murmurs of admiration from Peggy's friends, and she would laugh along with them and comment, "If only he was a little Black boy fanning me and feeding me grapes." She incessantly talked about men and flirted with our male doctors and nurses, asking them if they would examine her the way they examined us.

I watched their reactions, too young to understand the context but absorbing that shocking people was a great way to get a reaction. A neglected middle child with ADHD (which would remain undiagnosed for decades) needs attention and stimulation, and during the time we lived with Peggy—where I lived in a state of hyperawareness—and the years Peggy spent living nearby after, I used her behavior as a model, having no real understanding of what that meant. I thought her wild nature was fearfully animalistic and entertaining when telling the kids at school about her. I mimicked her to get laughs for years to come and to ease my inner pain.

We preferred spending time with Grampa, but too often "the old battle axe" got on his nerves, so we spent far too much time under the influence of our grandmother. I distinctly remember playing alone outside and wondering if I was losing my mind. I felt like Gramma made my head swell inside and hurt. But what recourse was there? Peggy was a whirlwind of sexual jokes, stories, hypercritical judgments on other churchgoers, and a magnet for soap opera like drama. If soap operas weren't playing on TV, they played around us.

Peggy and her high school–aged daughter compared romantic fantasies and gossiped about who wanted to have sex with whom in their Baptist church. This was so typical that it only stands out in my mind because I was met with utter silence (a rarity) from both Gramma Peggy and Rona when I repeated verbatim a conversation the two of them had about a high school friend who contracted herpes from her boyfriend—who Rona had rejected, of course. When Mom found out a great deal of time later, she was flabbergasted at the vulgarity planted in my prepubescent mind. But like I said, Mom found out a great deal later.

While we were in Maine, John was arrested for going AWOL and both he and Mom were accused of child abuse. This meant more time in Maine living as wards of the state (at least that's what Peggy said) and more interrogative attention for "the abused kids" as we were referred to by Peggy, her daughter, and their church friends. Rona's boyfriend (and eventual first husband), Chris, sympathetically took us three kids and Rona to see Disney's *The Little Mermaid*. It was my first time in a cinema, and the five of us shared a bag of popcorn my aunt smuggled into the movie under her coat until we entered the dark room with the dry November air and sticky floor. The movie played, and there was a cartoon version of Gramma on the screen in the form of the sea witch Ursula.

Peggy looked, behaved, and sounded just like her except the villain was less sexual and more subdued. The resemblance was uncanny: the way the two women ate, the pronunciation, the makeup, and their squishy, fatty bodies. While John was scary and mean, Peggy possessed a special talent for being boisterously humorous and frightening. The bawdy woman was sloppily overweight and exercised deception and manipulation like a body builder. I found her stimulating and funny. I was afraid of her. I detested the burn of the wooden spoons she used to slap us if we didn't clean our plates or wash the dishes the right way. My face burned when getting "jack slapped," as Becky called it. I knew Ursula, this other Peggy.

When we drove home from the movies, I noted that Ursula looked like Gramma Peggy. Chris and Rona laughed heartily. "The hair is different," he joked.

Becky innocently added, "Ursula lives in the water. If she made us scratch her back, all that skin wouldn't come off under our nails." Peggy's love of having her hair pulled and her bare back scratched until dander collected under our fingernails was disgusting.

Rona snorted. "Ursula never had electroshock that made stuff leak from her ears and probably wouldn't put you kids in dumpsters to look through trash." Clearly us kids held no position in the house. "Don't tell any of this to Gramma Peggy," Rona commanded, but keeping secrets turned our world upside down.

We weren't allowed to go home or talk with our mother and loved ones because the explosive secret about the child abuse had detonated on us, and the trauma from that devastation left me crying in the night for a mom I couldn't have. I for one was too shell-shocked to keep even healthy secrets. So I tested the waters and told Gramma Peggy that she looked like Ursula but that Ursula didn't make anyone scratch her back. Peggy reprimanded me, telling me that I needed to be a good girl and that God was watching everything I did. Having heard this before, I felt with certainty that she was right. There would be no mercy, and between domineering Peggy and Daddy John, home was not only an unsafe place, but there was no escape. Conforming meant survival even when I felt madness taking over.

I disappointed myself if God saw me not on my best behavior and felt often anxious if grown-ups were present. Peggy emphasized a need to be unrelentingly well behaved and took major pride in showing off our Southern manners while any deviation met with punishment. She brought us to her church where the children's group further cemented that kids needed to be good to have value in God's eyes. Although I've never come across Christians who believe this incorrect instruction in my adult life, it was pervasive in my childhood. For some reason, bad influences on many levels weaseled into my upbringing.

I knew from the Southern Pentecostal church in Georgia and Peggy's Baptist church that I needed to be a good girl and a servant. The servants I saw were not people who volunteered or were missionaries loving on others but characters on TV and in books like Cinderella. Those were the models who were always called servants. I learned subservience from my biological dad's family too. It was just the order or caste to which we belonged. This order marinated around me. An example: Years later when I was around fourteen, a woman returned me home from babysitting. She wouldn't stop talking, I "knew" it was wrong to interrupt her to tell her I needed the bathroom, and my pants were dark, so I did the polite thing and peed myself. The woman didn't have to know, and I wasn't being rude.

Because people in my youth enforced a twisted servility and oversight in teaching, Christianity—or at least the church—also became perverted for me. Adults trying to get kids to behave often oversimplified teachings to our detriment, and though many in the church likely knew my grandmother was not of sound mind, they helped enforced incorrect dogma and my negative self-assessments that I could never be good enough—not until death, when I could enter heaven and be perfected. But I wouldn't fall in love with suicide or death for a few more years. Living with Peggy wasn't a time of reaping but of sowing.

I'm unable to put into words how damaging my grandmother and her church circle's hypocrisy was, but my grandmother's church was the predominant church in my young, impressionable life. Though we remained in attendance for a few short years, that church was where my spiritual life was molded and where a fear of church and Christians started. I was so vulnerable and wounded that my experiences simply lived in me as fact. Becky still dislikes Baptist churches to this day and struggles to set foot in one not because she remembers that Peggy and her people were horrendous to us kids, but because she remembers through the lens of her wounds what it felt like to be a little girl constantly forced to dress and act the way a religious fundamentalist made her. The soul-crushing fear and powerlessness affected our lives.

We couldn't complain or frown because at one point, Mom was living in a homeless shelter in Maine trying to regain custody of us kids, and we knew we had been told by many people we were lucky to have food and shelter when no one else wanted us, but acting good all the time felt like not being real. If I cried, Peggy said I was "seeking attention," which was shameful. So much of being good was dependent on a woman who was too volatile for me to read, so I tried never to make mistakes and did my best to have perfect manners and posturing. Being performance ready all the time is just PTSD in the making, but kids don't know that, so we kept trying.

I remember a nice red-headed guy in children's church telling us to love God. I wrote on the side of my KJV Bible, "I love Good." I meant *God*, but it just slipped out. I closed my Bible after the group and joined Peggy, wondering when we could leave. Gramma Peggy was talking to a few church people, and I learned from her that the red-headed teacher was "a molester" but he seemed nice to me. Peggy had more to say to a friend and Rona about the man going to hell because he used to be Catholic or something, so we walked to the Farrington Elementary playground next door.

The adults walked off to the far side of the playground where they referred to the pale red head as an albino and some other things while Becky and I tossed rocks through an open mailbox attached to a playhouse. I lowered myself from the top of the playhouse through a pulley hanging from playground equipment. I quickly became tangled in the chain, which was wrapped tight around my neck. I was stuck. The grown-ups were too far to hear screaming, so Becky stopped trying to hold me up while I hung and ran to get them.

With the chain around my neck, it was hard to swallow against the python pressing against me. I could barely make a sound beyond a whimper. I hung there, no voice, looking at the sandy, pebbly dirt, around the empty playground and at the fluffy white clouds floating across the sky fast on the wind. Time didn't stand still for me and neither did Becky. It took a long time for help to arrive but not my sister. She ran right back to me until the adults walked over and I could be released from the coiled chain.

It wasn't until Mom got custody again that I would see a doctor for painful neck and head aches that have stalked me ever since that day on the playground, but she didn't have custody for some time yet. When Daddy John's court-martial for going AWOL started, we kids were simply shifted to stay with whoever would have us without anyone evaluating, it seems, the safety of our new environment. When my seven-year-old neck became permanently damaged with what I call migraines in the neck, no one noticed. I mean, grown-ups would give me an ice pack or pills, but I needed to wait until Mom was available so she could cradle my sobbing head in her hand, providing gentle traction and a neck massage. The relief rinsed away some of the ache, but the stain of the injury could only be treated through letting a chiropractor twist and crack my neck.

Around the time of the neck injury, the court-martial, and the mediocre child play therapists, we got reacquainted with our real dad and his side of the family, the Vigues. Dad's deep brown, silky-soft hair had such a dark shine it looked black. More than one of the Vigue family members said he looked like his father. Unlike Grampa Vigue, raised on an American Indian reservation living so hard on the bottle that he never learned to read or write, Dad was able to hold down a warehouse job driving forklifts. He was fun and felt like a dad should, when he wasn't with his ultrastrict, prudish second wife. There were spells when he entered a room and made us feel like the sun was shining and the day was gorgeous. We didn't mind his missing front teeth. The only thing we minded was when he grew out a mustache that somehow made him look like Jon Arbuckle from *Garfield and Friends*. We had a blast teasing him and so did he, but Dad's wife would unfeelingly comment on the scene before her that we were being immature and childish.

"Kids that age should respect their elders and speak only when they are spoken to."

"I asked them what they thought of my new look," Dad said, defending us. "That Jon Arbuckle must be a handsome guy."

We smiled and climbed on him, and he wriggled around on the floor. We called it wrestling, but the only other move besides trying to knock Dad on the floor through headbutts was to put a smelly foot near his face. He exaggerated a smell, following with gagging coughs, declaring, "PU. There's a skunk in the house. You win, agh!"

His wife discouraged this behavior and disliked how wound up we were. She especially didn't like Becky and me. "Girls are too hard to raise. They can get pregnant and they're emotional. That's why we can't have this."

Dad would not be seeking custody or letting us stay with him beyond a weekend. His wife wasn't bad; she just belonged in the 1800s and not in 1989. Dad could be a fun dad for a weekend—he had potential—but he wasn't ready to be a father.

There we survived, missing Mom (who was trying to regain custody of us while juggling life with John's family, who started to scatter when other abuses and rapes within the family and community were murmured about) and our home but adjusting. Presents from Mom back home (dolls, pretty bathing suits, and even a Barbie case) were exceptional—unlike presents we would have gotten while still in Georgia. Mom must have really missed us and gone without to splurge on such nice gifts. The problem was that they were all taken from us and given away. Us three kids were back to our threadbare clothes. I wondered why our cousin (the bratty girl everyone referred to as spoiled rotten) got to have our nice things and not us. Peggy's son had a daughter who was a favorite and everything went to her.

"I can't find my Barbie case. How did it get lost?" I asked Peggy one afternoon.

"That wasn't yours. That was for your cousin Christina," Peggy stated.

"No, that was mine from Mom for my seventh birthday. It's hard but squishy and has big bubbles on the outside, not the kind you blow because they're plastic. The case is purple, and my Barbies and doll clothes are in there with pointy shoes that make the lady feet really high like this." I plopped my body on the floor and mimicked Barbie's stiletto-shaped feet, pulling hard against my bare toes. "Mom wrote about it in my letter, and it was in that big package with my new bathing suits," I earnestly explained.

"Those toys weren't meant for you. Christina's mother gave her those. She's supposed to have those. Your mom hasn't sent you anything. She doesn't write to you."

I didn't understand what Peggy was doing at the time. My fancy toy was gone, and it wasn't fair. On the times we found out that Christina got our toys, she didn't even know they were intended for us unless we confronted her. "Hey, that's mine."

She would holler back, and Peggy would come to Christina's defense. The only thing that worked was when Becky fought back. Though only four years older than me, she fought back hard. I was simply too sensitive and internalized not being good enough to have the presents. My bathing suits went to Christina, even when they were way too tight for her body. I remember seeing her wearing my clothes or getting to wear them after she had stretched them out and feeling my spirit resign. It hurt to feel empty.

When it came time to fly down to Georgia to testify against Daddy John, I wasn't ready, but I walked into the courtroom as directed by adults after getting just a few short minutes with Mom, the first in months. Peggy had scalded me with hot shower water that morning. She wanted me to be squeaky clean, but it was a shower she couldn't operate well, so she turned it on hot and I screamed a scream that echoed off the copper-colored stone floor and grey-tiled walls. She was so mad at me for piercing her ears, but Grampa called her a numbnut for having a kid stand in a stream of hot water.

"I didn't know it would be boiling hot," she hissed. She was always hissing like a snake, even when she laughed. "Besides I like it scalding. It's good for your skin."

I walked into the courtroom feeling electricity on my still tender skin. I stole a look at Daddy John with his head hanging. I was told not to look at him, but like my skin, I was sensitive to everything. Too sensitive to share the sexual abuse when I took the stand but strong enough to say, "There was sexual abuse and physical abuse with hot pans and hot spoons and the knives."

When pressed by the military lawyer for details on the sexual abuse, I just sat in silence. The lawyer prodded me for more information. I felt the nervous energy in the courtroom though most of the chairs were empty in the audience. Honesty meant so much to me: I had to state again that there was sexual abuse because it was the truth, but I was humiliated by it. After much pressure from the lawyer saying that what I described wasn't sexual abuse, I just shook my head and let the man say what he wanted. He was a grown-up in charge, and my people taught me subservience through dominating me, so I couldn't state the sexual abuse. Failure is humiliating, even when you should be used to it. For going AWOL and abusing three children, Daddy John was sentenced to fifteen years in prison, and that's all I heard.

During this time in my life, my brain slowly started passing along to my heart collected moments that would eventually build up to formulate reasons to feel and act. What I mean is, unlike other kids, I watched and absorbed life incessantly, but I couldn't always make feelings come out of me. It's like I was just taking things in, storing them, and not speaking up or reacting (the way my sister did) until years later. Becky retorted and pushed back when needed, whether she was successful or not. I didn't have this in me. So many adults didn't really see me or pull anything out of me. Could they have? I simply knew there was a barrier of some sort and have only in my adult life heard autistic-type people say they remember, before being medicated, being trapped in their bodies. I just got stuck.

The grown-ups around me had forgotten what kids feel, and they went about their lives. I often looked at grown-ups with their unseeing eyes and wondered at my own dead eyes looking back at me in the mirror. My eyes looked different from what they used to. I didn't see anything in them that other peoples' eyes had. I was numb throughout. Between hiding from Daddy John and Peggy's demands for perfect performance, hiding in plain sight was second nature. Even if hiding wasn't needed anymore, it takes years for life blood to circulate back into your spirit, healing traumatic numbness. Only then can emotions trigger normal human reactions. Child abuse and poverty delay the ability to become a true human and not a dazed creature.

More mental conflict brewed when my biological dad commented and guffawed about what the narcissist Daddy John would experience upon being sentenced to prison for child molestation: "You know what happens to those people in prison." Adults forget that children are smart little sponges. I knew what he meant, and it broke my heart. Dad was the one who brought John into our lives, and now he derided him.

Remember when Daddy John taught "compassion" for others? "You better tell people that you love them. Tell them Jesus cares or they could grab a jar of pills and kill themselves like Annie in the Petra song." The thought of Daddy John being molested by grown men made me intensely sad. The feelings flooded over me and joined with the guilt I felt over testifying against my stepfather in court, sending him to the same shame and pain I understood. And Becky's testimony was what "put John away" as I wasn't strong enough to speak up. Instead of taking away someone else's burden like I was commanded to do, I was forced to share mine with John. This was the last thing I needed.

At the time of my biological dad's comment, my brother, sister, and I were trying to acclimate to cold, dry New England. Through bloody stools; nosebleeds; cracked skin; and the sicknesses attached to threadbare clothes, malnutrition, and dietary changes, we had no healing. This worsened when Peggy, who played the part of our guardian, drank our medicine. It was a confusing time. Why would Peggy drink the medicine that tasted like burnt butterscotch when the doctor told us kids to drink it? The medicines with fewer flavors were still manna to her hypochondriac mind. This life with people who lacked any form of character or sensitivity only accelerated my internal conflict.

Starved for love and attention, I needed security, safety from bullying, and justice, not revenge. I had to settle for Peggy and an aunt who was as pretty as a princess but as spoiled as a thousand-year-old egg.

"Close your eyes. I have a present for you," Rona said one afternoon.

I was shrewd to her game. No way was Peggy's daughter going to give me a present.

"No, really. I have a present for you," she said again. "Close your eyes and hold out your hand. Come here. I don't feel like getting up."

She was leaving high school; I was entering first grade. I knew my place.

Holding out my right hand, I felt the saliva and sticky clump land in my palm. I opened my eyes as my half aunt laughed, then repulsion hit me as I realized she had spat gray chewed gum right into my hand. My "present." I ran to the trash, threw it away, and scrubbed my hand clean.

Ugh, I should have known!

Bearing the brunt of "games" like this might seem light compared to serious bullying, but it wasn't. It left its mark, and even the smell of gum still turns my stomach, especially because there were other instances like this. Some people in my childhood were just gross and were allowed to control far too much of my life.

After nine months that felt like two years, Mom was allowed custody.

Some don't understand why my mom lost custody since she wasn't an abuser. Mom says she was told she lost custody but was lied to by Peggy and the social worker. Did our little family slip through the cracks and suffer needlessly? Did military involvement make things more complicated? Did a very manipulative grandmother who wanted money from the state to look after kids scam the system? I've heard worse stories than mine, so my response is: Why would anyone be surprised that three unwanted, abused kids were left in crappy circumstances, and who would have taken us in anyway? We weren't wanted by anyone other than Mom. You can do a lot to unwanted kids, and when they don't have resources, they don't really have a voice or, as the Vigues would say, they don't "have a pot to piss in." So once Mom got us back in 1990 and our second dad moved to prison, it was just the four of us, and that was exactly how I wanted things to be, though we lived in the same low-income apartment complex as Gramma and Grampa. But I had Mom back, and I liked to talk to her. She was my everything though she was juggling work and raising three kids as a single mom while her husband was incarcerated.

When the year 1991 had already peaked and 1992 was turning heads away from the now useless year, I told Mom how I felt about Dad's comment on what happens to pedophiles in prison and about Daddy John having to go to court and jail. It was in this dialogue I felt another imprint in my life forming when I started questioning how unaware someone I love could be. My mom was unaware, but she recognized my precociousness (having developed certain abilities at an earlier age than usual) and could provide me with answers and context that helped me understand situations better. She reached out to her child, who knew too much.

"You kids didn't need to testify. The case workers and John's brother gave enough information."

"Why did we have to go through that then, Mom?"

"Because you kids weren't being protected! I was so angry that Peggy created a circus and wanted you kids on the stand! I wasn't allowed to see you or do anything about it because she said I knew about the abuse."

"Yeah, I heard her telling people that. You didn't see what we wanted you to see. When we told you John was mean when you weren't around, you told him what we said."

"I didn't realize." Mom wasn't making eye contact. "I had to bathe you kids in brown water at the last house, and I never had to do that growing up. I was provided for, but I thought I could take care of you kids and work and go to school like my mother did. She could do everything, and John was my soulmate. I trusted him."

"I know. So one of Daddy John's brothers said something? To the court?" I asked.

"Yes. John's mom and sister said something but not in court. Sister or not, her brother did something to her toddlers. John's aunt was at the house when this came up. We were talking, and she said something in front of her husband really quiet. He raped his aunt. His mom made a comment once too."

This was news to me, but Mom wouldn't tell me more. I was too young at that moment to hear about Daddy John's own child abuse being discovered. Mom left off telling me that John wasn't a pervert as I parroted Peggy's description of him, but Mom simply explained Daddy John "had a demon in him." She said this a few times because she missed him, writing letters to him in prison. Through the lens of distance from Daddy John, I realized with both heart and mind that there was another kid out there with no protection and no voice; he'd just grown up and that was all. That's what John was to me—my daddy but dangerous.

In a later conversation, I asked about our toys, since when we left Georgia, each of us kids left with a suitcase and nothing else.

"The neighbors stole everything from the trailer," Mom said. "When we went to court, they broke in and stole the TV, your clothes, and toys. We'll see if we can find some of them through Avon and get you kids new ones. You've been through enough. That's why I was so upset when I found out Peggy was giving all the toys and clothes I sent up to Maine for you kids to Christina."

"Yeah" was my forlorn reply. "I really liked that Barbie case. It was purple and had shiny dark pink bubbles on the cover that came out like this." I started gesturing with my hand to show the exterior of the portable doll house.

The next part of the conversation involved an animated child describing toys and bathing suits to the very mother who had bought them for her. She let me get lost in the excitement and expounded on why she got them and how I would have matched my stepcousins back home.

Money was still tight since we were three kids and a single mom. Dad's child support was meager and unreliable, so we learned the monotony of poverty and how it forces you to live. A life of routine simplicity with untreated ADHD makes your brain buzz with boredom and a lack of vitality. Sometimes, the buzzing was audible. This made for an overwhelming force to fight simply to feel normal. If I had been diagnosed and treated, maybe sitting around in front of a TV when we visited Dad wouldn't have felt so draining, but I remember feeling like someone cut me and my life was draining from me and that my soul, whatever that was, would eventually be empty. We moved around in the apartment complex but stayed in Augusta, Maine and still attended Peggy's church from time to time. Our roles were either victim or survivor, well behaved or frustrated, hopeful or stained. But we made life work. Mom would read to us three kids at night, and there, snuggled together in her bed, we found the *Summer of the Monkeys* and *Where the Red Fern Grows*.

The story time stopped when Mom married her third husband (Mark) in 1993. He wasn't her soulmate, but after her romance with John turned into devastation and judgment against her from everyone in her family, she learned that marrying a safe man who could provide financially was what she should do.

We still saw Dad on some weekends. He'd buy us each a huge Pepsi, and we played games and watched a lot of TV when with him. Once he divorced his second wife, he moved back home with his mom, sister, and nephew into a two-bedroom trailer. It was cluttered with junk and an addition had to be added, but we made it work. We didn't have our older stepsiblings to play with anymore, but with Dad's last wife gone, he had more vitality. He told us kids we should move in with him, but we looked around at the disheveled, cramped trailer and the abandoned school bus on the lot where he stored his things and the small couch where he slept. There was no room for us kids. So we stayed with Mom and moved to the country to a small Maine town called Litchfield with Mark and his two wild sons, a place where solitude intertwined with isolation and nature nurtured adventure.

With my dad and former stepdad in my memory, I struggled to match my mom with this third man. He looked fresh from a remote mountain with scraggly facial hair and lines on his face like an old-time mill worker. His face was somehow like crinkled paper. Mark was gross with constant and loud flatulence from mouth to bottom. Farts bubbled out of him like boiling-hot mud. The burps of steaming tar pits on TV shows about ancient times always reminded me of him.

But at least the loneliness in my chest was assuaged when the two new stepbrothers entered the scene. My sister was boy crazy and always off with her friends, my brother had some neighborhood friends, but I always felt so alone. The stepbrothers were unclean and unruly, used to living on the untended farm in Litchfield or being with a babysitter (they were close in age to us) while their gruff, Homer Simpson–like dad worked two states away, spending nights in Massachusetts and only returning to Maine to care for his kids on the weekend. He was verbally abusive and ignorant, and his sons had nasty personal hygiene I'd never seen. Their diet consisted of fatty sausages, leftover lard, and bloody, red cold cuts—nothing like the lean turkey pastrami deli meat or the chicken and spinach roulade Mom preferred to buy when she received food stamps. But together we grew a large garden, and there's nothing like vegetables fresh from the garden!

Becky had been diagnosed with bipolar when she was in junior high and remained out of control, so the move to Litchfield was supposed to pull her away from bad influences in town, forcing a fresh start in the country. The remoteness was too isolating for me, but it was what Mom thought Becky needed. What manic depressive entering high school wouldn't struggle with the change? But she didn't just struggle.

A couple years later, a failed suicide attempt would splice through our lives when Becky swallowed all her pills. Therapy based on recounting the child abuse over and over again impeded the healing process—Becky still talks about how infuriating the repetitious therapy was and that her medication didn't stabilize her at all. I wondered, *Will she stay lost in this mental anguish . . . gone? Couldn't anyone help her?* This and the clash between the two sides of our family certainly added fuel to our scorched past. My sister recovered, and family blending counselors started working with us for a time. Miah was doing pretty well and flourished in sports. But I still yearned for the home of my past with the first stepdad's family and the creepy trees that acted as canopies along the Southern roads. Just because times were hard in Georgia doesn't mean I didn't consider Daddy John's family my own, and it was the first place I ever really called home. I missed my granny, classmates, and cousins, and I was only eleven when we moved to Litchfield, still young and dependent.

How do you take a break from life and go to a place where sisters don't want to die? You mentally retreat and yearn for a place that you know. Even with only having lived in Georgia for a few years and even with the abuse, there was less chaos in my life and more tenderness from family there, and we missed that warmth and being in a place we called home. What I knew there filled all my senses, and I missed every corpuscle of comfort and identity found there. Identity juggling was exhausting! *Who am I, where do I belong, who am I supposed to be, and who will I be?* These thoughts echoed in my prepubescent brain as often as did, *You're walking the line between sanity and insanity.* That old familiar warning seems to have started well before I entered double digits and stayed with me for many years. It wasn't about to leave just because I was older now. What could I do other than pull away from the mental line that meant danger? *I'm overwhelmed! Can I just go home where I belong? I belong in the South with friendly family around me and not starting over at yet another school with kids who make fun of me.*

My young mind wrestled its own thoughts, but was John's family, left behind in Georgia the summer of '89, any better than Mom's family in Maine? *They are no different and I know this, but I feel closer to them and never got to say goodbye. Did all the Georgia family fall apart after John's arrest, or are they still around? There can't be anyone left, and there's nothing left for me. All I can do is move on, but to where?* During this season of life, the Oklahoma City bombing made the news, Mom had married the second stepdad, and I disappeared into books, trying to escape my life.

One weekend, Mark asked Mom where I was, and she realized she hadn't seen me for a few days. Physically, I was in my room, still dressed in pajamas, finishing a Christian fiction book series. Mentally, I was in a world where I was free, and that's all that mattered. Also, people come and go in your life, like characters in a book. But when you close the cover, you still have the option to return to that time and place, sort of.

In my life, there were several moves and beloved people leaving without return and with plenty of dysfunction. This meant no returning. Visiting a former housing complex or school resulted in seeing empty places or new faces, not in a reunion or anything that provided closure. When a friend or I moved, they were gone for good. So I cried when my books ended because life overlapped into my fantasy world and my book people were gone, not quite ever to be the same. Even when Mom saw me in book-induced comas, I couldn't react to her glances.

One day, I stared vacantly out a general store restaurant window, ramrod still (like I had left my body) except for my moving lips silently mouthing what characters in my mind were saying to each other. Mom started mimicking me and chuckling. She thought I was being silly, not that there was something wrong with me like an undiagnosed disorder. When I accidently started up again—no doubt my rabbit-like brain was bored from waiting for food—she mimicked me again. Embarrassed, I planned to dive into my books as soon as I got home to be with people who wouldn't mock me.

I related to the love and shared the pain of my book family, especially in stories about small-town living, historical fiction, and slave narratives. They dealt with hard living and trauma like I had, only their settings were different enough from my life. Therefore, I had a reading addiction. People need community and freedom, and I had to get these from books even though they only existed in my mind. I certainly didn't trust the Pentecostal church we started attending since the Baptists warned me about them and their hell-bound, modern rock music. And now living in a family of seven on one income (Mom hurt her back and couldn't work, but Mark still worked in Massachusetts as an engineer and we had some child support money coming in from Dad), I was afforded few opportunities for emotional health. Living in a dream world helped me to soldier on through life, which has both negative and positive attributes.

Sometimes, you can't soldier on because you need help, and that's where I was. After turning twelve, I twice felt a layer of depression cover me like a cloak that I couldn't shake off. I explained to Mom that one layer could be from the child abuse and our lifestyle. The second layer could be from becoming a teenager. All we could do was ask a neuropsychologist to evaluate me.

Chapter 5

Puberty POW

Fathers, do not provoke your children to anger.

—Ephesians 6:4 ESV

In the waiting room at the neuropsychologist's office, a frail young girl stood next to an aging woman. Her frizzy permed hair rested on her awkward young body. In an instant, I marked the older woman as the girl's grandmother and guardian and focused on the girl, an easy target who would break with very little effort on my part. She was so weak. A wild mustang stallion will savagely kill the mare's young if it's born weak. In fact, if the newborn colt doesn't learn to walk within hours, you might see a mare hiding it from the stallion before he can stomp and shake the colt to death. That primitive charge was in me.

With gritted teeth like fangs, I focused on that girl who fit the profile of prey. I couldn't fight this laser-like awareness. The ache of abuse imprints in a survivor's mind so she learns to regard the abuser's triggers as survival mechanisms. See what he sees or else you'll be caught unaware. Unfortunately, the very adaptability that allowed me to endure the viciousness of child trauma deeply marked my physical body to react like my abuser.

Using these predator lenses, I knew this girl had no chance to escape what could be done to her by bad guys. The girl wasn't very different from my sister either, just younger. I simultaneously wanted to sink my fangs into her and cover her from the attack. Wanting to slap or bite her isn't dark to some, but it's a feeling that a compassionate kid finds repulsive, and that nastiness was amplified because I knew it didn't belong in me. My gut wrenched at what the eyes of a predator showed as they aggressively wrapped around my once humane, bleeding heart.

Abuse teaches survival of the fittest, but the inhumanity of such an abusive theory clung to me. Learning to see people the way your predator did is so instinctual and is *very* hard to fight. There has to be a demonic transference at some level, I think. But I believe this was my first overwhelmingly large dark moment like this.

This supernatural, evil overflow just sticks to you. It's not something I chose—it chose me. I wonder if this dark spirit transferred from John to me and I was left to battle it as a child. My choice was to keep the nastiness there inside my body, radiating but locked tight away from hurting anyone but myself.

In the neuropsych's office, I spoke with him (as I had with others) about this feeling I had regarding the girl as I had done with others as a means of searching for help. There were past events like this that I fought, testifying to grown-ups what I felt. Once the abuse was made public, I had few secrets I could keep. My body ricocheted secrets, which mostly proved helpful, except for developing a reputation for having a "big mouth" and, of course, with these predatorial eyes. No one seemed to do anything when I shared the darkness in me. I concluded to the doctor, "I don't hurt anyone, but I still feel this need to hurt. I know who's weak. I can't get it out. It's just in me and part of me."

The doctor thought I was fine because I was able to use reasoning to not act on my feelings. My brother, sister, and I had already gone through play therapy as kids, so I thought that if this doctor decided I was just very self-aware and mature enough that I could outgrow these disempowering goggles, then I would.

The doctor's findings after running several diagnostic tests: "Sarah's memory is highly elevated, off the charts. Congratulations. She also appears to be left handed. Twice she caught objects without hesitation. Great reflexes and no problems with her mind."

Sigh. I played baseball a little as a kid so as a right-hander, I learned to catch with my left. So his comment (despite my corrections during the test) frustrated me, and my loneliness—feeling like I didn't belong anywhere—and my sadness made his statement confuse me like a mosquito at an off-season nude beach! What was I supposed to do? What about the pressing I felt affecting my whole life? What I now know to be depression was a physical pressing down of my body, like gravity was my enemy, in addition to deep sadness and feeling unworthy. Who do you turn to when the helpers can't help?

The double-layered cloak stayed on, never leaving. But if I couldn't keep the depressive cloak off, I would at least fight the makings of malevolence when it appeared. Every ounce of perseverance in my life was directed to the fight against becoming a predator, someone who wants to lash out at others—a very real and sick threat even if the only ones who understood that were the actual abusers themselves. One of my many mottos was, *I might be a witch, but I'll be a good witch!*

Feeling weighed down by the world, I tried to turn my melancholy and turmoil into motivation to strive for better, fighting through life. However, I craved people who burned deep inside like me, the ones who burned for a vitality they couldn't outwardly feel, burned with hunger, impassioned to be lost or saved. The ones living in the margins knew how I felt, ones who quietly wrestled with the frenzy or boisterously sunk their teeth into our inanimate lives; they were my desired people, and I sought them through any medium, whether in fiction or in truth. With no relief from the blaze inside us, we lived in broken desire, but there we'd have each other. My mental frenzy, the offspring of childhood sexual trauma, caused my body to wrestle itself because love had been awoken "before it is ready" (Song of Solomon 8:4 CEV). This Bible verse isn't saying that all sex pertains to love but that sex triggers feelings and reactions that should happen only in loving situations at the right time. Instead of entering the gateway into healthy, beautiful, intimate love, abuse victims are pushed through the gateway of darkness where deception pervades.

I took solace in dark places, comfort in the shadowlands. They were relatable since I felt as cold and dark inside as they were. So, who prevents this? Who arms us, protects us? What are we to do? What person will hold your pain in sacred confidence while looking out for you? My answers were to walk the streets of hurt in the dregs of life, mindful of the safe shadows that hid me from dangers while reaching the sparse light, hoping that some misplaced savior would see me, love me, clean me inside and out.

Sometimes, I got lost in the darkness. Each time, I didn't recognize my own face. In panes of glass or mirrors, I didn't just look like a stranger—I was. An image often came to me of a death that would be caused by my own hands. I stared into this vision where my body lay in a field. My right side lay in view in lush green grass with my blood returning to the earth where it belonged. Both beautiful and peaceful, this image gave me hope for release, and I kept this option in the back of my mind as I resigned my suicidal fate to a day when it was only absolutely necessary.

Puberty needed my attention more than this forecast. Anxiety came to me when boys and men took more of an interest in me. I learned to arm myself with acting clueless to their advances. Flirtations from boys or men ogling my body made my face burn crimson. If playing dumb didn't stop the unwanted attention, I learned that acting abnormal, almost crazed worked. Fighting back or speaking up, even after being groped, seemed mean, so giving an attitude was reserved as a backup for when flirtations turned into outright harassment. I struggled with laying down these defenses until necessary as I had post-traumatic stress in my past, a crude home life, and kids who labeled me as the weird new girl at school. There I talked incessantly or not at all, I spoke with an accent and about odd things for a child, I teared up if someone was kind or included me, and I spilled secrets and opinions without employing a verbal filter.

In the meantime, fantasyland, stories, and music were safe zones. We couldn't afford a flute, but the school had a free clarinet. I fell in love with it and played it often two hours a day, though when playing at home, I often whispered out the notes or simply fingered the keys without blowing so no one would hear me in the house where I inherently felt unsafe, even when the yelling and fighting took breaks. I was a fearful little mouse, afraid of being discovered squeaking out what felt like were expressions of myself. Unlike my sister who carved scars on her arm, I would squeeze a knife blade, not enough to draw blood, but enough to feel pain that I could fight against, feeling brave and strong at what I could tolerate. Oftener though, fear beat me from within. As a Christian now, I realize that something else was present. Through the Holy Spirit's wisdom, I see now that escapism and creative outlets were also seeds of hope.

I've also learned that if I had hope in my life in the mid-'90s, I must still have hope now even when the world feels heavy. When hope feels missing, it has simply been misplaced. When something is misplaced, there's a chance that it can be replaced. Moreover, when the Lord gives you this wisdom, the reclaiming and healing is already starting! The more we Christians are progressively emptied of guilt, fear, and other fleshly problems, the more room we have for the pieces of hope we've collected.

In the next few years, Miah excelled at sports, far outshining me. My efforts were on social climbing and grades. We made big strides, but my brother's progress grew almost exponentially while I eventually lost my social grip. I'd been running on fumes and fell so hard from social graces around ruthless kids that I often ate my lunch in the bathroom, not in the school cafeteria. I knew my place—a place that didn't exist. My former friends and my grade, even maybe the school, would be better if I wasn't there. With Becky now an adult on her own and Miah doing well, that absolutely necessary time to leave life brushed against me, much more intimately than before.

What does it take to deeply fatigue and depress a teen? Let the world chip away at her piece by broken-hearted piece until her soul aches. With eighth-grade bullying leaking into ninth grade at a larger school, my feeble hope turned into a romantic pining for a natural way to die. *Maybe I can waste away . . . It's not suicide if you simply stop living.* My *soul could float away on a cloud. That's how I'll get home.* And that's what I started doing. Coincidentally, an opportunity opened around this time for us to move again.

A day after my sixteenth birthday, Miah, Mom, and my youngest stepbrother (the eldest also moved out immediately after graduating) went to live near the second stepdad's job in southeastern Massachusetts. Many houses were actual estates with manicured lawns and nuclear families clearly upper middle class. They didn't have acre upon acre of land like we had in Maine, but these people didn't live on their grounds rent free as had been our situation. These people were big-time fancy.

My real dad wondered, "Why do you kids want to move all the way over to Massachusetts with a bunch of flatlanders?"

"We're fifteen and sixteen. Miah and I live wherever Mom does." I couldn't believe he didn't understand.

Dad implored, "I don't know why you don't come live with me and work at the warehouse."

"Dad, you hate your job. You always say how horrible the people are and that the office guys don't understand you or your work."

Apparently, that didn't take root. When we talked about the shock of living in a "rich" suburban area after barely getting by in a small town, Dad would reiterate, "You kids could come up here after college. The office jobs at work pay a lot! Take a dump before you clock out, and you get to sh*t on the company dime."

I laughed at the way Miah and I had chosen a different path from our all-talk-and-no-action dad.

Moving into the home we now shared with Mark's morbidly obese, hoarder mother, we did our best to settle. I avoided the maggots under the living room sofa and positioned my sleeping bag at night in bunches, trying to provide cushioning over the cat litter smeared across the carpet underneath me. I couldn't eat or drink in the house. A can of iced tea needed to be wiped down and drunk outside or I wouldn't be able to swallow the liquid that seemed to absorb the smell and disgust of the house. We unpacked the best we could in the cramped quarters.

"Mom, where are we going to put all our stuff?"

"We'll make room. Just keep unpacking, and we'll cram it all somewhere," she said.

I opened a box of teacups and started unwrapping the ceramic, my mouth dropping open. "You're not gonna believe this. No way!"

"What?"

"Come here. Look at this!"

"What—" Mom stopped mid-sentence when I handed her one of the ceramic cups wrapped not in protective newspaper but explicit pages from a magazine. Her eyebrows shot up as I uncrumpled the naked French maid photograph.

"They're all like this," I said with force. "I don't know whether to be upset or laugh because it's so hyperbolic. It's like a bad joke showing how trashy we are. I thought Mark got rid of the car full of porn back in Litchfield."

"I thought he had," she said.

Why are we always fresh meat for hungry men? Being female is awful, I thought.

Making a new start would be momentous and defying. I chose to be my own person, not surrendering to my home life, instead developing a thick streak of perfectionism and athleticism to avoid the meanness from Mark and his mom. Self-help was my idol for recovery, and I used it to stomp on my sorrows. I waterboarded them with tenacity, but my sorrows were masochistic and enmeshed with me tighter and tighter. I fought back, thinking that a muscular body would protect me from perceived danger when my powerful, sharply manipulative words failed. My brother and I became close companions, sharing the same friends and classes. I excelled in school, sports, and music, gaining grants and scholarships for college. Time moved on, and my graduation approached.

It was rare for Dad to go beyond the borders of Maine. But he picked up Becky from work, and they carpooled for four hours, not stopping for dinner, to attend my graduation. After all, why would they need to stop when he had a cooler full of his standard bologna sandwiches?

Dad and Becky arrived in a disheveled state. Hearing Dad's outburst and catching a glimpse of Becky's battle-fatigued face through the truck window, I handed her the Cup of Noodles and drinks I had bought. She breathed in deep, exiting the truck and tasting freedom. With relief, gratitude, and a weak smile, she walked with me into the house to eat something other than Dad's standard-issue bologna sandwiches.

"What happened? You're frazzled!"

"I don't know! Dad complained the whole way, but when we got to Boston, he got angry at all the traffic."

"Yeah, it's pretty bad at this time."

"He hates Boston. We got to that big tunnel, and he went off!" she said.

"Really, why?"

"Beats me! He just kept mouthing off to it, swearing at Boston and giving it the middle finger."

We had no idea what to think. He hadn't been a drunk since we were young.

Confused, I said, "He was in the military. He lived in Germany. Why can't he handle a tunnel? He's spent way too much time living in the middle of nowhere!"

"Yes, but your dad was a barracks rat in the military," Mom explained as she entered the room. "He didn't leave much."

Dad's mood lightened during the ceremony because graduating from high school was something he understood. Plus, we used the local concert arena and that had him floored. He was so excited at graduation that he hollered, "Who's your daddy? Who's your daddy?" when I crossed the stage to get my diploma.

The crowd laughed, but I cringed along with my classmates, thinking about the sexual innuendo that people meant when saying that phrase. I plastered a smile on my face and kept walking across the stage. He is so lucky I paid for him to stay in the nice hotel room and not the maid chamber! Money saved from my summer jobs paid for Dad's visit, but I didn't think my bribe would result in a malfunctioning dad. I just wanted a dad to acknowledge my accomplishments—not that I graduated but that I became normal enough to have friends, to pick a future, to survive this long.

Chapter 6
Hidden in Plain Sight

"I have become a foreigner in a foreign land."

—Exodus 2:22 NIV

COLLEGE CAME IN the next season, and autumn in western Massachusetts at UMASS Amherst stuns with beauty. At nineteen, I ran the 2001 Olympic Torch Relay and dreamed big dreams. Unfortunately, the heaviness of perfectionism literally broke my back. Pushing myself too hard in sports, at school, and at work—beyond what was healthy or safe—led to debilitating back pain. Home during college break, I got out of the shower and bent over to wrap my hair in a towel. When I straightened, sharp, burning pain fell on me like a heavy anvil and I couldn't stand. I desperately clung to the sink and a towel rack, holding my body weight, unable to control anything from my waist down. In the background of the moment while I dangled helpless in the bathroom, the television played, and the noises of the house continued like my life wasn't altering.

It's odd that I captured my environment during the greatest physical pain in my life, especially when my frantic thoughts screamed, *I'm paralyzed! Paralyzed but I can feel the pain! It's over. I can't stand. I can't...* Isn't that how trauma is? The severe pain distracted me from my fatiguing arms and upper body. Gingerly, I tapped my feet to the blue and white tiled floor that felt so alien to my touch. Sweating, heart pounding, and breath heaving, I balanced on my feet, wincing not with every dragging step but with every movement as I tried to stand. The walls, then doorframes held me as I gradually passed from the bathroom, across the hallway, and into my bedroom. I laid my body onto the bed, gasping for air. When my stepbrother walked by, I asked him to get Mom. I told her what happened, and she sympathetically said that maybe I had a pinched nerve.

"Do I need an ambulance? This isn't normal. Something is massively wrong!" I whimpered.

Mom really had nothing else to say and she hadn't been a nurse in years, so she offered condolences and went about finishing chores. Miah and my stepbrother were preoccupied, and Mark was watching TV. Everyone was going about their day while mine was imploding.

Throughout the year, I saw everyone from chiropractors to physical therapists, nurses, anesthesiologists, and doctors—all had different opinions and ideas while nothing helped ease my now crippled body. Everything but breathing hurt; walking to class, sitting, putting on socks, leaning, picking up things. After seeking help from twenty or so medical people, a sports medicine specialist ordered an MRI that finally revealed what other tests and x-rays apparently had not: three herniated discs and sciatic nerve and sacroiliac (SI) joint damage.

Next, testing various prescriptions and injections around my spine started because I was dismissed as "too young to have back surgery. Wait until you're in your thirties."

Another spine specialist advised, "The procedure for correction is too complicated. I'd have to go in through your abdomen. The way the herniations are located . . . It's not worth the risk."

The doctors had no problem with me getting a disability placard for my car and recommended I file for permanent disability. It made no sense to me because they made surgery sound like the answer except for their statements as to why they wouldn't do the surgery, which indicated a fear of risk and not understanding how awful my quality of life had become.

I felt like I'd slipped through a crack and was still falling. This coupled with a recent breakup from my first boyfriend ever had me looking at the stars in the night sky and wondering if I could go up there to join them instead of living a life that had me wondering, *Is this as good as it gets? Is there anything more?*

Fear and a lack of direction or structure in my life bowled me over. Misery then took her fleshy pale bottom and sat next to an ever-growing beast of despondency that overwhelmed my life. I threw away a box cutter an uncle had given me to cut luggage tags in a desperate attempt to protect myself from clear signs and thoughts that I could drain my life with it. I've always watched myself like this, mothering myself, correcting myself, guiding a life that seemed to be unseen by anyone else, and at this time in my life, self-harm was intimately close.

Through great strides of will and learning how to live with a disability (and no doubt from the care of doctor after doctor, medication, and injections), I decided to study abroad in France, possible because of grants, scholarships, school loans, and work study. You better believe I used my rugged independent spirit and resourcefulness to find work scanning gym memberships and washing dishes rather than "giving up" and becoming morbidly obese and disabled like so many of the other people in line at the pharmacy and in the doctors' offices. My thighs—once so muscular they started developing tiny stretch marks—shrunk, and my body slimmed. Yet I was like a gas stove: Some of my burners had gone out, but the pilot light deep inside was still lit, and I clung to that passion for life.

In Paris, I also found freedom from family. Alone for a month before school started, I lived in another world. Like my dad, I didn't always know how to live, so I wandered around Parisian museums and parks trying to learn the culture. Metropolitan life was a culture shock, but I ticked off the days until I forgot about the countdown and Paris became another residence like any other place I knew. But imagine the adjustment of not being allowed to walk on grass anywhere after living in the suburbs and in the country, and using broken French and body language to tell flirtatious men that you're not interested in giving them your contact info or personal attention. Once school started, I had to make even more adjustments, but I adapted and found my way.

I met some Chinese friends in Paris. And after visiting them in Scotland, which only cost the price of two dinners, my school workload and the clash of all the cultures encountering mine hit me full force. I rushed back to my dorm like a rat escaping a sinking ship. The sudden rush of anxiety overcame me. Awareness that I was in a foreign land trying to live with trauma made me realize I didn't belong. I was drowning. I breathed, facing fear one inhale at a time, allowing myself this retreat. I self-parented, "Everyone panics. Just do what you can do when you can. There's always tomorrow to start again." So I did.

Some surplus student loan money and a decent grasp on handling finances (absorbed from all my book reading in personal finance and self-help) enabled me to live a little when studying abroad in college. When I was a twelve-year-old, I remember how visiting a Pizza Hut to redeem Book It! pins for personal pan pizzas almost brought me to tears of joy. This hadn't entirely faded when I went out with high school friends, and so even in my early twenties, going out with others and trying novel things brought me new delights—often to the point of not being entirely sure what to do with myself, especially in Paris. Many feel like this in college and especially when living in a foreign country. But I had felt like a foreigner my whole life, so when I was an official foreigner, the "extraness" of it made it hard to grasp. In this regard, it was nice to get back home to the USA because unsure footing is better than no footing.

After graduating in 2005 with two bachelor's degrees, I accepted a job in insurance near Boston to earn the salary I was "entitled" to make with my college education. I had squeezed so much experience out of college, I thought I could do the same with work. I soon discovered being in the corporate world wasn't the community I craved. I found I certainly didn't belong in such a sterile world. And with Mom's dramatic neck injury, the resulting personality change from the brain trauma, and her divorce from Mark, I had to keep checking on her though she was such a handful. The only warm thing in my new world was my first corporate stalker who started off as a friendly IT guy and morphed into someone who crossed boundaries to the point of showing up to my house unwelcomed.

    I had much to learn about countering harassment in this landscape, how to set expectations of how I should be treated, and how to act on telltale signs of upcoming problems, but I eventually learned how to hold my own and to put up boundaries. How people act and react in white-collar environments and situations is different than in the blue-collar world. I relearned how to profile people and behaviors and adapted by relying on some old survival mechanisms from the abuse and childhood bullying. Trusting instincts while learning how to leverage corporate culture and rules challenged me. Protecting yourself and navigating a new class is still a form of fighting; it's just a gentleman's fight like fencing and not a street fight with balled fists and bare knuckles.

    Simultaneously, the façade of living in my own apartment, all while having privacy and safety, still could not make me feel like I had gone home. Reality finally hit: Home would not be a place to which I could return. Calling "Sanctuary!" would not provide protection from muscle memory, and my muscles knew to soldier on because, for me, there was no returning home; it didn't exist. The irony was not lost on me when I moved to Home Street. My focus became doing my best to start my desired adult life the right way.

    Before going out for a walk one day, I noticed an odd shape pushing through my Salvador Dali poster of *The Persistence of Memory*. A closer look revealed the outline of a face. I tried to lie to myself that it was an optical illusion. *Maybe a fold hasn't been smoothed out.* I ran my hands along the smooth poster, making sure it was flat against the wall. As the weeks went by and I grew tired of aimlessly walking around town (the only exercise that didn't hurt), I poured through resources for disabled people. Sitting on my futon, I happened to glance up at *The Persistence of Memory*. Once again, I saw the face jutting out from the wall. This time, the protrusion was more prominent, and the face now had horns. *Coincidence? It could be the light.*

    Then I noticed that even when the shadows from the light moved, the image did not. I chose to ignore it. I now lived next to Salem,

Massachusetts, full of people not just practicing but living out the occult. *I'm not getting involved with that creepy stuff.* I decided to concentrate on my health. My thigh muscles had become so skinny I could fit my middle fingers and thumbs around them at mid-thigh. I knew I needed to implement activities to get stronger. I began to focus on a strategy for improved health.

A week later, the image in the flat poster caught my attention again. Not only did the shape look much more pronounced, but I could now see a fully formed demonic face with thick, curved ram-style horns. The cyberdemon-like face remained supernaturally embossed on the poster. I took a picture of the raging beast and sent it to my family, asking what everyone saw.

The family all called back at once. My mother looked at the image on her computer and commented on *them* as opposed to the one that I could see. *They*, as she called them, looked like the demonic bad guys in a computer game that she and my second stepdad had played in the mid-'90s. I was further confused when my sister also said she saw *them* and had even counted five.

Puzzled by their responses, I magnified the photo I had sent to them only to see the body of another demon in the mouth of the beast. "Oh, I see it! But where are the other three?"

Mom had been scrutinizing my snapshot of the entire poster, and she had focused on a spot beyond the clock hanging in the tree at the side of the artwork. "There's another one crouching down. Do you see it?"

I did, and then I saw the other two she pointed out.

"There's two more," Becky added.

Miah agreed.

"How did you even see these?" I asked. "The poster is right in front of me, but I didn't realize how bad it is!" Fear and rationalization (which I assumed would protect me) had allowed a demonic presence to grow in my life. I guess I needed something more.

"I think it's time to pray over your place," Mom said. "Get some blessed oil."

I grabbed olive oil, and we prayed over it on the phone, making it blessed oil. Going around the apartment, I asked the God of my childhood to protect my home by dipping my fingers into the oil and drawing crosses on all the windows and doors. We prayed for evil to stay out and for strong guardian angels to come in. In the bedroom, we rebuked the demonic images on Dali's work in Jesus's name.

The poster now looks like a normal poster with the demonic images never having returned. Rebuking in Jesus's name and praying worked. The ability we have to do something like that says much about the power and holiness of the Lord's name. Unfortunately, moments like that also became fodder for the illusion that I was already in Christianity, so I believed that what I had was all that God had to offer me. I thought that if you've said the sinner's prayer with a sincere heart and can rebuke creepy things in God's name, then you must surely be a Christian—and that's all it took, right? The truth that there was more simply evaded me.

As true rest and recovery also continued to evade me, I wandered and wondered a lot. I wandered through life with no goals or direction, belonging to no one and a member of nothing. Not knowing how to really live, I stumbled through job after wrong job, wondering why the corporate careers I idolized always brought such dissatisfaction. Secretarial jobs were the wrong fit, and I hadn't discovered how to penetrate more creative and analytical jobs like marketing yet. Jobs that boasted of great benefits didn't provide healing in any way, jobs with a full team and resources still had horrible morale, and everything in life seemed so sterile and dead. In what could I put my faith if not my career? What else could give me security except for money? I took worldly advice, trying to blaze a trail that I could call my own, and just hoped that being spiritual not religious would steer me in the right direction eventually.

I felt I didn't fit in anywhere except in nature—traipsing through the woods. Plugging into the spirit of nature served as a pressure valve release much like humor does. Communing with nature released some pressure, but it still couldn't provide me with something real, something that would never let me down. The boulders I scaled were not rocks of salvation but patches for deeper wounds I didn't know how to dress.

So often, during different periods of my life, I felt like prison doors had been thrown open—there was no more child abuse, I was free from my stepdad Mark, my disability was more manageable, and I was almost out of poverty. My only perceived problem was that I had no idea how to walk out the prison doors or what to do with myself after I made that choice. A normal life could not provide the way to learn how to live like I should. I had too much stirring beneath my surface. Life coaches were too expensive, and I tried a few psychotherapists that weren't the right fit. I hit dead ends despite my best efforts. Though everything still felt meaningless, I could feel an absolute truth flickering within: I was meant for a better life, and pinpoints of hope would crack through my dark nights.

Chapter 7

Clouds Without Rain

You, God, are my God,
earnestly I seek you;
I thirst for you,
my whole being longs for you,
in a dry and parched land
where there is no water.

—Psalm 63:1 NIV

"I JUST PURCHASED THE iPhone, and look what it can do." My much older coworker had found a new reason to stop by my cubicle. He wasn't flirting with me again or telling me about spending hundreds of dollars on a haircut. It was 2007 and he had bought that new technology, the iPhone. He pinched the screen in and out, then made a ball bounce just by moving the phone.

"Oh, look at that. So fancy!" I said.

"I've got the whole weekend to figure out the programming," he replied, leaning over my cubicle. "I'm going to make my own sausage, have a nice dinner and . . ."

My attention wandered. He had a bowl haircut and looked so much like Tweedle Dee and Tweedle Dum that I couldn't stop thoughts and scenarios from playing out in my brain. *Is the haircut a foreign style? How could a man's haircut be $300 when mine is a tenth of that?!* I pictured him bouncing around like a cartoon character until I realized there was silence.

"Am I free this weekend?" I asked. "No, I'll be with my half brother. I rarely see him since he lives in Maine with his mom and she hasn't been married to my dad for years, so I've been planning an excursion where we dress up funny and go to the Maine State Museum, minigolfing, ice cream, and stuff."

"You mentioned your mother is single now that she's divorced. Does she look like you? Would she want to go out sometime?"

"I did mention to her that I had a coworker who likes nice, fancy things. Maybe you two would hit it off. She loves British humor, but I don't know . . ." I didn't like where this was going, but I didn't know what to do, possessing the insecurities of a young adult.

"I'd rather have the daughter," he said with a leer.

I froze.

Another coworker jumped in. "Sarah, I need your help looking at these keywords over here. Can you come over here, right now?"

The iPhone guy left after I unfroze and went to see what John needed.

"I don't really need you," John said. "He's just very creepy, and he's always talking to you even when you are clearly uncomfortable." John shook his head, making a disgusted face. "He's going over to Roseanna now."

Roseanna was gorgeous. "She's out of his league and she's not single. She's safe," I said. "This day needs to be over. I'm driving up to central Maine from here so I've got to get through north shore traffic, NH traffic, then I should be clear."

My boss came over. "Aha, discussing plans for the weekend?"

"I'm just having a quiet weekend with my wife and getting my car fixed," said John.

I said, "My half brother and I are going to wrap aluminum foil around our heads and wear 'Beam Me Up, Scottie' T-shirts that I made and wander around Augusta, Maine, to various sites to be silly. I've got a pair of shorts I also made that say 'Aliens do it in black holes.' "

The guys snorted with laughter.

"Someone's a *Star Trek* nerd!" said my boss.

"We're not Trekkies. We both just like doing random, weird things, and I want to make a memory with Sam. He's twelve years younger, and I never see him. He's growing up like an only child."

We palled around for a little while; my coworkers were really the extent of my social circle.

Driving from the start-up job in Andover, Massachusetts, with ridiculous weekend traffic on Route 95, I chugged water and sipped hot chocolate coffee from work. I hadn't yet been diagnosed with ADD, so I hadn't learned the effect of dairy on an inattentive ADD brain. I sipped away in a reverie. The caffeine was supposed to make me more alert, but the milk from the packet of hot chocolate just set me off down a rabbit trail of thoughts, like I needed any help there!

Rather than focus on the extreme traffic, my cloudy mind got a little stormy. I struggled to save money and had planned the weekend to spend one-on-one time with Sam so that even though he was twelve and I was twenty-four, we'd have something special to share. Sam was just a baby when he came into my life. He was still just too young to deal with sexual trauma when he turned five and he had a sexual act performed on him by a cousin older than him. Sam's mom had told me Sam was "catatonic" when he got home that day. Her words still echoed in my mind.

Sam had been near Gramma Marie's trailer while Dad and his sister April weren't present, probably watching TV or crafting, not aware despite our cousin's extreme behavioral issues. This cousin was terribly unsocialized to the extent us three kids and the other cousins hated being around him. His wild jumping attacks would send fists winding through the air at us, and he emitted a nonstop stream of conscious, slurred speech. He wouldn't calm down and bombarded into your life like a wild animal that needed to be trapped into a room when someone visits. If the cousin wasn't so much younger than us three kids, we wouldn't have been able to get him away from us. I'd be sitting on the floor when he would enter the room and jump on my head, bending my glasses out of shape and hurting my damaged neck. He wouldn't stop unless I maneuvered my legs under him and pressed him away. He kept getting removed from school for his behavior. He was such a forceful and spastic creature to be avoided! I do remember hearing about a neighborhood boy bullying him. *Was that how he learned sexual abuse?* I hoped time and again someone got him help because far too often, sexual assault is learned behavior.

Sam's mom (Carol) said an investigation with social workers revealed that the cousin, who was maybe around eleven himself, still slept in a bed with his mom and that it appeared that's where the abuse was learned. This hurt my heart. I knew Dad never had money, but he had four kids, which should have meant something like finding his own place or keeping the cousin away from us. He didn't need to live in the shoddy trailer with his mom, sister, and nephew. *Grown-ups have options*, I thought, and I always remember rooting for things to get better, but they never did.

Poor Sam. How sad. Alone. Unlike after the abuse with us kids, external things for him didn't change much, from what I saw. Sam still visited Dad some weekends per the custody agreement, like us kids had. Gramma Marie owned a pop-up camper, so Sam would come for a visit and stay in the camper from that point on, after the abuse. It made no sense and felt so unfair to me. When I first discovered this, we—all four kids—walked up the driveway with Dad and had started on the walkway through the heavily cluttered lawn, past the lawn ornaments, when Dad indicated that Sam would go to the trailer.

Dad explained that the cousin was home and said begrudgingly, "Well, Carol and the state want it this way. Sam can't come in and watch TV with us and relax, so he's gonna relax in the camper." Dad wasn't a fan of the cousin either and couldn't hide his annoyance.

Us kids waved to Sam and said we'd be out soon. I watched little Sam walk into the camper and waited my turn to shuffle into the trailer, very confused. I guess I was stunned. I walked into the trailer and didn't even go to the bird cage. For years, I'd go to that bird cage with those tiny, bitty birds and deliberately think, *Two weeks from now, I will be standing in this very same spot thinking this very same thought like I never left this* time. *Two months from now, I will be standing in this very spot, different but still in this spot, and though it's a different time, I will be the same having this thought.* Playing with time, I called it. I didn't play with time then; something had shifted.

"Sam's not coming in at all? He's just going to stay out by himself while we're all in here?"

Aunt April chimed in. "It's foolish. He could be in here with everyone else but . . ." She said something inconsequential to me. It didn't matter what she said: It's that she said anything. She was my aunt, and I respected my elders as always and cared for her.

However, I was a high schooler now and was tired of feeling sorry for her. Whatever her rebuttal was, it wasn't right, but before I got a chance, the cousin immediately chirped in like one of Gramma Marie's birds and parroted exactly what his mom said, adding a smile, spastic gesture, and "Yeah!"

"I'm going out with Sam," I said as I left for the camper. "He shouldn't be out there by himself."

Sam and I hung out. He was a good kid. He said he'd usually be in there for a long time, bored. After some time, I said I was going back in the trailer, but Sam pleaded for me not to go. I didn't really know what to say to Sam, and I used to incorrectly think what a boring person I was, so I couldn't imagine why he'd want me to stay.

"There's nothing to do out here, is there?"

"No," he said. "And I want to spend time with you because you're fun and it's more fun when there are people."

"Well, I'll come back. I'll send Miah or Becky out."

Only one of them joined us before I moved. Then the next sibling came out. Becky was sunny and checking on Sam, and Miah was joking with him and revving him up. It was a good time. Dad came out, and we made it an early night, all of us making room to sleep in the camper. The weekend went in a similar way. We took turns with Sam in the camper, leaving shorter periods of when he'd have to be alone.

Gramma Marie was sweet, but all she offered was, "Boys will be boys." I loved her so genuinely that this sentiment didn't smack me then, but it did in the future. This also wasn't a situation where an adult attacked a boy (there were likely two victims, after all). I disagreed with everything I saw and tried like I always did to bring reason, but there was no reasoning with that side of the family. Counseling, improving behavior, living like healthy people: That was a dead end.

Dad had thought I was "fancy" and putting on airs because Miah and I lived in Massachusetts. We had moved there with Mom because we were literally kids and she still had custody, but Dad's people just hadn't understood my culture and lifestyle. I did understand them, and I didn't want to be that way. I just wasn't certain what to do and how to lead myself.

Now on my way to meet Sam, I lowered the car window, breathing in deep, filling myself with air, feeling the heaviness of my thoughts lighten as my lungs expanded. With the schedule I had planned, I was going to make the most of this long trip! When traffic lessened, I stomped the gas pedal—and my concern—until I reached my little brother and his sociable mom.

We had a great time, from the food we ate and how we ate it to physically goofing around and a slumber party. During the weekend, we visited the Maine State Museum, minigolfed, and went around dressed in our random, weird outfits wearing aluminum foil hats just because we could. I made a bunched up mohawk rooster helmet from my foil only to turn around and see Sam took his endeavor seriously, crafting a German WWII spiked helmet. Brilliant design, such a talented kid. We switched hats, tickled pink by each other's creation. People enjoyed our silliness as much as we did, and we relished the friendliness.

We detoured to Whipper's, a family favorite sub shop, taking our sandwiches through Cony Circle to the playground and Kennebec River boat landing. The aluminum foil hats were sweaty hot and put aside. We demolished lunch and wandered over to a maybe twenty-foot embankment. We liked investigating striated rock, peeling layers of mica, and walking in the silt and sand with bare feet. Sam found a stream and created a little dam. My brother, a beaver, was so in his element, I didn't want to interrupt him—until fifteen minutes of moving dirt mounds and rocks became much longer.

Sam did not, could not stop. "I didn't take my OCD meds. I can't leave this stream like this," he explained, hyperfocused on moving the earth where he needed it to go.

I'm an observer; when Carol and Sam had showed me the night before this cutting board Sam made in school, I had felt its smoothness and saw the worn sandpaper as Sam had started sanding the clearly finished project.

"Stop sanding it. Sam, that's enough!" Carol had scolded. Sam had already sanded the board over fifty times.

Standing at the foot of the embankment, I said, "Okay. That's fine. It's our time." I loved that quirky, little kid, and I was different from others too. I daydreamed, sauntered, and chatted with Sam.

Forty-five minutes . . . an hour . . . I watched Sam reroute an entire stream and its branches from the top to almost the bottom of the mound. I can't remember if at that point I had read from self-help or learned from my therapist that OCD is often a result of trauma or if I recognized the compulsive gnawing in the body from my own traumatic experiences, but as I watched my baby brother act in such an "I need to control this" way, I further believed Carol's sentiment that it stemmed from the sexual trauma. Sexual pleasure forced on me and my brother as children damaged us so thoroughly.

I had Sam finish the rerouting, and we did enjoy our time. However, something broke in me that weekend. An internal cloud cracked, and raindrops of empathy poured out. When you grow up used and ignored, it's hard to feel empathy for yourself, but seeing it in someone else, so precious and young, it just doesn't feel like they deserve hurt. I felt piss poor and worthless, but my empathetic love compelled me to throw my weight against the silencing that happens when one is violated and against acting like it's fine to not prevent abuse or ignore awareness of high-risk situations and people (like the abusive cousin). Love for Sam looked like breaking apart from a blood is thicker than water culture that professes blind loyalty to family. My empathy watered the truth that confronted me: I needed to do something.

That's when I started pulling away from Dad, the one who brought his friend, John Herrin, the sexual and physical abuser into our lives; Dad, the one who introduced us to Paul, his buddy and boss who had a baby with his own seventeen-year-old stepdaughter; Dad, the one who knew how his nephew was and still left Sam with him. Reading these people, these hurtful, damaging people, was so easy for me, and I was just a kid. There was no longer an excuse for Dad.

Fathers are needed. I needed that man. I guess he needed something else. Funny thing is, even after I phased him out of my life and no longer spoke to him, he could have ignited a wildfire of healing just by looking into me and responding to a daughter who wanted a father. He could still only give Christmas presents to my sister because he felt she needed more help. Fine. Just him reading me a little would have given me hope. Even grown kids benefit from halfway decent fathers. Relationships matter and ours was dying.

❦

"Yeah, I mean, I'd see him some weekends and holidays, but I don't consider him my dad. He didn't raise me," explained Miah.

That caught my attention. I had no idea he felt this way.

As we were standing in a sunny parking lot with a friend, the casual afternoon conversation made me do a double take. For years, it was like I'd been anxiously holding my breath in front of a closed door, but Miah's words cut through my tension and opened the door to freedom. The freedom to agree: *Dad doesn't feel like much of a dad.* Being a good girl certainly hadn't provided this validation of my own feelings.

Allowed to admit the truth, my mind pictured Mom. *She struggled to raise us. She couldn't do it alone but showed that she wanted us by her actions, though flawed. Dad told us, "I don't know why you kids don't come live with me," but he never showed that he wanted us. Besides, even after Gramma Marie put an addition on her two-bedroom trailer, there were four people crammed together with Dad sleeping on the couch. Where would we stay, on the floor with the animals or in the camper, a tent with wheels, in rural Maine with heavy winters?*

It's freeing when your brother/friend confesses his similar feelings, and my brother was "the man in my life," a safe, loving support. We'd talked in the past about not living with Dad, even if Dad got an apartment and even if his latest wife was decent. We'd read the signs since childhood. Dad could be fun and loving for a time, but he just didn't know how to be a dad. Though only in his forties, he spoke like he'd already given up on life, talking about when he would die and how old he was. In his mind, he'd lived a long, full life and seen enough; he wasn't expecting more but existing until he died. Limited people, those who live with limited thinking: Why are they so hard to reach? If none of his three wives, grown adults, could help him, how could I? His goal was to live as long as his father had (age forty-six), that's it.

His attitude would slice my heart. One time, I think before this conversation with Miah, I saw a horrible gash from a chainsaw accident on Dad's shin bone barely healing. Dad couldn't trouble himself to go to the emergency room for stitches. The slice turned into a scar as I saw that Dad felt trapped in a warehouse job that he hated when a better job with higher pay and more benefits was only a few miles away. My dad acted like he belonged in the book *Life in the Iron Mills* and continued living with his own open wounds.

My dad with perfect hair, beautiful blue eyes, and so much wasted potential once wanted to brag to an abusive boss about suing him.

"You have a lawyer?" I asked.

"No!" he said. "I just wanted to sound important. Like I was somebody." He laughed and shrugged, not thinking anything of it.

I didn't laugh. I thought plenty of it. He WAS somebody to me. What a powerfully lonely moment, to watch life pass you by as you regard it from a distance because life is for "fancy people" and not you.

Watching his life felt like a time in the woods when I saw a strangler fig wrapped around a healthy tree, slowly squeezing the life out of it. I couldn't help but uncoil the serpentine vines from around the victim tree, so how could I stop trying to motivate Dad to have some sort of gumption to change his lifestyle, show up for his kids, and take ownership of his life? Professional counseling wasn't viewed as something people did, like seeing a physical therapist or even a dentist. It certainly wouldn't be known as a preventative solution, teaching communication and behavior modification that could restore and protect relationships. I'm not sure Dad thought his life was worth improving. And just like I couldn't completely unfurl the strangling vine from the tree because of the extensive height of the strangulation, I couldn't reach Dad either.

I also couldn't trust him to understand that I didn't want my niece, nephew, and half brother near people who might hurt them. With my brother's sentiments in alignment with mine and my experience seeing my traumatized half brother, I didn't feel like one person's detachment from life exempted him from protecting children, his children. This good-looking, funny, everyday man now looked to me the way he appeared to his ex-wives. He gave up trying in marriages after the weddings because he had accomplished the goal. He even thought it a wasted effort to put in his front teeth dentures. "I'm married. Don't need my teeth." I saw what the wives saw, only I felt helpless because I had no other healthy father figure, and it wasn't fair that blood was no thicker than water.

Our text messages and calls became spartan after the visit with Sam. On the rare occasion when I had to communicate with Dad, he needed handling in a distanced, firm manner, sure to see my unwavering discipline toward his behavior. "I will not have a relationship with someone who refuses to break the cycle of severe dysfunction. There's no excuse." He was no more aware, and family discourse didn't start occurring.

It was awkward when someone at Thanksgiving would whisper, "Sarah can't sit near Dad. We'll have to move her placement."

I'd breathe, not wanting to feel like the pariah, but wasn't it the truth? It didn't matter; I couldn't stop standing for what was right. I expected and hoped it would only take a few years of cutting off my relationship with Dad for change to occur. I guess when you're suffocating in your own life, it drains you from the spirit until your body stops keeping the score and you, like my dad, have a stroke, ending up on a gurney with machines breathing for you until there's nothing left. But I'm getting ahead of myself.

~☙~

In May 2008, I was washing my niece's hair in the tub, deliberately showing and telling her how easy it was to love her and all the reasons why. I wanted to pour love into her to cover any love deficit. God poured out his love into Zoe, my sweet three-and-a-half-year-old baby girl (my sister's daughter)—love he had given me for her—but she and that amazing love wanted to pour love into me too.

I started to usher her out of the bathroom so I could bathe.

"Auntie," she said, "I want to stay in the bathroom with you."

"Okay, sweetie. Here, you can play with this comb and cup in the sink. Don't use this knob for the hot water or you'll get burned." I demonstrated a mock-burn scenario, crying "Ouch!" when I put my fingers under the hot water.

Zoe, with her squeaky-clean face and wet hair draped around it, looked up at me with something else on her mind. "I want to wash your hair." She really meant it.

No one renders me speechless and flabbergasted like my niece and the Lord God! Zoe's dad was very absent (choosing time with cannabis and friends for days at a time, even during holidays and birthdays), and her mom was just as dysfunctional (with untreated bipolar, post-traumatic stress, and rage) by withholding love from Zoe, so I needed to hop in the tub because someone needs to show love to those who don't have enough of it! Helping and loving others starts with us. I realized Zoe needed to express her love by caring for me.

Of course, an insecure, young, single woman accustomed to washing in privacy wants exactly that. I admit that I strategically placed bubbles around my naked body, but I didn't want my niece to learn shame from me. I'd seen enough of that. So I let her wash my hair while I sat in the tub feeling oafish and awkward but, nonetheless, tended to lovingly. She did a great job with her little-girl hands and arms and told me when to tilt my head up. She was so gentle and didn't get soap in my eyes or anything!

This moment with my sweet baby girl Zoe was a lesson in both sacrifice and love. With some humility, an ego check, and a hop into a soapy bathtub, I knew I was giving my niece something that she needed. I found consenting to her request worth the effort. Zoe had at least some love poured into her, but whom was she getting to pour her love into in return?

We need to express emotions like love. God starts forming ideas in our minds, then mentors us using real-life examples that teach us how love and relationships work. Love is like a circuit: I must express my love to my niece, and I must let her express her love for me or the circuit isn't complete. Replace the word *love* with the word *relationships*, and the concept still works.

Learning this multifaceted lesson is excellent for understanding how to have an interactive relationship with the Lord, which for me was still farther down the road. The concept of transactional love birthed the understanding and acceptance of the sacrifices that people like my sister made. I had to accept what my sister's sacrifice (being abused more frequently so that she would be the scapegoat rather than the rest of us kids) meant because her love transaction would go beyond providing simple answers. Her sacrifice would provide a love that mimicked the sacrifice of the Last Adam who was marred beyond human form and murdered so I wouldn't have to be.

Cursed with navel-gazing, I was unfortunately oblivious to this truth at this point in my life and searched instead for answers all around me—only in the wrong places—and fell into new age practices until life spiraled out of control.

※

Even in sorrow and dysfunction, joy's effervescence rises to the top, its spicy bubbles popping into a fit of giggles as it spills onto your life.

One day while appreciating the versatility of a spork (the Bart

Simpson of the spoon world), I heard that in addition to Noah and his family, the Islamic faith believes that seventy-two other people were in the ark. Wondering if this claim was true, I turned to the person in my life who I mistakenly considered a religion buff. I called Mom.

"What's up, doll?" she asked.

"I wanted to ask you a religious question."

"Okay. Hang on a minute . . . I'm putting you on speaker phone," she muttered. "Now where is the speaker? Oh c'mon, you stupid phone press-on. Oh drat! Hang on a minute, sweetie. The phone is not cooperating."

"It never does," I mumbled. *Those super smooth touch screens are annoying, especially if you're not wearing your glasses.*

Mom returned to the conversation. "Okay, I'm ready now. Sorry about that. Oh, I must tell you about something funny that happened. Obviously, I was very sleepy when I read the weather report today. I thought the news said that it will be 'clear with probiotic clouds.' It really said 'periodic clouds.'"

Chuckling, I replied, "You know I'm going to hold this over your head and bring it up in public some time, right?"

"I have always said that the news headlines are better when you misread them!"

"You never say that. And as entertaining as your gaffe was, I called because I have a question about something someone at work said was in the Bible. Here at work, someone wrote an article about Noah and the ark based on what they said Muslims believe. My coworker is vetting the article and he asked me for help since I've got degrees in English and comparative literature and know some things about religion and church stuff. You got some time?"

"Oh, okay." Deafening hound-dog barking interrupted the call. Mom, trying to wrangle her dog, commanded, "Get down, Duke! I said get down. I'm on the phone. Can't you see that? Sit, sit."

Used to this phone routine, I sat in silence, waiting.

"I said sit, Duke, sit! Oh no . . . That's not what I said. I said SIT." I heard a muffled holler. "Dave, I need help cleaning up after the dog! Oh, drat!" Uncovering the phone, my discouraged and harried mother started to explain to me what I had just heard. "Hang on a minute, Sarah. The dumb dog, he always wants to bark when I'm on the phone even though I keep telling him again and again that I'm on the phone! I just told him to sit, and he just took a big—"

"Ayuh! I got that, Mom. If you want to put the phone down and go handle business, I'll wait."

"Okay, hang on just a minute. I'm putting the phone down." Noise, male and female voices, shuffling, more barking, and the phone was back in play. "Okay, Sarah. I'm back." Catching her breath, she continued, "Dave's taking the dog out to the smoking room. He likes to sit out there smoking and watching TV, and then I don't have to listen to the barking."

Wanting to correct her grammar and partially joking, I asked, "Is the dog sitting out there watching TV and smoking . . . or Dave?"

Confused, she said, "Yes. Why? What did I say?"

"The dog, Mom. The dog . . . Never mind. So, you're all set, the dog is out smoking, and Dave won't interrupt?"

"Hahaha, yes!" she replied good-naturedly. "Dave, Sarah just asked me if you and the dog are both out there smoking cigarettes and watching TV."

Without missing a beat, Dave (Mom's fourth husband) replied, "Duke's keeping me company so I don't superglue another cup of coffee to the table!"

"Did you hear that, Sarah?" Mom asked with a loving smile in her voice.

"Wait, what? How did he do that? Oh! Was his blood sugar low again, or was this just a Dave thing?"

"Just a Dave thing." Her tone was a vocal shrug, and she finally gave me her full attention. It takes a while for us middle children to get and sustain attention.

"So, Mom, did you know if Noah's family was all alone?"

"No," Mom said. "How did Noah make a wireless phone?"

Laughter jumped out of me, and I couldn't catch it to bring it back. "No, Mom. You never listen! I said *all alone*. Were Noah and his family alone?"

The brain fog started to clear. "Oh. So, there was no phone?"

"No! Mom . . . this isn't *Gilligan's* friggin' *Island*! No one is making technology in the middle of nowhere." My eyes rolled all the way to my brain. "We're talking about Noah and the ark and whether or not they were alone . . . like, aloooone."

"Oh, I get it! Ha! I thought you said that Noah made a—"

"Yeah, yeah, yeah, I know what you thought. It was funny." And that was her strong point. She had a sense of humor and was daffy enough that humorous moments happened often. They acted as opened pressure valves to life. But it's a lucky thing that Google grew in popularity or I would still be wondering about those seventy-two others. And no, they were not on the ark.

Chapter 8
A Sheep Tangled in Death

> *Some Christians try to go to heaven alone, in solitude. But believers are not compared to bears or lions or other animals that wander alone. Those who belong to Christ are sheep in this respect that they love to get together. Sheep go in flocks, and so do God's people.*
>
> — attributed to Charles Spurgeon

THE CHURCH DOORS were locked. Again. *Why aren't churches ever opened? The only thing worse is having to pay for parking. You'd think accessibility would be a priority. It's not like there's anything worth stealing inside.* I pursed my lips and exhaled. Sometimes, I just wanted the comfort that religion could bring. Not a commitment, just to stand in the periphery. Between toddlerhood and pre-teens, I'd spent maybe eight years collectively in churches. I considered myself spiritual not religious and looked toward church establishments as dried-up lemons that were hard and unyielding, but if I tried hard enough, I could squeeze out some spiritual juice. I yearned for deep spiritual connection but mostly with God since people, churchgoers included, were so hurtful, like Daddy John and Peggy's people.

Too wounded and bruised from trauma to handle even light judgment from religious people, I stayed in the religious periphery, which protected me from church gossip, denominational infighting, awkward and forced get-togethers, and domineering men who made the women around them do all the work. However, I missed the sacredness of God and his church because even through my spiritual wounds, I sought Truth.

I left the locked Protestant/Reformed church and settled for ducking into a Catholic church because at least those were open, even at night. I cautiously walked in and sat in the pew to pray, just breathing in the holy nature of a high church with incense and stained-glass windows. Footsteps entering the sanctuary echoed over to me, and I bolted, thinking I probably wasn't supposed to be there.

We had been taught, and Gramma enforced, that Catholics go to hell because they worship Mary. A childhood friend had explained to me once, "I'm not Christian, I'm Catholic." Catholic high school and college friends had some religious events like getting confirmed, but they were just religious actions that we hadn't talked about much because they were just "things you do." There had been an invisible barrier that existed, so we respected it. What seemed like fruitless social constructs didn't appeal to me.

The footsteps sent me fleeing from the Catholic church I had temporarily infiltrated out of desperation, so I settled for what felt like an interrupted battery charging. This was how I navigated religion as a spiritual but not religious adult in her twenties.

Without a personal connection to a church, outreach signs weren't enough of a welcome either. I remember being very interested when I drove by a healing service banner at an Anglican Church. *What do Anglicans do?* I kept thinking about how the Baptists and other fundamental denominations I heard of attacked charismatic churches and supernatural healing. Then I remembered the Pentecostal and Assemblies of God church experiences where people were not what I now call biblically anchored (following Scripture), acting wild but calling it being "Spirit led." *Is it safe or not to go to a healing service?* I had no reference point for Anglicans. No approval or disapproval. I didn't attend their service.

I needed some churching, a holy community, but I was afraid of it. Church, without the fullness of God, isn't a haven for the broken. *What're the rules? What's the right thing to do?* I needed spiritual guidance, but unhealthy church experiences and secular judgments against the church (like Christianity is another pointless religion, it's about taking money, women are inequal to men, etc.) left me confused, unfulfilled, and dangling over a spiritual swamp filled with dangers beneath the surface.

Unwittingly, I pushed through the surface and discovered energy healing, a new age concept combining science (supposedly) and spiritualism. A coworker enjoyed "polarity" and other energy healing sessions. When we were laid off, I wanted peace and good energy. Why wouldn't I splash around this likely innocuous practice?

When we hear that people are in a cult or playing with the occult, we may be surprised or judgmental. But we respond with more sympathy when we hear exactly how people fall into these dark and desperate groups. It's commonly a victim or orphan archetype that just wants a place to call home but is led astray. Sometimes the victim is passionately misguided, like Saul before his road to Damascus experience in the New Testament. You can see how I fit into this formula. Someone with no roots will fall and land hard.

If joining new ageism was seen through clear vision, I cannot imagine there would be much interest. Any new age and occult events I attended always had meager attendance. Quite pathetic turnouts—which should have been an action-provoking sign! The work was iffy and damaged; hurt people were the "healers." None had concrete answers. The problem with people who have not found health and healing who try to help and heal others is that they only know hurt and pass that along. I wish that I had seen beyond "a glass, darkly" (1 Corinthians 13:12 KJV). But honestly, I was so smoothly swept off my feet and was an easy target, despite being cautious because I was so broken that I pursued healing over having discernment.

When sparring in martial arts, it's easier to learn how to sweep kick the sparring partner off their feet if baby powder is sprinkled under the partner's feet. There must have been spiritual powder all around me! I went through the air and landed hard and dazed, just like I was when I was age seven taking judo. My foray into the occult ended up with me unknowingly channeling and having one-person (and sometimes group) séances at one point. How did this result from visiting a metaphysical bookstore after a devastating layoff? Well, positive testimonials about relaxing polarity workshops, a welcoming environment, free services, and compassionate support acted as the invitation. It was 2009, just a year after the economy had collapsed, and new ageism offered hope.

∽

While I still had a gym membership, I used the hot tub to massage my neck and back muscles. One day, a miserable acquaintance castigated the place as usual, then mocked a woman changing in the sauna. I felt awful and guilty by association. The next time I saw the changing woman, I commended her for switching from a cold bathing suit into nice warm clothes in the sauna and told her not to let anything she might have overheard get her down. Significantly older, she may have needed the support. We became friends, and she invited me to her church. I didn't know what a Congregational church was, but her description of it was positive, so I thought I'd attend. I paralleled attending this religious institution to practicing energy healing.

A few months into awkwardly attending the church (the first church I attended as an adult), I remember my new gym friend talking with a group of church women, questioning if she should date a man who belonged to an Assembly of God church. "What is that?" she asked.

All ears, I heard more confusion than answers. "I'm not sure. I think they still believe in God," said one woman. The consensus was that it wasn't Unitarian Universalist where Jesus was just a man, so it might be okay. Unfortunately for my friend, her boyfriend ended the relationship with her after *his* church friends warned him that my friend was a Congregationalist. No doubt, they were looking for someone "Spirit led" (believing in signs and miracles from God) and not too fundamentalist and "religious." It might be funny or sad now, but it was hard being in a group where none of us knew our church identity, what our faith options were, or even our identities within denominations. Maybe churches need to address church history and improve relationships within the church body. When I asked a church leader about the Anglican church, he told me something I didn't understand and equated it to a branch of the Catholic church. I guessed it must not be good.

The next time I saw the Anglican church's healing service sign, I was on my way to the new age bookstore to which my former coworker had introduced me. Dismissing the sign, I drove past. The metaphysical bookstore was like museum gift shops except for angel or oracle cards (similar to tarot cards with angelic portraits, though I didn't know that at the time), Tibetan chimes, incense, spiritual multicultural meditations, and music. I loved science stores and museum visitor shops. My early education in Maine included environmental stewardship and earth appreciation (e.g., counting the age of a tree by its internal rings and learning about rocks and minerals). Naturally, I felt at home amongst the crystals and geodes.

Without my health, chronic pain was heavy all around me. Fairweather relationships revealed how alone I was until medical bills were my only company. Without job prospects for large stretches of time (I identified myself by my career), I honestly believed I had zero value, and I got desperate. Metaphysical bookstores are intimate, warm, inviting, and very real. They are not the obligatory friendly that I remembered in churches and around the social class of my twenties. I grew up in severe environments, grew up hard. Middle-class people at school and work were not entirely relatable to me yet. People from the culture of lack fit more into my comfort zone and those people, my people, me: We belonged here in spiritual brokenness, searching.

I thought I could be classless or live a healthy existence where people mattered more than things with the new age group. There I found myself, sitting in a new age room with others searching for—well, we didn't know what, but we weren't alone. I became initiated into reiki, an energy healing practice where the master prays something quietly, then breathes into the hands of the initiate, who experiences supernatural heat and a feeling of awareness. The initiates practice healing each other, saying, "I call upon reiki masters past, present and future to" heal or whatever is desired. It doesn't matter, as the whole practice is just a séance with a presence that is not of God but is supposedly neutral and not evil. The presence shares the person's body. For me, the energy provided a supernatural ability where I was still able to control myself if I wanted, but the energy, or spirit, moved my limbs. During this, I was told that energy healing can only do good things and is never painful. I was skeptical but not enough. My poor boyfriend at the time experienced something very different. He grew up repeatedly traumatized and didn't want *anything* controlling him, let alone a presence and pressure that invited itself into his body through manipulation.

How sad it was to not really understand that we are in our bodies for a reason and can't give ourselves away—not temporarily, not long term, not to spirits or sexual partners, not anyone. We, as humans, are so important that we need principles, set standards, and discipline because they safeguard us, and we are worth the attention, effort, and love. Having a biblical anchoring helps us to understand the Holy Spirit so we can be Spirit led and learn this. Anchors protect us from the jostling of an "everything is relative" world. Relativism, the concept pushing the practice and religion of new ageism and occultism that teaches that there's truly no right or wrong, is so dangerous and never ends well, as I have experienced and have read about in scholarly works. But how could I have been reached to understand this then? I didn't know about, let alone understand biblical living and using the Bible's teaching so I could use its anchoring (disciplines) to learn how to live, which would teach me a new way to handle freedom.

I tried rationalizing at every step and making logical decisions with an open mind—I wanted to protect myself from anything in the energy healing world that was too bizarre but still be accepting of new things. How pointless! Problems grew because I lacked any true and meaningful standard Christians know as biblical standards. For example, the Bible says to challenge each thought, to hold every thought captive, and this is precisely why: Our lifestyles, histories, current setting, and genetic makeup affect our thoughts, which affect our decisions. That doesn't even include any influence from the spirit world. We need God and his biblical truths so desperately because any one of these variables (especially when inflamed with dysfunction) can render us completely vulnerable and about as useful as the walking dead.

The metaphysical workers could explain how unhealthy emotions cause negative effects on the body, but their knowledge ended there and a part of me remained skeptical. I knew abuse and feeling unworthy could cause depression, which would lead to becoming more lifeless. This could lead to low back pain from depressed posture and weakness and feeling the heaviness of the world every minute of each day, so depression could equal low back pain, but this rationalization didn't provide a cure or tackle bigger truths. We were taught love and energy heal, but where was the proof or healing?

I pressed through this time by trying to create a more structured environment and working with a good therapist, hoping my mind, newly diagnosed with ADHD-PI (attention deficit hyperactivity disorder predominantly inattentive), would also be helped. My desire to simply disappear lessened with nature walks—except nature was sparse. The resources I loved (going grocery shopping and devouring books, movies, and audiobooks) offered me a reprieve. They gave me something to do with myself when unemployed or if I was having a sciatic flare-up that resulted in debilitating pain. I could lean over the grocery cart and slowly make my way down the aisles or get lost in a library. My extroverted self felt energized by the people around me. When I couldn't stand or even move much, I escaped to library books, wishing for bodily muscles and adventures beyond the mental realm. None of that felt like real progress. There was more depression than hope. I needed other tactics to put into practice. Swimming in the pool and long showers to feel cleansing hope or wandering through any place open twenty-four hours when insomnia hit at least kept me from lying around feeling empty.

As I became deeper involved with reiki, I'd wake to spirits touching and moving my body, so my relationship with sleep became complicated. When it wasn't safe to sleep, I in turn haunted the only local place always open—the well-lit, friendly Walgreens. I walked the aisles directionless, listening to the upbeat music, which was safer than being on my own in the dank, musty basement apartment. If there wasn't chronic pain crouching at my door, there was a ghostly attack waiting. I had no clue what to do.

❧

I was wandering through life and in desperate need of a shepherd. I felt like such a lost sheep. Growing up in Litchfield, Maine, we lived on more than sixty acres of land with the best grass a sheep could eat. One time, someone tethered a sheep gifted to us with a soft cloth rope to a post. The sheep mowed the backyard with ease—until the next morning when we found the rope so knotted and tangled that it had strangled the sheep to death. I still have no idea how that could have happened unless the sheep twisted several times, double knotted the rope, tangled some more, then was lifted and wrapped, and the rope pulled tight.

Whenever I think about sheep references in the Bible, I remember this sheep and its death or the ever hungry and dirty sheep I cared for when I volunteered at an animal reserve in high school. No matter how one thinks about them, practically, sheep are dirty and dumb. Romantically people think, *Aww, they're so cute and precious.* Or they think the way I do: *They are dumb, dirty, and precious . . . and they secrete lanolin found in body lotion, so if I rub myself on them, it's like getting free lotion samples! YAY!* Regardless, sheep don't fare well alone, and they are completely lost and in immediate danger without a shepherd.

I was grappling to find my way through life, but I hoped to be found through persevering and self-help. I was self-sufficient and very resourceful after all. Those attributes never failed in surviving abuse and neglect and were thus the best ways to get help, right? But no matter what methods or changes in energy healing I tried, the treatments would help a little, then grow into something dark. Because the treatments helped some, that gave merit to energy healing as a whole but proved I was trying the wrong healing, I hypothesized. This wasn't just my mindset but what healers, psychics, "medical intuitives," shamans, and Indian mystics told me. Only the rude people from the International Reiki Institute called me a failure and denied any wrongdoing that resulted from reiki—even when that was my only new age practice at the time. They were so angry and mean and ended the phone call with "Good energy and love are the same. Dizziness and sickness doesn't happen. It can't hurt."

But love can be painful. It must be given in proper doses. In a conversation with my sister around this time, she told me that during her abuse, "Sex was always painful, but I thought, 'If he's doing this to me, at least he isn't doing this to the other kids.' " The love my sister showed me and my brother when she thought that she was preventing us from being hurt was her practicing straight love. The straighter and purer the love, the stronger the sacrifice. Yes, that's painful, but the love expressed to Miah and me wells up into a wave of gratitude that someone could consider a tatterdemalion like me so precious. However, in this moment, before this godly wisdom, my sister's good intentions/sacrifice had me feeling like Miah and I were forced to act as burdens. A lie—but not entirely. The taste of guilt and shame that I couldn't be rid of mixed with the new age practices, and it was starting to go beyond sour to rancid despite some of the truths mixed in with these deceptive arts.

Yet still, I wanted to be open minded and had no idea how too expansive my spiritual boundaries were. Christians are called to be "in the world, not of it," but that means that we are to be strong in our beliefs, firmly planted in the Word, and thick skinned to the shock around us, so we can help and serve. Had I been a Christian and meditated on that, I would have corrected the poor design of my spiritual boundaries. Who am I kidding? I'd have still been too wounded. But without contemplation of the Word, I was like so many so-called Christians who played the part of a boomerang in church: Screw up out in the world, then fly right back into the church. Repeat. Sounds a lot like the behavior of an addict and not someone living free, doesn't it?

Can you see how someone enters the new age world through a gateway that escalates into something worse? My first purchase at that bookstore was a handful of minerals and crystals. They surprisingly emitted a quiet chatter after I set them down and walked into the next room. Someone must have put a spell or some other bad thing on them because these were simple lapis lazuli and rose quartz crystals, and before I fully entered the occult, this had never happened. The experience was odd and interesting. The crystals sounded like people quietly whispering to each other. I only noticed the sounds when I really listened to them.

Can angels be attached to these angel crystals? Most people (churchgoers, neighbors, new age practitioners, etc.) responded to this odd supernatural crystal experience and to my questions—*How is this possible?* and *Is this good, do you think?*—the same way so many would respond to *Can smoking some pot be healthy for you?* I got some earnest responses that were akin to *I'm not sure, Maybe, That would be nice,* and *It seems harmless.* I kept the crystals while I started my metaphysical search for healing, like a drug addict feeding her desperation.

When presences manifested as "archangels" that guided the angel and tarot cards, it wasn't scary but more interesting, like reading about magic and mysteries. There was some interesting information by Doreen Virtue (a massive name in the new age world for years; she's since become Christian too) that was hokey, but I read her work anyway. I certainly never protected my mind or sheltered myself, as I thought exposure to the world would make me stronger and wiser.

I liked Louise Hay (another celebrated new age leader) because she was a relatable woman. Her practice seemed much more rational than Doreen Virtue's, which swam with mermaids and channeled angels that wrote self-contradicting books for her. I wasn't looking for that. Louise Hay's teachings discussed metaphysics and things like how negative emotions affect our health. If you had low back pain, that would show you had money worries. Shoulder pain would show that you were shouldering hard-to-carry life burdens.

I felt like there was enough science to connect some dots. When doctors are treating kids with otherwise unexplainable intestinal pain, there are specialists and researchers who have found that there is more to the kids' stories. Abandoned, insecure kids have more accounts of sickness and weakened immune systems (including problems with the small intestines). Anything can be rationalized, but doesn't this smack of truth? So the roles of emotions in physical health were discussed in this spiritual practice unlike in the one-size-fits-all sermons that still retained the shape of the can from which they came.

There should be a safe way to explore mind and body wellness in Christianity, but I had never experienced this or even heard of it being touched upon by Christians. A common complaint was that churches never explored treatment for sexual trauma either. Imagine my utter joy at finding later in life that there are churches that don't just discuss big topics like this but get involved in praying and healing for those impacted by trauma, the occult, etc. When I was out in the world, it seemed hard to find Christians who had the courage to talk the talk and walk the walk—whatever the subject might be—so I continued on my way into the occult, my only perceived option.

Around this time, I met Andrew, who started off as a friend. His kindness was tangible, and I wanted him as a friend or colleague. He wanted to date me and kept trying little ways to sneak into that role. I'm pretty blunt and made clear and repeated statements that we weren't a good fit for dating. Finally, a confession tipped out of Andrew and spilled everywhere. He shocked me with revelations of violent Black children and their parents attacking him as a young mixed-race child, being thrown out of a tree house and permanently damaging his knees, traumatic bullying ending up with him in a dug grave, and child sexual abuse from an incestuous family with Andrew's predator ending the abuse to go study being a Catholic priest. Andrew needed a friend, I thought. He wouldn't see a counselor; I guess like so many others, he thought that meant talking about the abuse and that's it. And Andrew had another secret that he couldn't hide or share with anyone else.

People tell me things, and Andrew had horrific trauma he further spilled, staining me. As a young adult, he and a friend received a ride from a guy who offered Andrew a drink. Andrew ended up drugged and unconscious, taken into a house where awful things happened to him. The friend stayed in the house guarded by a mentally disabled man. Eventually, something happened to Andrew where he started urinating and fighting. The predator gave the van keys to Andrew's friend, and they left. I left out some of the details, but you can still see from just this account that it's a heavy story.

Maybe, then, you can see why I got sucked right in thinking from one trauma sufferer to another, "Poor guy. Maybe I need to give him a chance." We started dating. Yeah, terrible idea; the guy needed healing from the Holy Spirit and trauma counseling, but hindsight's 20/20, right? He told me about experiencing trauma so horrific that I needed to share it with others because it was too much for me to process alone. I really needed to set clear and healthy boundaries with him, but I had not learned that yet. Andrew's confession of blistering rapes throughout youth and adulthood was an accidental confession that cried out of him and soaked me in the process. I felt I had to give him a shot at a relationship because someone owed some kindness to this guy. Because I wasn't worth anything, really, I didn't know that I had a choice in remaining only friends with Andrew. Anytime the relationship was draining, which was frequently, I felt I needed validation and permission to end the relationship because otherwise I was giving up on an innocent victim. *Don't I owe people who suffered, Becky and Andrew? Isn't it true that if they weren't hurt, someone else like me could have been?* Our pain kept us together.

Now, all relationships are precious, but an intimate relationship with someone is sacred. No one with a healthy mind should enter a romantic relationship with someone out of kindness or this accidental manipulation, but neither of us had a healthy mind. He would make angry barbs, lashing out as if I was his toxic mother, and I'd push him away from me, feeling like I had to turn off my own personality just to be with him. I became codependent and miserable and trying to find the right antidepressant for my own depression was unsuccessful and expensive!

Andrew joined me during the reiki experiences, though. His mother practiced it, so he knew that world. Though he disliked it, he tolerated the energy-healing experiences with me because my depression, neck, and back trauma continued and because he still lived with pronounced (though undiagnosed) PTSD—even when the presence of the practitioner felt like an intrusive, intimate physical violation.

After we broke up, freed from our unsuccessful relationship, we would see each other once in a while. Sometimes I needed computer help, maybe he would need shoulder manipulation (he couldn't let strangers, even a female masseuse, touch him) after work, or I'd need a talk walk, working out a child abuse quandary.

For example, when my siblings and I discussed an FBI report on our abusive stepdad John, his lack of activity stuck in my craw and I could not get it out. The report stated John spent four hours sitting in a chair outside of his home, went inside for lunch, and then returned to sit outside again on the porch for four more hours. I desperately needed to know why he was doing this. I could not stop my mind from fixating on wondering if he'd had a stroke. Was he doing this because he did this in prison for fifteen years?

Everyone else told me to move on, but they didn't realize that I was having an obsessive, compulsive type moment stemming from the trauma sown into me. I was outright disturbed and had an anxious fear that I needed help squashing. Andrew told me that the stepdad deserved the behavior, but I told him, "Yeah, I know, but I need more. I need to know why so I can stop this feeling. You get this because you've been through it. Plus you're a thinker and you're analytical like me so you can reposition this for me like I would for you. We can analyze the behavior and play therapist a bit."

I hate to say someone needs experience to understand something, but sometimes it's true, isn't it? Sure enough, Andrew theorized that there could have been health issues and that a specific substance could have been used to keep John from molesting anyone else. Based on our conversation, I went home, looked up these possibilities, and worked through the mental jam.

When I see others processing things in this fashion, things that seem small, I can't tell if they have a traumatized brain or a disordered brain like mine, but I try to help them work through it. They may not have a fellow trauma brain person like I had. Andrew and I could occasionally support each other, and that's important when you've had trauma.

※

On my own I went, aiming to answer my own questions and fulfill my own needs because I felt that I could only trust myself. But some wounds just can't be dressed without a loving touch from someone else. There was a moment in my local gym's saltwater pool where, for no apparent reason, I couldn't swim even one-eighth of a mile as opposed to my usual mile. I started grieving. There was no open wound gushing blood from my belly, but I had to keep looking to double check. Trauma and pain had me certain something was happening. I felt so wounded and anxious, not just to the point of thinking that there was a large gaping wound in my body, but to the point where I started suffocating if I was under water for several seconds.

I kept trying to soldier on, but I eventually gave up and used the salt water to muffle my howls and sobs. The chronic pain, depression, and rejection won out. No one can ever say that I am against expressing emotions or that I am not resourceful! Water is an excellent source for muffling sobs and hiding traces of tears, and my teardrops filled the deserted pool—no one was the wiser.

When recounting this experience to the friend who invited me to the Congregational church (where I tried to be a good churchgoer despite demonic attacks—dabbling with demons who fought to control my body as I vacillated between feeling relief and fear), she and a few others didn't really know what to make of it.

When speaking to my cognitive behavioral therapist (she and my affordable gym were made possible many times by credit cards), she had a sympathetic response, but she had no definition of what was happening or how I could use this pain and sorrow to travel to a healthier state. Our focus was for me to learn healthy boundaries with unhealthy family members and to avoid suicidal leanings and unstable working conditions: my ways of coping. Life had been painful and arduous. My responses were that of a worldly person reacting to trauma. Could a therapist or these church acquaintances give me unconditional, restorative love that would never fail me? Who could teach me about spiritual fighting or protection?

At this point, I'd had about four years of counseling and been diagnosed with ADD and depression, so I was at least more functional but still so isolated and broken. I still had great pain in my life, and I needed something more. Who and what would give me answers to whatever I was searching for, like how someone who had debilitating pain, was often out of work, and had dated someone out of coercion could get relief, security, and freedom from pressure? Instead of showing exasperation with life, I would walk around feeling unworthy. My life goal? Just exist until life ends naturally. All I really knew was that whatever I was supposed to do was intangible and overwhelming. In the end, I knew that God existed and so did I. The moments of "God, this hurts so much," "Take away this pain," and "The world feels so heavy; help those of us who suffer" came, but there did not seem to be answers from God. The more I saw others around me hurting, the more I plummeted.

Daddy John had sexually assaulted me and my sister. However, the fact that she had to be the one to admit the sexual abuse in court, in front of actual people, just to imprison him beyond his military desertion (AWOL) charges felt awful. He didn't even get charged with the physical abuse. Yet here I was suffering and experiencing life with a deeply traumatized sister. I wanted the emotionally satisfying answer to *why* instead of the logical answers of why bad people do bad things. Emotionally, life still hurt! And I still felt like I had to mention everyone else's suffering just to validate how bad life felt so I could prove that it wasn't just me but that all of it—abuse, hunger, shame, chronic pain, poverty—was too much! I needed another approach to soothe the never-ending burn that this doomed identity made me feel. What more intimate place than the shower? I needed to feel and express pain. Signs of agony are less visible after submerging yourself in water, so I planned to have a grief session in the shower.

Did I have an excuse for the pain I was in, though? Plenty of people grow up with abuse, neglect, and poverty—so what if there are brokenness and hard times? While my thoughts fought my need to confess all that I was feeling, my spirit fought the burning imprint on my marred character. Telling myself to march on no longer meant to ignore pain but to face it head on. I focused on how the major traumas (except for sporadic job loss) in my life were over, so I needed to be healed already! I couldn't be avoiding humanity because I had a face swollen with grief.

Authentic confession results in freedom or an action to take. Confession, for those of us not Catholic or Orthodox, gets a bad rap and is often misunderstood. In my younger years, I thought confessing meant admitting guilt. It made no sense to admit guilt if you weren't guilty, and what victim's defenses don't shoot sky high when someone says, "Confess your sin"? It doesn't matter if the sufferer is a rape victim, an abandoned single mom, or whomever. *Confession* was a sensitive word like *Jesus* or *submission*. But facing how you feel and admitting that feeling counts as confession. It is a noble way to both heal and build character, which leads to hope. In the shower, I needed a confession.

I confessed the pain:

1. People brutalized and beat Andrew throughout his life. Others got to be safe in the moments he was abducted and ripped apart.
2. He and my sister had developed addictive personalities, and both made that hand to forehead gesture of anxiety when I mentioned these abuse topics—they're still in raw pain! Their lives, their skin, their self-care, and their relationships show the resulting post-traumatic stress.
3. Someone brutalized my sister, and it's almost impossible to admit to myself that I was violated too. She was physically violated more, and I felt guilty that I couldn't help her. She was hurt needlessly, my adult mind thought, but my inner child felt guilty as it wasn't Becky's job to stop a serial abuser.
4. The adults in my life were clueless and acted powerlessly. There was so much silence. Nothing but silence and ignorant ideas.

I could not even bear the burden with those who had "worse abuse," which made me worthless in my mind, not someone struggling with PTS. Me, what I experienced, didn't matter to the world around me, so I internalized that and both it and I did not matter. I could only feel for them. *Is that enough?* What they went through was a sacrifice! I knew real victims, and I knew what was in the back of their minds: They know they are fighters. They have memories of choosing to be a substitute for others and have said to me that even though sexual abuse broke them, they would bear it again to keep it from happening to others. I couldn't bear this sacrificing; it was painful like authentic love and sharp like truth!

A sweet gift—that's what this confession was. Somehow it helped communicating with myself. I received some seeds of restoration just from letting myself feel.

Once I learned the whole definition of confession, I started explaining it to people as confessing out the poison. With snakebites, you can expel the poison by flushing out the blood. Confessing this poison left me drained. However, I had intentionally set aside private time to do this: I made sure the water was a hot massage against my muscles and that I could sleep in the next morning. Looking out for myself like this allowed peace to grow. My ADD mind relaxed some. I could learn from God's still small voice, but at this pre-Christian time, I only knew that my twenty-something-year-old mind was working things out.

I started developing a definition for sacrifice: authentic love in action, so pure it fights against our fallen flesh, leaving us undone and closer to God. It leads to an unconditional love that hurts at first—you only allow that pain out of bravery. At a later point, there's more pain, but you know it will get better. Then comes the craving for more sacrificial love; the more you feel it, the more you want it and appreciate what it means. The secular world tries for this and ends up with a perverted view—nothing but sadomasochism.

Meanwhile, part of me wished the sacred name Jesus did not still feel like a derogatory word. That same part of me got anxious walking into a church full of church people. However, change has to happen with someone; why shouldn't it start with me? So I continued churchgoing with the Congregationalists.

Walking into the typical white church building with bald white pillars in the entryway, I figured continuing to attend couldn't be worse than fighting the battle I was still in. Being welcomed with that *put on your Sunday best* disposition and guided through the vestibule, outer sanctuary, or, even worse, narthex—whatever term the church society had given to a carpeted, painted mudroom with hangers—wasn't worse. An oil painting of a bald white man and a copper bust of some even older figure of the church's past tied in nicely with the corporate workers dressed in business casual far more than I did, but it's not like I hadn't been in plenty of other uncomfortable situations. The men and women had perfect hair, well-prepared faces, and ironed clothes. At best, I smoothed my clothes by wearing them and hoping my body heat would smooth out the wrinkles! More frequently, I wore used attire, compelled to use them up and not let clothes—just like food—go to waste. This higher class of people didn't possess that proclivity.

Sitting in an ultrastiff, painful pew stuffed with people with a wide array of obvious medical conditions and various discomforts made me think they were as delighted to be there as I was. Doing a deep eye roll, I retracted the leash on my attention. *C'mon, lady! Going to church is the right thing to do. Sickly Christians or not, you gotta start somewhere. It's just like being the new girl at yet another school. Grab a Bible or something!* Yet there were no Bibles, only hymnals. Sighing, I stared at the ceiling, then windows, then walls. The whitewashed barriers were holding me in this great sterile space like a hospital room you haven't yet been cleared to leave. Humiliation is easier to hide when you're alone. Feeling it with others who are also hoping to find basic spiritual provisions is excruciating.

Breathe, girl, breathe. It's just another "face your fears, food bank" moment, and you don't have to go there anymore. You're okay. I simply exhaled in disappointment and embarrassment: I had forgotten to wear church clothes and showed up in how I normally dressed—track pants and a tank top—so I felt further disconnected. I was hoping for the church to be as inviting as the new age places and to feel like home and family. I was hoping to not see so many broken people and to get real direction from someone instead. I loved eccentricities and wished for colorful, healthier, normal people with a blend of oddities—anyone you would find on the street—but not people letting all their problems be known just because it was a Sunday. I didn't expect a hospital.

Maybe I should just leave, I thought. I just felt religion there, not hope. I felt overwhelmed and alone because, inside, I was. I saw everything through the lens of my own woundedness. Like so many people who had some church experience growing up, I had almost every fear- and hurt-based reason to avoid narrow dogmatism except a mustard seed of truth that knew the only truly narrow object in Christianity is the gate that every Christian must pass through to reach the kingdom. Anything else is temporary or illusory, so we can't let religious roadblocks trick us or prohibit us from going through the narrow but sacred gate of salvation.

For example, it was awkward listening to comments from the pulpit and the after-service fellowship gathering about women being prohibited from teaching from the Bible or preaching. I often heard, especially from women, that "the Bible makes it clear that women can't lead men" and "this is the only solid view; people disagreeing are pushing an agenda. It's false teaching!" Some said women couldn't share testimonies either, and others wouldn't let new Christians or female missionaries speak about major Christian events, not even to those local outreach events in Salem, Massachusetts. A husband had to stand at her side.

Well, I'm single. What if I'm supposed to say something? Why can't I talk to a church group, but I can effectively lead men at work? This made me uncomfortable because the men and women espousing this viewpoint acted dominating and rarely discussed alternative arguments. If this was predominately what I saw around churches growing up and was seeing again, what was I supposed to do? It was all the more irritating when some guy stole my visitor information off a sheet and started contacting me because he said he fell in love with me and my eyes. I wasn't there for this. I just needed help.

Learning about being a Christian is hard when questions to leadership are shut down with force or even when there's simply no dialog. Sharing different views might seem like exposure to faulty doctrine, but how could I know what evidence to look for in the Bible to examine it for myself if I was kept in the dark? Don't we have to make up our own minds on what we believe? If we're wrong, can't someone right engage with a fellow Christian or church attendee without fear? It's easy to get leery when a pastor says, "Church, we believe this . . ." Oh, how many times I've heard this! Did I believe the same thing, though? Is wondering allowed? I wanted warm, nurturing people to engage me like a family.

It seemed like women's roles were not up for discussion; females were apparently not holy enough. *What about those church ladies who were barely literate but showed me such tender love as a child?* Clearly, they prayed for us three kids when they saw our skinny, barely covered bodies. I didn't know what to do!

A few months into attending the church, I suggested a Jericho march, only without knowing the official name, I called it a type of conga line to "Blow the Trumpet in Zion." My suggestion was "ill suited" for a Congregational church. How on earth would all those claims about the church being the place for help come to fruition if churches didn't know about spiritual battles and couldn't explain something as simple as the differences in their beliefs? *How did I end up in this place?* I was the sheep my family received when I was in junior high: tangled in confusion and in the wrong place.

Past life experiences crashed into my present reality. John's humiliating, controlling mind games; our legalistic, churchgoing grandmother's soul-crushing behavior; Mom repeatedly showing up to junior high sporting events to pick me up hours after everyone was gone because she was stretched too thin—I learned that I didn't matter, I was the junk fish Dad threw back in the water because pickerel were all bones, no meat. In post-traumatic reveries, I'd remember coming home from school and warning Mom and Mark that the upcoming storm in Litchfield meant we should bring the dogs inside. But our dogs were outside animals and not trained to be in a house, so pregnant Lady, our Lab, remained outside. She gave birth during the storm, and her puppies froze to death, making it hard for my stepbrother Robert to shovel their tiny corpses as their frozen skin stuck to the ice. But Lady at least got to stay in the unfinished garage after that. My mind would play these moments on loops. Can hope exist when your past is still working in the present?

Presently, it wasn't even that long ago Becky was shoplifting diaper rash cream for her babies in one moment and blowing her tax refund money on tattoos the next. She looked like the other chain-smoking, low-income women around her, and all I could do was offer her exhortations (to which she wouldn't listen and stay by her side, being there for her kids when she and her husband couldn't or wouldn't. It seemed like I was needed there, not at the church, some impersonal, corporate gathering to fulfill religious duties. But could I help anyone if I knew I didn't belong and wasn't appreciated anywhere? Was it all just smoke: my value to the family as the voice of reason, my identifying as a Christian while feeling awful anxiety in church, realizing how little I knew the Bible—having mistook Bible stories for knowing actual Scripture? I was a wreck.

Chapter 9
Drive-Through of a Glass Darkly

And so, God willing, we will move forward to further understanding.

—Hebrews 6:3 NLT

I was so entangled in ungodly things that even though I saw glimpses of the way out through praying to Jesus and trying to turn from the energy practices, I started wondering if maybe my caustic wit and begrudging need to survive were not enough to get me where I needed to go. Yeah, I was pretty friggin' resilient, but the journey was so lonely and that's how the demonic world further hurt me. I really do not want to describe my experiences with the demonic attacks that resulted from energy work. It's embarrassing. Maybe it seems like a churchgoer at a Congregational church who idolized the rational mind would stop creepy practices or that a woman in her late twenties would have more sense, but life is messy and real.

Demons sporadically hounded me daily and jerked me awake at nights. Months of this escalated, greatly affecting my sleeping and impairing my judgment. I can't even remember if I kept a journal about the new age stuff, but my emails reveal some pretty bizarre things. When, for the first time in years, I could skip and jog, I reached out to any and all of my helpers to thank and learn more from them about relieving chronic pain.

Even though the energy "healing" occurred around 2010, the time the Affordable Care Act launched, I want to backtrack yet again (sorry!) for a few pages to explain how disabilities frustrate and prime one for the occult.

I don't have a clear answer on how I became disabled/developed chronic pain. Was it from waitressing long hours in high school/college, constantly on my tired feet, fresh out of school for the day or just after a track meet? If there was no track meet before, I would jog two hours after my shift, come rain, shine, or night. Was it powerlifting too? Maybe leg pressing four hundred pounds at the gym played a large part in herniating at least the discs in my lower vertebrae. The SI joint damage, I just don't know—arching my back when I jumped across a finish line? What I do know is that I'd do whatever it took to live differently from my mom, who conformed to her husbands and their lifestyles, which meant at this time (college) she was so morbidly obese that the five-pound tumor in her abdomen wasn't even visible. If it had been malignant, I would have lost my mom. I needed to fight back by performing—overperforming—athletically and scholastically. Sweat drops were my tears.

At some point, though, it's time to acknowledge that not caring for oneself leaves its mark. I had lost myself years before. Part of me died from all the trauma. So how could I have cared for myself when I was no longer living? Internalized abuse and listening to who your world says you are make working with yourself chaotic, so fighting for a place in that world and trying to earn a modicum of respect is like earning a spot at the table of adulthood. You might have earned it, but will you be accepted when you get there? Are your accomplishments measured in their depth, sweat, and truth or by what people think?

My goal in high school/college was to counteract the dysfunction of being a female by turning myself into someone strong by worldly standards with beautiful, powerful muscles that earned acceptance and gave me the same competitive advantages as men. While a little girl part inside me still dreamed of creating and being beauty, I more frequently thought of the little victim girl stunted and imprisoned in me that feared what men would do to me if I lost my muscles and the only strength I had except for my sharp tongue.

Self-reliance was the closest thing to intimate love I had known. A problem with self-reliance is you don't have someone else looking out for you, and in high school, I had a negligent mom and a verbally abusive, extremely chauvinistic stepdad, so my guardians didn't care enough about me. In college, I was the one checking on Mom after she separated from Mark, who had punched my brother and been forced to physically leave the house but contacted her despite the police order. Someone had to help her remain strong. However, I couldn't live her life for her. Then she broke her neck after falling off a ladder she placed on a floor far too slippery and lost her mind for months upon months until she eventually had two surgeries at Mass General in Boston and Mark divorced her. I was needed. No doubt extreme exercise and not knowing how to properly care for myself caused my back pain, but the root of the problem was so much more. I had no idea who I was and tried to form my identity on social constructs since that's all I had.

Naturally, energy healing couldn't reach this deep parasitic root in my body and spirit, but it did lessen the side effects of back pain. Even though I still had to massively overhaul my behavior and militantly guard my lower back, I actually had moments of freedom. To an injured person, this probably makes sense, but when a person becomes disabled, there exists a completely new way of living. When the scales of disability/chronic pain tip further by the weight of subsequent injuries, life quality plummets. Let me give an example so there's context.

Diabetics don't die of diabetes but of complications. They get a small cut that resists healing, that injury becomes infected until surgery and eventually amputation happens. When that procedure doesn't heal entirely, another amputation happens. More medications are given, and the diabetic becomes as sedentary as a sloth because the weight gain, frustration, and pain seem to land on the person in heavy heaps. All these problems keep happening. These sins beget other sins while the diabetic is trying his or her hardest to juggle these burdens that seem to fall from nowhere (unless some of these come from bad genes or bad habits, in which case, self-blame develops and jumps on the pile of problems too!). No one ever officially dies of diabetes, but if you "take every thought captive" (2 Corinthians 10:5 ESV), you know different.

One of my subsequent injuries was after a nasty flare-up in 2008, two years before my foray into energy healing. Doctors still wouldn't operate on me because I was "too young" and the surgery was too complicated because the procedure requires access through the abdomen, so I delt with epidurals and prescriptions that weren't enough and became so immobile that I was worse off than when I had been in college just a few years prior. It hurt too much to exercise, so the only workout I got was walking and I couldn't do much of that. I tossed my disability placard for my car and didn't bother renewing it. I needed walking; it was my only source of health.

But soon, I needed a knee arthroscopy because my thigh muscles became so thin and weak. Several times when I stood to get up and pushed against my left leg to lift my body, hoping to relieve the back pain that felt like both a flaming wire and a broken knitting needle, my knee popped out of place. My knee would feel like a fingernail being bent backward but much worse. I had to reset my leg into the socket multiple times as physical therapists and I looked for solutions. I hate having to reset my own bones! It looks cool in movies, but in real life, it's so easy to cause further damage. Living with the consequence of long-term abuse and neglect, growing up hard, made it frustrating to stomach more subsequent damage, physical or otherwise.

I eventually got a referral to an orthopedic surgeon and an MRI. The result was a badly torn meniscus that needed an arthroscopy and not physical therapy, yet insurance wouldn't cover it without physical therapy first, which just created further damage. Whatever—same ol' story, but at least I was getting somewhere.

While I was anesthetized for surgery, a nurse forgot to ground the scope, which resulted in a nasty second-degree burn into my thigh. It's very easy to fall through the cracks in hospitals or even when you're unconscious getting a simple arthroscopy. The nurses pretended no one knew how the wound occurred when I woke up with a burning thigh and tights covering the wound.

It took months of trying to file complaints and get wound treatment just to find out what must have happened. Of course, the medical lawyer my therapist recommended wouldn't take my case because he said, "Negligence can be proven with the details, after care and lack thereof. The photos and the report from the hyperbaric wound center will help, but at most, you'll get a few thousand dollars and that's not worth taking on. It's too hard to sue doctors, even making a complaint to the physician's board is just going to result in a slap on the wrist by his peers."

Outside I tried to be normal; inside I was on fire and that internal burn was a bonfire. My quadricep was covered in pain, and it took specialists scraping away at the wound and shots just beneath the remaining transparent skin to get the wound down to a palm-sized scar that people often comment on to this day.

Some ask what happened, and I have to give an appropriate, short answer. Some relate to it or mention how they know someone badly marred too and feel sympathy. Another response received is "What a waste of a leg," and I smile and say, "But there's all the rest of this to look at," and laugh. I'm grateful for what could be taken as an insult of me being soiled goods because at least that person understands that, yes, I am damaged and my appearance was greatly affected and it's not fair. The response that makes me cry: When little kids trace the scar with their baby fingers and look at me with sweet sympathy or walk up to me and kiss my scar, trying to make it better. Sometimes my teenage niece will still come to me at the beach with a handful of sand and rub it against my thigh because she remembers me for years "working on my scar" trying to fix it in some way and even using the sand at the beach to exfoliate.

My story isn't unique. Some would say it's an inconsequential narrative. After all, everyone has a story and substories. Some scar stories are symbolic of a life to come (like the curvy mustache scar on my face). They hurt differently than the multiple ways a loud, distracting scar like the one on my thigh does.

The thigh scar was an embarrassing "gift" that kept giving because it was an awful start to my new permanent (finally not another temp job) career with crutches and a weeping zombie-looking wound. Letting it breathe means nothing should touch it, so the healing wound is visible, awkward in an office setting. You can't cover that up when you're in the women's bathroom re-dressing the wound. I would grow faint and pale, sweating from the efforts and trying to move fast so no one saw what I was doing. It was humiliating, like I was showing proof: *See what someone did to me? This is the value I have, and no one cares that I'm left to clean up my body that just gets used and discarded.* And I had to keep from throwing out my back with all that leaning.

All that to say, the consequences of the serious lower back flare-up in 2010 scared me! The root cause was back pain, but it led to all this. With Mom being a nurse and me growing up around the medical community, I loved it, but because of my experiences, I did not want to rely on it. So when the "Oh no!" panic at all the complications that a flare-up could bring me hit me, I panicked. *Do nothing—waste away. Do something—be in pain. Do more, trying to live—more pain and maybe further, uncontrolled injuries.* I never collected disability because suing to get it was something I didn't understand was common at the time and because I knew I couldn't settle for living like this. There had to be another way. This is how my disability and fears of resulting injuries transported me to occult practices that showed me what looked like hope.

When a coworker at the company, Helium (now out of business), talked about something called *polarity* and feeling good from this energy healing offered just down the road at a metaphysical bookstore, I checked into it. After Helium laid off most of us, the free services at the metaphysical bookstore were the right price, plus the place just seemed multicultural. Reiki and crystal healing were introduced to me there, but I drew the line at Kundalini yoga with the overt spiritual nature of channeling/visualizing a serpent wrapped around me. I couldn't see how that would help anything.

The crystals were the real draw. How beautiful the rose quartz, sapphire, and pearl entwined necklaces were. These items on their own have always been safe, but I was told that they had healing properties. Well, count me in! I didn't think that entailed anything demonic but simply that the crystals would possibly improve something the way some people claim copper bracelets help with arthritis or magnet therapy improves something. The metaphysical bookstore sold a lot of things meant to help people, stuff for hippies, foreigners, spiritual people—all things I had seen before at museums, American Indian events, and college. The only thing I had found that had a negative effect on me were dream catchers. They brought nightmares, so I stopped having those in high school. Surely, I could ignore the tarot cards and dream catchers and accept that the metaphysical store was a place that housed mostly good things.

Therefore, these crystals were most likely good and the specialness of having some angels attached to these was divine. Did the bookstore clerk tell me these were angel crystals or someone in passing to whom I recounted this experience? I don't remember, but my family found it interesting and I felt pleased with the purchase.

I looked for more places like the metaphysical bookstore in my town so I didn't have to wait for the Andover Metaphysical store but could check out some "spiritual" places on Cape Ann, right smack in Gloucester, where I lived. I thought I was so fortunate to find so many energy healing places near me! Reiki was practiced a lot and involved healing through laying on hands mostly. I was told Jesus did the same thing, and like I said before, it helped with my pain and I saw that it was offered to cancer patients in the area for free, so I continued to practice it and become certified.

My emails from this time remind me that after doing the reiki exercises during our initiation and certification, I told the women in my group that my bedroom lights started flickering and my hands started moving on their own just like they had in class. Apparently, this along with dizziness was normal for the reiki master. She emailed back explaining things even freakier would happen to her. I know, I know—WARNING! I acted naively, but this was something I could try with measurable results. I figured I was doing something wrong as a beginner and that I needed to correct the situation and that's what I was told, so I doubted myself and continued looking for direction while I persisted in attending church.

Sometimes I stretched my palm to the congregants and could feel their ailments, and some I tried to heal. I could feel prickling sensations from a nervous church friend and cramps from someone else. I felt like I was a part of something. When the church mentioned outreach for elderly shut-ins, I remembered being recently snowed in, unable to leave my apartment because I was on crutches and a Gloucester plow encased my car with snow. I didn't have the bandwidth to care for elderly shut-ins when I myself was in need. I was so empty, looking for help, and when you're in that state, you're deeply compassionate toward others at first. But then when your own needs get ignored because you live twenty minutes away (too far) or you're young so people assume you're fine, compassion evaporates.

When the solitude around me was too much and I lost my next job (after Helium) to layoffs, I watched videos of Christian leaders, hoping it would fix me and teach me more than the tiny bit of Christianity that I knew. I owe so much to them, even the ones with major struggles, because I could relate to their messiness. When I needed company, my mom and sister would be on the phone. Since Mom had broken her neck, she became disabled and eventually could sue for disability, which meant she didn't work nor did her boyfriend/next husband, so she had time for me. My sister had young kids, so they provided entertainment and distractions.

When times were occult scary, Mom would stay on the phone with me. I remember one time nodding off and I woke only when I heard Mom say, "Are you still there? I think you fell asleep, so I'm hanging up the phone."

I said, "No, I'm awake." Other times, I'd wake up to the dead phone.

Speaking with my brother and sister-in-law about occult things, since they said they used crystals and angel cards, may have added fuel to the spiritual fire. They lived in Connecticut and my sister-in-law had "Catholic" chiropractor energy healers of some sort that she and her mom loved seeing. Maybe it was seeking the Way of the church instead of being content with the occult.

Either way, the occult experiences continued while one nasty attack left me driving home feeling as if an invisible cloak of fear was on me. Gang members don't like it when you hang with others. Demons are the same way and any angel not from God is demonic, so this behavior is what one should expect if he or she is involved with occult practices and also trying to learn about God. I had just always thought of angels as positive, light-filled beings from God.

As I was driving home, I was overcome with dizziness. Hoping to escape the feeling, I tried calling someone as a distraction, but the buttons on the phone wouldn't work. Pressing the buttons, any one of them, made no impression. Rationalizing that there must be a problem with the battery or something, I plugged the phone into the charger when I got into my apartment. Giving the phone a few minutes, I tried praying to the God I knew existed but did not yet fully trust. I sang worship songs with raised hands to the God who had my attention but would not sustain it. Hours earlier, I had felt one of the spirits near me and my friend in church. However, I thought that the imp was left behind and I would not be pestered so soon. I tried denying the fear that a demon could harass me in a church. Further rationalizing hadn't stifled the fear that grew on me as I had driven home because I had been a truth seeker since I was a kid. How could I deny what was happening? I wasn't even safe in a church! I knew I was scared and lacked confidence that Jesus would cover me. I could not move on.

Side effects from a new antidepressant started around the same time. Could I connect the left leg tingles, dizziness, and fear to the medication? Sure, that's how the Enemy works—by confusion. However, at that moment I felt an entity embrace me and sway with me as if there was a person standing behind me, mimicking a soothing gesture. I needed truth. The spirit rocking me was a goblin poorly pretending to be something comforting! It gave off a feeling of climbing horror. I broke away from the embrace and grabbed the phone. The phone still wouldn't work when I pressed the buttons, but it was on! I couldn't stand it, and the residue of horror was still present. A chill shot through me when the numbers 88888 jumped on the screen. *Okay, a delay, right? The phone will work now* . . . No. Something was pressing the number eight when I would pick up the phone to use it. I froze, but I knew I wasn't going to go over the edge of fear because it wasn't three sixes. It's odd that came to me, and I'm far too pragmatic to let such superstition bother me. However, these weren't exactly normal times. All I could do after seeing the eights appear was read my Bible while the demonic attacks came and just keep rebuking them in Jesus's name.

All other times I wanted to call someone in the midst of an attack, the phone would not only work but would have enough power to remain on six hours into a call. I'd call Mom after an attack and be so tired or wounded in need of a little long-distance comfort. We would talk or I would just listen to the goings-on of my mom's day while we used the speakerphone feature for all that it was worth. Mom would leave the speakerphone on so she could be present enough for the conversation. Sleep took over when my cheeks bumped the hang-up button. Sometimes, I would hear her talking in the background to someone else, but I still needed her on the phone because that connection was enough for me not to feel alone. A persistent spiritual attack might mean waking up every few minutes during the night and into the morning so that I could hear Mom making breakfast. I know on some bad occasions, my sister and mother felt manifestations of evil energy in their own rooms while we were on the phone. Awful.

In between Bible studies, church, prayer meetings, and work, I kept searching for the Lord. If the church was right and he was the answer, I wanted to research him through multiple mediums like I did with everything else. I read the Bible, asking God to give me a desire to read it and to help me understand it. There were insights when I did this. However, Scripture hadn't yet been illuminated the way it would be in my future. I was simply giving the Christian religion another shot because you can't judge such a huge enterprise by *some* of its people or even *some* of its ideas, right? I had always been a truth seeker and legalist to a fault, painfully honest and always trying to look beyond perception to truth. I craved searching for meaning and finding a place in this world from when I was young through now in my late twenties. I needed to keep searching for spiritual truths, so that meant including various church events and churches into the mix.

The Congregational church where I went said spiritual warfare existed, but it seemed none of the several hundred attendees had experience with it. No one discussed it. The church's belief was that we all have spiritual gifts. Sermons on what that meant or how to use them were "not necessary and will bring up confusion." Until a female Presbyterian pastor joined the church (given a new title, of course, since females weren't allowed to be pastors or preachers there), even small group studies weren't done on spiritual gifts and any gift pertaining to spiritual warfare wasn't elaborated on, so I wasn't sure how to counter demonic attacks except for what I came across online or remembered from my childhood. Often, I had to guess.

I was always told and outright pressured to stay with a church organization, so even when I wasn't sure it was the right fit for me, I stayed and listened to teachings that were edifying but were also not helpful like, "God may or may not heal people; we can't know." Personal testimonies of amazing experiences that were medical successes were applauded, but supernatural healings of someone praying over a broken bone were met with silence or "We don't know why that happened" and "Praise God. We're glad you figured that out. We can't know God's mind or explain why that happened."

I felt like I couldn't go to that church for help; it was the only church I had been invited to and had come to know as an adult. In fact, I wrote a note and asked the pastor if he would discuss healing. He said in a gentle way, "We don't talk about that." He did recommend a marriage counselor since she was the only Christian psychologist he knew of, but she either wasn't seeing new patients or insurance wouldn't cover her. It's hard to trust something confusing, conflicting, and unable to meet you where you are. I've since found several churches that believe God still heals and know Christian counselors. Maybe it's my job now to spread the word that there are good Christian resources out there if you just don't give up.

However, since I couldn't rely on that church to meet my needs, I continued exploring energy healing, tailoring it to be more Christian influenced based on advice from fellow church members who showed interest in it. Though, with my lack of spiritual experience, of good or evil, discussions that really struck a chord with me were not had inside the church. Since I was living near Salem, Massachusetts (the witch city with heavy occult traditions including a Satanic Temple), and the church was near the actual witch trial location (Danvers), plenty of neighbors and colleagues on the North Shore found energy healings interesting. Many of us had encountered spirits in our two-hundred-plus-year-old homes, so a place ripe for new ageism was not countered by the church.

Someone on a whim recommended that I make sure I was doing my energy healing in Jesus's name. "And make sure the practitioners are praying to God." That was such a good idea! How sweet for them to look out for me. I took their advice and ran with it. I then learned that *praying to God to do ungodly things won't work.*

After several more moments like this, I learned that it might be okay to go to a church that was more appropriate for me. Churches push for you to commit to them and take membership classes as opposed to church hopping, but I've heard a pastor decree that you really need two years at a church to know if it's a fit, and I heard similar sentiments from Christian books and videos about how people would just leave churches for a place with better music instead of investing in the church. And the inner talk if someone broke the rules and left the church for another—I wasn't ready for that confrontation! But I was at least learning that the truly biblical and Spirit-led church is without walls and without borders. It might be difficult for a church like that one I was attending to reach people like me. But at least they got me studying the Bible and offered the invitation for my messed-up self to be included in their mission. It wasn't a great fit for me, but thank God for the people there willing to pray for me and tolerate such a mess of a human! Run-down churches, beautiful well-funded cathedrals, and megachurches—they can all reach someone. I simply tried to be less awkward, prickly, and wounded so I could have connection more to the church as a whole. I also wished that a self-professed, Bible-believing church with a few hundred committed members knew much more about nurturing new and troubled members.

I wished they knew how to confront the unseen world. I hadn't yet found church to be a comfortable home, a place where I could get low and fight against the tide, then rest when done. With a jumbled mind and no clue what to do, I stumbled forward.

⁂

I eventually discovered there is something called biblical living. It's how to live in a way that takes the scales off our eyes so we can see true humanity and reach what the Koine Greek in the New Testament calls *metanoia.* We are supposed to be changed by love as the Christian platitude goes. Unfortunately, at this point in my life journey, I was what evangelist Ray Comfort calls a "false convert." I did not put *complete trust* in the Lord into practice, which in turn hampered the final step in turning from worldly ways and turning to God's ways (which I also subsequently learned to define as *repentance*—who knew that's what people meant when they yelled at you to repent?).

Planted seeds became sprouts, and theories started developing. I couldn't change the past, so I looked at it through the lens of what I experienced with my niece when she washed my hair in the tub and what Christ did on the cross, then applied the church's answers about why Christ died to understand why I needed to love my sister's child abuse sacrifice for me and let it be felt within. The equation worked out like this: If I did not accept her love and that she did what she knew how to do, I would be judging and rejecting her actions. Often people think that their actions define them. Perhaps my sister would also feel like I was rejecting her and her innocent, sacrificed body. Enough people already did that to her; I certainly wouldn't. That is where I have never budged. Ever. Whatever insight God was giving me, it was helping me but not in a way I expected.

Did any of this directly prepare me for the spiritual battles I was in? Not a whole lot. Interestingly, it armed me for the war and a sneak attack that became my first real temptation as a Christian later on. But for now, along with many other God-given spiritual insights, I was experiencing the start of being in relationship with the Lord. Funny, this bonding was so tender, gentle, and light that I had no idea an intimate and divine relationship was starting. If this relationship had started with anything beyond a loving brush of the hand and a sacred friendship, my thin skin would have jolted back at what would have felt like a burning advance. I didn't know what healthy relationships were, but I knew what they were not. The challenge was navigating life through this single negation. So far, most advice had been to read the Bible.

Turning to the Bible is as important as prayer and following the Lord. It gives us the fundamentals to build a spiritual foundation. Using J. Vernon McGee's *Thru the Bible* series gave me support beams as I tried to taper off the new age healings. Because the demonic attacks would make me too dizzy to stand, I had to lean on these beams. It wasn't a pretty sight. I looked so foolish trying to heal the herniated discs, sciatica, and my SI joint with new age practices that I almost didn't care how I looked anymore. If I was willing to tackle reducing the scars of long-term child abuse, neglect, and poverty, why not become a brave, Jesus-committed, Holy Spirit–following, Bible lover that leaned on spiritual truths and principles that would protect me from demons? It was better than where I currently was standing!

Various energy healings and worldly methods had simply opened pathways into the supernatural world that never needed opening. There were no other viable options for help except for completely embracing Christianity. Even praying to Jesus before energy healings didn't work, but then, why would it? His name is powerful, but I am almost certain now that one cannot pray to the Lord to do godly healing in an ungodly way. "No one can serve two masters. For you will hate one and love the other; you will be devoted to one and despise the other" (Luke 16:13 NLT).

In retrospect, I was picking and choosing parts of Christianity to use without honoring the rest of it. I was behaving in ungodly ways, showing a true lack of commitment to a relationship of which I thought I was a part. Sections of Christianity were good, and I figured what I had with God was personal enough, but I hadn't fulfilled my part of the relationship. I stank of untrustworthy character, but I didn't know this. Good character was not a concept in my mind, but something I would have defined as a description of someone. I would say, "He or she is a good character," like a hero. Character was not something one had. Defining quality character—noble principles in someone that result in noble and godly actions—was foreign.

At least I could self-advocate a little. I knew I needed to find some relief for the physical and emotional pain that changed my lifestyle and crawled into everything I did. It was better than giving up at least, but I was barely living. When I was laid off from yet another job, I held myself in even less value than before. People need work, to earn in order to appreciate what they have. However, I was not thriving in any way. I had slipped into existing in life, idolizing work and bodily health, sprinkled with tired attempts to survive this phase.

Bragging about being a bad victim but a great survivor was still a backward self-compliment I used to bolster courage to get through each day. It's not a land in which anyone should be. If living in Victim Land is symbolically a place where humans are only meant to exist short term, then the next stage of living in Survivor Land is long term, but it's still only temporary. There's no *metanoia* and permanent residency in serving as a victim or survivor. There's no honor in outstaying your welcome in those lands. I was starting to become aware of this, which is a great direction for life and a good step, but I was still moving between these lands despite this new perception.

Chapter 10
Wrangling Demons
(or Spiritual Warfare in Christianese)

For our battle is not against flesh and blood,
but against the rulers, against the authorities,
against the world powers of this darkness, against
the spiritual forces of evil in the heavens.

—Ephesians 6:12 HCSB

IN LATE SPRING 2010, the backyard grass and flowers smelled sweet, and the afternoon sky was gently sunny. I was still exploring healing outside of church since it wasn't offered, but I was trying to follow what I was absorbing through Bible reading and sermons and people who called themselves Christians who practiced energy healings. I further explored a method of healing with angels who worked on behalf of God—or so it was said. It was a Christian slant to a channeling prayer I hoped would bring more dazzling manifestations that made me feel something good.

I was lounging in my backyard asking for the archangel Michael to provide healing. It wasn't him, of course, but that's what I was told. I felt the demon's stern presence. Within minutes, a raven flew near and crowed and another spirit joined, clutching my heart with an ice-cold grip and making its introduction via speaking through me. I've heard stories like this from people who were trying to communicate with spirits or help them "pass over to the other side." That's not for me, though. I didn't even know what to do in this situation. Being a medium of any sort was never part of the plan, and I didn't like any of this. I got up and paced back and forth, rubbing my bare feet on the grass and shaking out my arms, trying to get grounded. Dumbfounded, I called Mom and asked her what she thought. She immediately went into mom mode.

"Umm, that doesn't sound right! Whatever you were doing, you're doing it wrong."

"But I'm following the instructions, and I'm only trying to heal! I wasn't trying to do any of this. This woodland spirit started speaking through me, and I could feel how cold it was in my chest. It said it is part of this territory . . ."

"Sarah, read off the reiki sentences that opened the healing sessions. I'll wait."

I walked into the apartment to get the paperwork, still flustered. "But I wasn't looking for sprites! I have never had anything talk through me like that before, Mom."

"Um-hm. What does it say?" Though flawed, she was still a mom and brought maturity to this occult situation I didn't have. Her daughter was little all over again and found herself in a mess where she needed Mom to help her sort things out.

I read off the script to her. She recognized what I was doing as a séance and told me to stop it and not to let that happen again because "messing around with séances is dangerous." She reminded me of her experience with gazing into a crystal ball with friends at eleven years old. I remembered the story with fear and understanding, but I loved that about Mom. It sounds pathetic, but when I think about these times, I revere and appreciate her. She knew exactly what was happening and what to say with complete authority; she didn't know God personally yet, but she knew what not to do. Even though she didn't and couldn't keep me safe from her second or third husbands, she tried to protect my soul.

If loving her for something that seems small is pathetic or is psychologically defined as a desperate need to love, well, I can honestly wear that label to my grave. Sometimes you just want someone to try.

Now, it's weird to have a one-person séance. I didn't go through that type of experience again where I felt the demon speak through me, but a one-person séance is exactly what the metaphysical world, Christian Scientists, and channelers (developed by Edgar Cayce, who considered himself a Christian) are doing. I had known that guided meditations/hypnosis was often used as a window to the new age world. I didn't think I was getting very involved with that, but neither did the founder of new age, Edgar Cayce. He was a churchgoer and fell into the occult, became afraid of it, then was talked into it and started the movement.

It was easy to use my angel cards since they weren't called tarot cards and used the guise of angelic images and platitudes. Eventually, I owned a deck of both types of cards and used them with my sister and sister-in-law. We would watch when one card was whipped out of the deck by something invisible and flung across the room. *How did I become that person?* All of my life, I was the exact opposite. What was next, a Ouija board with angels and Roman Catholic saints on it? Did I need to buy those too, using them to supplement what I hadn't yet found in the church? *Only* the Holy Spirit should be indwelling within us and providing healing, but I didn't truly know that yet.

I was so misguided and didn't know how to handle my spiritual journey. And true predators thirst to attack misguided, weak prey. I learned this from watching bullying stepdads, mean-spirited junior high kids, and other people or animals interacting with one another. I knew how to handle these predators. To get control of the new ageism, I looked for weaknesses, assessed observations, and trusted the rugged determination that allowed me to survive life up to that point. Information stored deep in long-term memory surfaced. The Pentecostal church from my childhood taught my family some decent things about wrangling demons like having the Bible open to Psalm 91, "the spiritual warfare chapter," and rebuking in Jesus's name. So I drew on their experiences and ideas.

Of all the things I tried, the tactics that protected me came through facing down my pride and fear. I continued attacking the Enemy with everything I had:

Keeping a Bible open to Psalm 91 (which discouraged the least aggressive spirits)

Rebuking in Jesus's name (which served to slap away the more persistent but still pathetic spirits)

What I call feeling the faith, picturing Christ as a real man who lived and dragged his cross to Golgotha and died for me (which worked on all demons)

After many days, then weeks of insomnia forced on me, my poor body would fall into a deep sleep. That's when a whole mess of dark angels showed how nasty they were. That's also when feeling the faith in Jesus Christ hit back at the dark spirits. A simple reverence for our Messiah is that powerful! In that moment of faith, the demons were wiped away.

You know something? This wasn't the first spiritual warfare season in my life, but it was the most visible and conscious one to me. I learned through trial and error how to handle the demonic predators. The confidence that I surely needed came from *epignosis* (Strong 1890, #1922)—God's revelatory wisdom or holy angels whispering insights into my ear. I still wanted nothing to do with ghosts and spooky, silly things. I was careful to not assume something ghostly was manifesting unless it was extremely obvious. By appearance, I was still trying on logical skepticism, but behind that façade was downright fear!

My sister would tell me to rebuke evil things in Jesus's name without fear. Even when Mom was the instructor, Becky was motivating me to fight back! My sister had spotty church experience like me, but thank goodness for it and for them both encouraging me and confronting my self-doubt. A strong woman has weak moments, even seasons, but long term, she has got to trust God and those who lovingly support her.

I put my mom's and sister's encouragement and motivation into gear. Learning the right formation for me to employ for attack and what position to take in my stance against the nasty supernatural world finally became possible. I was so much more effective once I had this epiphany or shift in perspective: Demons are no different from criminals and child molesters. They are still predators just without physical bodies.

That's it! I thought. Grasping this idea was a cinch! This was territory I understood, but I had been thrown off by the lack of the demons' physical bodies. I took this info and internally fleshed out what I had just learned: *Ghosts are like child molesters and other predators. They will attack you; you need to be ready. They are going to come at you when you are weakest; they won't fight fair.* This self-coaching solidified what was happening, what I needed to do, and how I needed to be. The intangible became tangible. I could take up my position with confidence. I needed to become a very real threat to the demonic presence invading my life.

Though I tried to pull out of channeling more than ever, several spirits started bothering me one night after a Francis Chan *Forgotten God* Bible study. After I went to bed, I was still thinking about the book topics and the class discussions, feeling great and excited. No one had ever talked about the Holy Spirit like this in my limited experience. Everyone in the little group wanted to become better Christians. We seemed to be on a roll.

Out of nowhere, I felt a very creepy presence. I knew something was coming. I got dizzy and felt that external fear manufactured outside of my own personal feelings. It was as if someone was placing something on me. The KJV Bible opened to Psalm 91 by my bed wasn't warding off the presence. This is why Christians shouldn't ever fall into the trap of worshiping the Bible itself. It is so precious, and the *contents* are sacred and holy. Really though, it's the God within that is what matters. Still, I looked at my old Bible and the paperback one I had started sleeping with and carrying on my person like a security blanket. Clutching the paperback NIV gave me confidence, and I spoke the words my sweet church music director advised, "I am bathed in the blood of Christ. You are not welcome here. Go." The creepy presence took its sweet time departing. Other dark shapes flew off. The external fear and awareness that something was there left after this rebuke.

With a drained and delayed mind, I didn't have time to register what was happening, let alone feel the faith. I had little regard for the few dark shapes gathering in the center of my bedroom. Like passersby ignoring a homeless man being jumped in a crowded alleyway, I continued as normal without consideration of being harangued by anything lingering. It was like this situation was just the quotidian instead of a horrid, unusual attack. Within minutes, I was laying back down.

I technically did not know the Lord, as I still had not yet been born again. This put me in the same situation as the seven sons of Sceva in Acts 19. The demons knew Jesus and that he protects his own, but they knew I wasn't yet his own. Some persistent, ugly, squat entity either wouldn't leave in Jesus's name or it returned. I woke with an alertness that came over me. You know, you are deep asleep, but you somehow become aware and then even wide awake. Well, I felt that unlike ever before. My eyes were still closed; I had not moved. That persistent demon had the gall to enter my head.

Having a disgusting ogre of a creature walk into me and put my face on like a mask shocked me. I had no idea that was even possible—never thought it would happen to me. I wasn't even standing but lying back in bed, thinking that the spirits would come no closer since I had Bibles. Now I understand through reading Acts 19 how powerful the name of Jesus is but that using the name, without personally and actually knowing him, imposes limitations. Something inhabited my face, and at the moment I became nothing more than a used object, I felt my eyes change in the darkness. In the past, sometimes the attacks would happen exactly at 1 a.m. or 3 a.m. for a few days in a row. Supposedly, it was the witching hour when the demons were stronger. This sounded eerie and I didn't like it, but I often checked the time because awareness leads to protection. I looked at the clock now, panicked when I saw 3 a.m., and froze.

My eyes focused. They zoomed in supernaturally on something. This was so much more intense than looking through the magnifying refractor used by optometrists where your eyes have to adjust from the change in lenses. The shifting was more fluid and quicker, the way a feline's eyes change when they catch sight of prey. It felt feral and demonic. Expecting a vision to come, I tried to keep my eyes closed, but they opened without my consent. I was through with self-negligence and deception through overanalysis, so I did not stop to think about what to do. Moreover, I didn't compare it to the séance-like encounter where a spirit squeezed my heart with ice and spoke through my own mouth. On my own terms, I sat up and opened my eyes. I would have control. Though nothing was visible, I cast out the spirit again and read Psalm 91 aloud as I got up and walked around.

I started feeling the faith while casting the thing out of my body in Jesus's name. I forced scenes from Mel Gibson's *Passion of the Christ* and various oil paintings—whatever images would arouse in my sleeping mind—quickly through my head, focusing on the Man who made history. The ogre left my face quickly, and the attack lessened but still continued for what felt like hours. The prescription medication I had started taking could produce side effects. A prominent question entered my head: *What if this is just a side effect?*

The demons were mimicking medical side effects and playing mind games with me. I had started taking a common antidepressant, which is acceptable for handling depression. Its sporadic side effects had been tingles in my left leg whenever I started to fall asleep or sometimes after lying down. The effects grew into light dizziness as well. I had been open with my therapist about these spirit visits before the medication. She also thought spirits like a "grandmother or those who have passed lingering around to guide and protect" were possibly around. I had explained that these beings were strangers. We essentially went on to ignore the spiritual activity and tried to address my need for selective serotonin reuptake inhibitors (SSRIs) to find a better antidepressant for me since that was all this particular doctor could address.

On previous occurrences, my left leg would tingle; a few moments of inactivity would pass. *Now maybe it is the medication*, I would think, then try to drift back into sleep. That is when a nauseating force would hit me so hard my head reeled. My leg would tingle from toe to hip like the whole thing had fallen asleep, and something would crawl up my leg and even try to crawl into my body. This part had happened before, but after the ogre put my face on, I threw rationalization and political correctness out. Perturbed, I needed to fight back without worrying about how I appeared.

At least these attackers weren't silver and gold sparkling in the afternoon sunlight. It's a horrible embarrassment to know that angels I had thought were good had been deceiving me so they could experience my body—and I didn't mind at the time. But now I decided I was so done with angels, all angels and their games. Whatever these creatures were and no matter how hard they wanted my body, or me, I was desperate and afraid, but I was as ready to call for help as I was when I thought there were monsters in my room as a kid. I got my mom.

When I called her, I'm sure I rambled on like an insomniac—not just tired but exhausted. I was in extreme need of sleep. Sleep deprivation affects your appetite, how nutty you sound, and how frustrated you get, but Mom understood. After I told her what happened, I fitfully fell asleep with her on the phone. I needed sleep and comfort so badly. When I woke to the sound of my mother's voice several hours later, a slow dawning came on me: She was still on the phone. This time, only my speakerphone was on while Mom had her phone to her ear and right against her mouth. She was gently talking about what she was doing, but her attention was on me as if I was right there with her.

She had no idea that I had awoken. I pictured her at her computer playing a game to pass the time while she spoke lovingly to me, and I remembered laying my head on her lap during a grown-up church service when I was seven years old. Instead of being dismissed with the children to Sunday school, I had gotten to stay with Mom. Sure, the sermon was too boring and I started to fall asleep, but I was an abused, neglected middle child and a momma's girl. I needed that time with her. As kids do, I lightly dozed in my mom's lap.

When a hand touched my arm, I pulled back with a start. She immediately said, "Shhh, it's just Mumma." I had plugged back into the comfort of my mother, and the comfort of the church atmosphere on that sun-streamed pew, and I had slept.

This moment with my mom always meant so much to me. Connecting with that time now allowed me so much gratitude that I still had Mom in my life. I always feared losing her. Though pain laced our relationship, I was so desperate for a mother's love and protection that having my own mother doing the best that she could do at that time was more than sufficient. I laid there during the phone call with Mom's love brushing my hair back from my face and the susurrations of her voice rubbing my arms.

I had my mother's love, but it wasn't enough. I needed something more. A tender moment and a break from our flawed relationship couldn't carry the weight of such brokenness. She'd often not act like a mom but more a self-destructive teenager. She'd had to vacillate between defending us from her third husband or getting lost in becoming more like him, and nowadays after divorcing him, she had her crude boyfriend/future fourth husband (Dave) to mirror. He was safe in that he didn't express sexual advances toward us, but Dave was just so extremely crude, like a homeless man yelling out gutter expletives.

Mom conformed to him fast. When I lost my voice from stress and not sleeping, Mom replied with an oral sex innuendo, a sign of complete decay from propriety that horrified me and my siblings. I mean, this guy still acted like he was fresh off the streets, so of course he influenced my malleable mother. Dealing with the swinging pendulum of Mom's personality was shocking, hurtful, and infuriating. We, us three kids and Mom, just couldn't become like the men, the dads.

There had to be someone else I could turn to. I craved feeling reverence for someone so immense that the whisper of his name or the thought of his expansive presence could hold even the ficklest attention span. I could feel that innately. But what was that something?

Who was it? I was pretty sure I was already born again, but I knew I didn't have that change and supernatural encounter that some Christians had. Ex-drug addicts on fire for the Lord always seemed to have a date and sometimes even a time when they confessed and repented to the Lord and gave their heart to Jesus. I didn't know what to make of that. I had never heard of a false convert, but I knew many others like me and we all called ourselves Christians.

How many personal prayers and conversations with God had I prayed and how many signs and wonders had I seen before? A handful of encounters with the Lord had influenced my life—even a sunset where the clouds had parted and a word had been written in the sky, in my late twenties. The small gaggle of people around me at the Gloucester High School football field had ignored the sunset, save the couple at the other end of the football field who excitedly pointed at the sky. They must have been as floored as I was. I felt plugged in, the way a person has a sudden understanding when Scripture is illuminated. That sign or miracle taught me a lesson on not needing another's approval for validation. *Hola* appeared in the sky like a mighty invisible being drew his finger through the clouds, and I had enough time to walk up the hill to get my camera and return to the bleachers and take a photo, but I did not. I've never hallucinated and knew I wasn't then. The couple at the other end of the football field and I watched the mystery appear and slowly pass as anything written on the wind would. It wasn't for others to appreciate the *hola* written through the clouds—they'd think it silly and scoff—but I had personal insight into God's humor. I had to be a Christian for God to have a relationship like that with me, right? It turns out, no.

But what about in the same timeframe, maybe the same year and before slipping into the occult? I had almost walked away from God, telling him, "I don't know if I believe in you anymore." I've thought of that as the day the world went quiet because I was lying in bed just after dinner on a Friday night and when I said that to God, whatever appliance running in the basement next to me stopped, the kid noises from Gloucester High School (just outside my open window) stopped, and I both saw and felt the lace curtain around my bed stir as something like a big wing took leave of me. Talk about unnerving.

Next came a weeklong separation where I thought I knew what it was like to be a non-Christian. Like someone recently separating from a husband and removing a wedding ring, I had felt anxiety, nakedness, and a lack of security. I felt a profound absence in my life. Within the week, I came back to the Lord on a white moon night, and I sincerely vowed, with too many tears and snot all over my face, to stay with the Lord. I would stay with him no matter how much lost romance we would have to face. We were partners and committed to one another—we could tackle anything together, although the honeymoon was over, and I didn't feel the same way about him as I once did.

Maybe these moments were rededications of faith and would make more sense had I encountered sacramentalism and teaching on what this all could mean. But I lacked a vast amount of information on faith and religion and had no discipleship, nor did I know what that even meant. I simply knew these moments meant something at a deep level and that I had a sacred relationship with God.

Once you know the real born-again experience, you discover God is desperate for an authentic, interactive relationship with us. But my experience is that he makes himself known and will help us before we truly know him. Even so, without surrendering yourself and desires to God and without trusting him like a real person who interacts with you, you are not yet a Christian and are missing out on the most fulfilling experience you could never even dream of. You are still destined for an eternal damnation—you miscarry the very sentience that allows you to even have life. How could I have known that this intensely deep and sacred relationship was what I really needed?

Chapter 11
Growing Discernment

And no wonder, for even Satan disguises himself as an angel of light. So it is no surprise if his servants, also, disguise themselves as servants of righteousness. Their end will correspond to their deeds.

—2 Corinthians 11:14–15 ESV

Several months had passed since the demon had put on my face, and I grew weary of reiki and wanted to feel more connected to God's spirit. The practitioners were more spent than a kid's allowance money. New agers were so open and giving, willing to give what little they had to whoever wanted it. Noble but sad. But I trusted them because I didn't have notions on how they should act like I did with Christians.

I misunderstood God making Christians perfect to mean mistake-free, completed, and holy like Mother Theresa or a wonderful person that after they die they take on a "can do no wrong" mystique. I couldn't yet identify a genuine Christian from someone who simply attended church, let alone reconcile that Christians can sin without being defined by that sin because Christ's pure blood covers them and that's why Christians are perfect, in the process of becoming perfected and further saved. I saw a ragtag group of people doing things differently than I would. Though Christian ways didn't make sense, there was some hope in the gospel and Christian messaging, so I kept with Christianity. It hurt when I read so many references to *brethren* in Bible studies, and I wondered if there was really a place for females to be valued in Christendom. Since I was not sure I belonged and was simply unable to trust Christians or God enough to let go of the worldliness of the occult, I juggled both.

The energy- and angel-related practices were not helping enough, but it seemed to me like I was going in a cleaner, more positive direction. Who wouldn't be open to angels, beings of the light, which simply must mean they're only good? I read in the Bible that Satan was a bright white light, and I wanted nothing to do with him or his own. But I'd be fine with angels because the occult teaches that your intentions matter, so if you only intend for good things to heal with you, that's what will be manifested.

It's Christianity that teaches true discernment to measure something by its fruit. That's still not so easy to comprehend either, especially if you're in your twenties and you haven't developed critical thinking. I did so much alone, lived alone, and relied on self-help so much of my life for guidance that I'd only known secular discernment to protect from bad people, not spiritual discernment that would be revealed by God or Christians and how to play something through so I could hypothesize the outcome.

Angels seemed like nothing from which I would require protection. After all, pretty angelic trinkets and healing music dedicated to angels seemed harmless. Then there were angel cards, interactive unlike the silent God who "doesn't talk to people anymore," which also seemed harmless. I'd found a concession between Christianity and energy healing, and this compromise seemed harmless—until it wasn't.

How did this occultism keep creeping into my life, and why didn't I have any control over it? What would an escalating drug user do to prevent becoming an addict and stop the dangerous drug use? She would go to a methadone clinic (probably one that people around her recommended—just like church) and eventually use methadone to fight off the other drugs. Thank goodness I don't have an addictive personality and that I was not a new age addict, but the comparison still fits so well. Here is what my "methadone" looked like.

I would receive healing from people who pray to "the God they know," aka the Universe, even though it opened spiritual doors and windows that did not need opening. For example, when you think about Buddhism, it's a form of atheism or godlessness, which doesn't seem fulfilling or end well. Using Scripture as a way to understand truth, one holds every thought captive to define something, then challenges every thought to examine the definition. In Buddhism, you start to see that "we are gods and god is everywhere; you can find god in a flower . . . god means beauty." This relativism translated means: "There is no God and certainly not a personal, intimate one." Thus, praying to the Universe because "we can't know God, we can't see God; there could be reincarnation and life on other planets" all starts to translate to: "There is no God. Heaven can't be big enough—I can't even fathom that. I must have the answers despite how I'm living. I must keep striving."

There is a connection between the Healing Touch (an occult practice like reiki) practitioners I would start seeing (they channel spirits and balance chakras and auras) as they also fall into this relativism, trying to find their own truth and to be their own gods. When I was still in this mindset myself, the most bizarre new age practices to the most established became possibilities because everything was relative—no standards, no right or wrong. So instead of completely turning from this world, I simply shifted my drug of choice while slipping deeper. My "methadone" energy healing evolved beyond healing work from angels into treatments from the doctors of the spiritual world, who performed surgeries with "guardians and guides from other dimensions" (Healing Touch and specific School of Healing).

That's right—I found a whole slew of people who worked with aliens. Odd but my brother told me he felt like he was sent to earth from alien life to live as a person with ailments he'd have to suffer with, kind of like a reincarnation experience. I wanted to do good work and understand what this meant. Remember the sheep getting so tangled? I grabbed a textbook on this energy healing, available at a public library like all the other new age books, to learn what I could do. The main institute I tried still exists, [founders name] School of Healing. The "guardians and guides" would operate on a patient's energy. If the patient's third eye chakra was injured, the spirit would operate on it and repair the incision made in the energy field. Coincidentally, my brother called me during this reading to say he "was predisposed to hernias" because he was "an alien from another planet."

The Congregationalist church I still attended held the belief that we are no longer of the age of what the Bible calls generational curses, so I had no understanding yet of what that could mean for my family. I was still thinking that we must be Christians (since my family knew the gospel of Jesus dying for our sins), so we were "free" from any bondage. I didn't think maybe we were under a generational curse nor was I aware of how much the occult is sprinkled around people. I didn't know that a Christian way to respond would be through spiritual discernment, renouncing the occult, breaking generational curses, and asking Christ to fill us and seal us with his Holy Spirit. I just felt sympathy that my family had been through a lot and that my brother was searching for something spiritually fulfilling. Though I thought the alien idea was ridiculous, I needed to be a good girl and keep an open mind about this alien clinic because that would be showing love.

Aliens being demons dressed in deception hadn't occurred to me. Healthy judgment and discrimination were still foreign, so I lived and accepted absurdity; I had no biblical standard or solid moral compass. What did I have? An after-work appointment with a part-time alien surgery practitioner who charged more than $150 for no-shows. So I told my brother I'd give this energy healing a chance, and he wished me well as I said bye to him, laughing and making the Star Trek Vulcan hand gesture. I was off to try something new.

Yes, energy healing is absurd because it isn't real science. It hurts wounded people. Nigel Mumford at a Christian healing seminar commented, "Hurt people, hurt people. Healed hurt people, help people" (Evergreen Covenant Church in Sanford, Maine; November 20, 2015).

I pray in Jesus's name that I remember not to laugh at the absurd things others find themselves in so I can tear down these deceptive things instead and that my experiences can be put to good use. It's one thing to laugh while I write this because I'm safe now, but the healing school is an actual institution with a few different established schools in other countries. There are so many wounded people looking for help and comfort. I wish they could turn to the biblical church more easily to find what they need. The frustrating truth I personally encountered was that the energy practitioners were easier to talk to about anything supernatural, including biblical miracles, than my local church groups. I appreciated the open door because deep down I wasn't just hurting in my back and neck but hurting from spiritual brokenness and loneliness.

Going to a practitioner of this school of healing eased my chronic back pain enough that for a half day I could skip and sprint across the lawn like a normal person. It also gave me a chance to ask an approachable and knowledgeable person about prayer, meditation, hypnosis—healing approaches. After a few other sessions, I also had happy, smiley moments and physically felt like other people got to feel after successful epidurals, though my physical issues didn't find such immediate relief from epidurals. These thrilling energy healing side effects didn't feel like I was under some generational curse, but liberating. But they didn't last long though. This energy healing failed like the others. I would soon learn that I was trying to cancel out the reiki experiences (what I call one-person séances) with a different spiritual tribe of equally bad things.

While I did a self-healing meditation (channeling energy), a male spirit glittered and sparkled around me. It was a beautiful sunny day only hampered by a little bit of sciatica, the three herniated discs that always suffocated me with pain, and what felt like a knitting needle in my spine. So just another afternoon, but I was home and hoping for a change. I was lying in bed practicing the technique that "only helps and never hurts people." Because Healing Touch, reiki, and other energy-healing modalities are currently offered to cancer and AIDS patients at numerous hospices and hospitals across the country free of charge, they must be true and good, right? I thought, *Some obscure but free or low-cost energy healing that promised love for extremely vulnerable patients certainly would not be permitted unless it was founded on truth and was in no way harmful.* I kept thinking this and continued, seeing beautiful shimmering silver and gold, starlike, floating over me. They were pretty and mesmerizing, but they weren't healing me. They just wanted access to a body. They could interact with me and touch me, but that was okay for me because I was living relativism; live and let live, just go with the flow, the original intention doesn't matter. Talk about being in a trap of seduction!

Apparently, the male spirit latched onto me and wouldn't let go. Persistent dizziness drowned me, so I sought the healing school practitioner for assistance. She told me to immediately stop reiki, explaining that it is unregulated and dangerous, which makes sense to anyone who knows its history. The lady explained how energy healing was like the Wild West and that the dark spirit attached to me was extremely malevolent toward women and children, likened to a sadistic rapist. She claimed he had ripped and bent something in my energy field and popped out some top chakras that left me open to other spiritual attacks. Bent on sabotage, whatever he did physically affected me to the extent that I got vertigo and fatigue and was massively dehydrated for days.

The practitioner had to have "spiritual police" types drag him away, she explained. This sounds funny to me now, but after the woman started repairing my crown chakra with therapeutic touch so my mind wouldn't be such an open receiver to the psychic world, I was okay with her getting rid of that predator. I certainly didn't look at this misguided woman as a predator or even misguided at the time. The churchgoers at the Congregational church and this practitioner both described thinking about God and connecting with him when they prayed over people in their minds, so I thought she was similar to a churchgoer and that would be fine. I verified again with the practitioner that she was "connecting to God as in Jesus; that God." Her explanation was "Yes, that's how I think of God." It was sufficient for me, but then, I didn't know what I didn't know.

When this school of healing, the magnified angel healing, and crystal healings were not helping, I allowed myself to drift further into new age practices like channeling the Akashic records. Wandering aimlessly into trouble is all people like me know. Whether it was from ADD, living with chaos, or a bad upbringing, I didn't know what my purpose was. I just hoped that I had one that I could find. All I had to do to find my life's purpose (past, present, or future) through Akashic records was to get into a meditative state and open my mind to information that came to me. It didn't matter if it made sense or was true or neither. I had no idea that the meditative state didn't mean a contemplative state but a hypnotic (more suggestible) state because I would be exposed to yet another thinly disguised one-person séance.

All I did was ask, "The energy of love, light, and truth, guide me in opening and reading my Akashic records." I liked research, loved libraries, and relied heavily on intuition, so finding records of my life and connecting unexplainable connections to places and people sounded informative. That didn't sound bad to me! Who wouldn't enjoy knowing what déjà vu moments are all about? *Maybe I have already experienced some of my life before?* Having depression and not being on a stimulant for inattentive ADD made drifting into a light slumber (like in hypnosis) a cinch. But hypnosis and meditation can have dark sides.

As your mind slips into this state, it feels the same as when you start to fall asleep in math class. I was aware of everything around me, but my eyes were closed and shapes appeared behind my lids. When I looked through my mind's eye, I was walking through a massive, grand library with cloudy great shapes. These tall people, including the librarian, looked at me as I walked by. I felt like a small child as I asked directions to my records. Everyone wondered at me until I found my row. Nothing else really happened, but there was no point in being a stranger in a strange land, so I stopped. My heart wasn't into this and if the man who created this practice (Edgar Cayce) was initially afraid of it, was it really what I wanted? I talked to Mom about my experience. She was a good sounding board even though none of this made sense to her. She sent me this email a few days later:

Hi Doll,

I woke this morning and had a thought about you. Maybe it was a waking dream or a vision? Anyhow, you and I were in a huge warehouse, shelves galore loaded with crates, boxes, and assorted sizes of containers neatly stacked along these very tall shelves. The aisles extended further than the eye could see with rows of shelves on each side. It appeared to be limitless. We asked a warehouse associate where we could find the Akashic Records, and he said, "Those are located next to the Map of Eden and are off limits to humans."

So I think that all your "troubles" started with you wanting to know something that "isn't allowed." Like you bit the apple in the garden and now you reap what you sow. I think you also came to this same conclusion days ago, but that's what my thoughts/vision represented to me and I wanted to share it with you. Since Edgar Cayce is the "father of the New Age," I think you are correct and this is a confirmation that what you're doing isn't Christian but is indeed New Age.

Having someone actively listen to me to the extent that she deeply thought about my situation showed me that I mattered. I needed that! Where else could I find this but from someone who loved me? This helped me pull back harder from new ageism. A resolve in me became a protective barrier from the escalating battle or wanting the good new ageism offered without the awful. No longer could I hear that muted chatter from the crystals I'd purchased months before, and my experiences with angels were that they were not beautiful and blessing me, as a medical intuitive (a new age practitioner) had told me at a free metaphysical event.

When I say I was done with angels, all of them, I meant it. I was really ready to quit them this time. I just needed an escape plan. Being done with angels, completely turning from them, meant that I distrusted them even when I felt I had to work with them. It was really a lot like the relationships with my stepdads. I couldn't and didn't trust them because they were dysfunctional at best. But I had to continue having a relationship with them. In my experience, I was pulled out of relationships or homes by someone moving me to a new place or being laid off from a job or a contract expiring—not quitting at that stage in my life because I was someone to be used, not someone who made rules about bodily autonomy or relationships. Quitting something meant you were a quitter and that was failure, so I couldn't have possibly had a choice in the matter of leaving a relationship especially without feeling immense guilt. This was a recurring pattern for me.

What is going on, and how do I get out of all this? I thought. I continued seeing the practitioner for a couple of sessions where she called on alien beings, then quit since it was the same old, same old. Why did I put my faith in people? I had no godly standard against which to compare my actions. I didn't know that I was putting my faith in people and their ways instead of the ways of the Lord, clearly mentioned in the Bible I was starting to read. Now, I realize that many church people have no idea how to handle abuse, spiritual warfare, and mental health, but that didn't make sense to me then because the church is referred to as a haven for the broken. If we are all sheep, or wounded, how on earth was I supposed to get all cleaned up, let alone transformed, without solid help?

The answer to getting out was almost as simple as surrender. Leave these other spiritual ways behind. Fall into the triune God like skydiving out of a plane, knowing my chute will eventually open. My mom loved the spiritual experiences she had with the pastor we had had in Georgia and that she continued to see after us kids were taken to Maine. She said he helped her hear from God and fight demons while she lived alone trying to get us kids back, make ends meet, and make sense of what was happening to her husband. She recommended that I track the Pentecostal pastor down and ask him what to do. I certainly couldn't go to my church leadership in my mind because we didn't have a great relationship. We were so awkward and different and it was a stilted fit, plus it would be embarrassing to admit to them how far I had fallen. I hadn't found a church that felt like a loving family, just a group of people that acted more as polite coworkers.

Thinking about the alternative to seeking church help had me picturing success at an all-female energy-healing event in Lawrence,

Massachusetts. An obese, abrasive woman had a bunch of us meet at her house to meditate and sway around a circle, singing John Lennon's "Imagine." It was not my idea of a good time, and I could see why the event was free. I couldn't try more new age, so relenting to Mom's suggestion, I looked up the contact info for the former church in rural southeast Georgia.

The town didn't look very substantial on Google Maps, so I was sure the place I used to call home was the right spot as it still didn't have many street signs and paved roads. According to an FBI report, our first stepdad had served his fifteen years and was back home, so with the phone number in front of me and that tidbit in my mind, I wondered if he had gone back to attending the church. Naked shame rests on victims, not the predators, so why wouldn't a vicious abuser rejoin the church? Are a bunch of church mice going to chase the cat out? In my experience, no. Our old church was where we sang up front, where our granny, cousins, aunts, and uncles (stepdads' family) went and was the last church before so much changed in my life. I had no expectations on my map and no bearing to follow for the next steps.

Chapter 12
Finding Thorns and Thistles

When the ground soaks up the falling rain and bears a good crop for the farmer, it has God's blessing. But if a field bears thorns and thistles, it is useless. The farmer will soon condemn that field and burn it.

—Hebrews 6:7–8 NLT

After a call to the church to schedule time to tackle the linebacker-sized spiritual warfare issues, I was able to first speak to the pastor (Brother Arnold) while I was on a work lunch break. Polite as ever, I gave him my full name and told him the names of my brother, sister, and mother, explaining our connection to the first stepdad, John Herrin. He remembered us. It had been twenty years since I'd seen him, but I imagine it's memorable when one of your members gets sent to jail for abusing his stepkids and people talked about his affair with his brother's wife. There had been talk, small town talk. And John was brazen. The pastor remembered.

We had some small talk and before letting the pastor know that I wanted to speak with him further when I got out of work to discuss getting rid of pesky spirits, I asked him, "Don't feel like I'm blaming you or the church, but John was a bad guy. Why didn't anyone ever do anything? He raped his own aunt and sexually assaulted toddlers and random neighbor children. Didn't the aunt give some clues to the church or something? This rampant rape of the grace the church offers happened for a few years, and John's personality was like a wild frat boy's. He had many problems, and some people knew he killed animals for fun. Forgive the term, but the guy was a jerk. It was *extremely* obvious to me. Why didn't anyone do anything except for us three kids testifying against him?"

"We didn't know," he said.

It does have to be a stressful job, pastoring a group of sometimes thankless people. It's a shame he let a wolf move into his sheep pen. Giving him a break, I scheduled a later call.

When we reconnected, he prayed with me and did what pastors, preachers, and ministers do—prayed a typical sinner's prayer with me. After a while, you wonder if all those genuine sinner's prayers are going to accumulate and eventually spill out results. Church people just seem to think that if you keep casting such a net, something, anything will get caught. But I wasn't looking for this catching. I wanted help, hope, safe and true intimacy, and healing. And Brother Arnold was no different than the fundamentalist church leaders he told me to avoid—they all had the same answers and the same techniques that weren't working for me. Brother Arnold told me something about me needing to spread the gospel and sold me a book for $35, saying it would tell me what I needed to know and that it would change my spiritual life as it had for so many others. He even tried to sell me a cassette tape. I broke the news to him that it was almost impossible to find a cassette player, let alone one that would play a whole tape before shredding the ribbon.

We could both agree that my current church wasn't right for me. The pastor advised I send him a list of churches in my area. He would pick one that would understand tackling spiritual warfare. He also had me cast the minerals and crystals that I had used for attempted healings into the sea. That was tough because they were expensive: I was essentially throwing away money. However, giving away something with demonic power could hurt others. Into the ocean they all went like the pigs possessed by the demons Legion. When I created and mailed the list of churches, had some time to think about Brother Arnold's conversation with me, and looked through the workbook he sent, I thought a few things: *There are tons of churches around me, interesting. The pastor seems out of touch. He didn't give me anything of substance that I haven't already gotten, and he didn't express any sorrow or understanding. I feel like he took advantage of me by selling me a shoddy, generic workbook on leading people to Christ that was half blank and meant for a group led by an experienced pastor. Mom's judgment is so poor and her standards so low that it wouldn't take much for her to think that this pastor was Christ himself. He's probably not all that she cracked him up to be.*

I had such deep hurt and frustration, fear and confusion. After this, I wasn't sure what to do. We didn't get a chance to solve anything, and my back throbbed. Was I supposed to abandon ever being able to sit how I wanted? Could I never wear a pair of shoes without having to worry if they were orthopedic enough to absorb the impact of walking? How long could I pick up my niece and nephew before they were too heavy for my weak muscles and burning spine? My physical and emotional challenges made my life miserable. Everything seemed to hurt all the time and I was so depressed. I needed to figure out if I was hereditarily depressed too for treatment options. Learning I had inattentive ADHD around this time was a relief so the problem could be discovered and managed, but it was also sad because it meant something else to manage and another embarrassing disorder. So how was I supposed to live—as I had been but with pain multiplying each year?

I continued going to Bible studies after work and navigating church, though it didn't feel like family, like the New Testament Christians coming together. I still felt spiritually hungry, trying to understand personal (interactive, transactional) relationships and how that should be our model for loving and relating to people, businesses, and groups. I was still learning that the biblical church was without walls and without borders. I also found Bible studies to offer several things, but none of them ever offered intense study or a real theology.

While this vulnerable period was certainly not rich with restoration,

I was confronting issues I had with the church by sticking with the spiritual disciplines of showing up, getting involved, and making efforts to learn. Feelings of awkwardness about needing assistance (what self-made person, who soldiers on through life, ever asks for help?) had to be bypassed to survive. Reaching out further to leadership at the Congregational church, where they prayed for me was extremely helpful and I was grateful, but it was so humiliating. The last time I had felt so much shame had been walking into a soup kitchen and food pantry as an adult back in 2008. I had walked into the building in my mid-twenties and felt the failure of my life weighing me down. Though it was an economic depression, being unable to provide for myself as a grown adult had burned every pore and tiny hair on my body with an electric shame and anxiety that those born to absolute insecurity and poverty know all too well. After a few attempts and self–pep talks, I had faced the bread line and knew that I could do the same with the church.

Now, I simply had to ignore the deafening sound of my actions and focus on the advice I would give myself. *I need some churching in an intimate way.* Growing up in and out of (mostly out of) churches, it was so natural to hear that Jesus was God. It's like I never needed to believe because that truth was obvious. Learning verses from the Bible through AWANA and Sunday schools had planted seeds, and maybe I needed to make my issues known like an addict at AA for something to happen. Worst-case scenario: I'd be led to say a sinner's prayer yet again, the current church would consider what I had done at the Baptist or Pentecostal churches before insufficient, and maybe someone would tell me that the baptisms I had at ages three and seven were insufficient too. I would do it all again, focusing beyond head and heart knowledge and looking toward a knowledge and experience that reached the soul. How would I get that from my church?

Obviously reading the Bible and privately studying the Word on my own and with small groups helped, but during the strong attacks at night, I was hoping for physical actions to take almost as a medicine for getting rid of my new age sickness. The Pentecostals that occasionally spotted my youth had action steps for people engaged in spiritual warfare to take, but some of the actions seemed too out there. The nonbiblically anchored church people that stick out in my memory were so interested in spiritual warfare that it was exciting for them in the same way an adventure is exciting. My life isn't lived for anyone's entertainment. So going toward what I considered Pentecostalism would not be an option since it felt wrong and some suggestions to counter the demonic attacks were too much like the disease and not the cure. I didn't need extremists way too interested in "demon hunting" and trying to "bind the strong man." I wanted genuine compassion for my plight and to get solutions.

The flipside was scaring the fundamentalists into paralysis with my bizarre experiences and feeling shunned by people better than I was but not better than whom I wanted to be. I had to try something. Yes, trusting the Congregational church leadership would be shamefully awkward, but I had to go through it. I was on my own, yet again, and I needed help, not pride. There was a real and adamant expectation I had that some condescending, frigid person might just tell me how stupid I was while rapping me across my knuckles with a ruler. Ugh!

But the churchy people would be no different from a stiff-necked, cold librarian who disliked foolish people, and I could handle that. I just had to butter them up by letting them know, "Yes, I went through child abuse, but I am insightful and healthy enough to function, knowing this pain is likely a root to many of my problems. I am also in therapy to learn healthy boundaries with family dysfunction. I am honestly trying in the church, reading my Bible, going to church regularly, and attending Bible study classes (even ones for parents just to get closer to God). I'm really trying."

Sure, I hadn't slept well in months and was a wreck, but I planned to confess everything to the Congregational pastor. I had a fantasy that he would have the right medicine and maybe even be a mentor. Imagine having a real mentor. I'd never had one of those before!

Chapter 13
Church Fright and Embarrassment

*For God hath not given us the spirit of fear;
but of power, and of love, and of a sound mind.*

—2 Timothy 1:7 KJV

K NEELING AT MY bed, clutching one of my Bibles—biting into it with my fingers—I listened to the tinny church voicemail tell me no one was available at the church. The pastor was on another vacation—one that would last five weeks. I couldn't wait that long nor could I keep ignoring my misgivings! With all the demonic encounters and my learnings from Bible studies growing, I was realizing that I was standing just outside the Christian camp, on demonic territory. This recognition scared me, and I knew I had better move. Clearly, the demonic world knew what my reaction would be, and I needed to rush the Christian camp faster than red rover at recess. I at least had enough sense for that! I went to every possible church event. After a few days, some demonic things didn't even bother with pretense but stood before me, emanating this terrifying energy. These entities were still transparent, but they exuded fear, so I gave up respectfulness and called the church at 2 a.m. on a weekday.

Of course, no one was around, but an emergency phone number was given on the recording. The number led to the very conservative Presbyterian pastor, Martha, who had transferred over to the Congregational church. She was not a pastor there because she was a woman (not allowed there), but she served as a Bible study leader and took on administrative duties. That had to be hard for her. She was the only one accessible outside of Sunday school hours.

I was still so immature and anxious about church things and people that I must hold the responsibility for any frustrations or nonloving words from what was my church then. It's got to be so difficult to handle people's crazy at the oddest times. Constantly striving to be purified like a priest entering the tabernacle of the Lord with the corporate duty of serving basket cases like me must have been a struggle. With no polish or pizzazz and with frustrating disorders, insomnia, and deep emotional wounds from a broken childhood, I was a tangled mess! Some people knew of my struggles and had a growing concern over my involvement with what I described as "conducting energy for healing others and myself." Several women were helpful in saying lovingly, "Be careful," and I know I was in their prayers.

However, after I confessed to Martha what was happening because I'd participated in new age practices, I felt ashamed and scolded by her. Weak and wounded, I felt like I was in the middle of a confrontation for doing something I knew was wrong when Martha prayed for me that night. She admonished me for getting into so much trouble: "What did you expect?"

It was 2 a.m., and she was a mature Christian living a strait-laced life and didn't come from a church that taught deliverance or healing. Her agitation was palpable, but I could feel in my embarrassment that Martha was trying to be patient. Her annoyance didn't change the fact that she was there and listening to me, which was a loving gesture. I sensed right away that the Enemy didn't like it any more than I did. I didn't like her chastising, but the evil around me didn't like the gift of time and listening she offered me.

While Martha was praying over me, a demon tried to replace the power of her prayer with what felt like a blanket of fear. I couldn't see any physical material falling over me as I knelt beside my bed. I knew I was being deceived and couldn't help but think, *This isn't my fear!* I started reading Psalm 91 quietly until Martha finished praying. I told her what happened halfway through her prayer, so she prayed some more. We scheduled a time to meet, and she didn't pack any hard punches, but she gave me the response I had anticipated: "What do you expect when you mess around with this?"

I felt like a failure when she told me that I had opened doors and now I had to learn how to close them. She even told me my experience wasn't normal. In her world, it probably wasn't. What I heard from that statement was that I was weird, like I'd been called my whole life, and idiotic. But what other choice did I have? I needed the church.

I agreed, promised to continue avoiding the energy-healing stuff completely, stuck my tail between my legs, and crawled back into bed. I was happy the cloak of fear was gone and was exhausted. So much had happened with spiritual warfare and a disappointing job that was mentally damaging. I was earnestly trying to serve the church in whatever ways were appropriate, but I was running out of gas and self-worth. I hung up the phone and went to sleep with my Bible.

When Martha and I met that week, it was July 2010. I had only entered into the arms of the occult in spring 2009, but it felt like years! I understood why reiki practitioners looked so run down even though the reiki teachings kept saying that the energy conducted through them should charge the teacher with energy too. Instead, they were exhausted like they had been giving away their energy. Now I realize that these practitioners were giving away so much that they dulled their senses. They gave away themselves as if they were worthless souls in clay jars that should be broken, swept away, and forgotten. These pathetic souls were in gnarled earthen vessels and so was I, but we were not made for abuse and neglect. We were made as gifts, presents that delight the Lord.

I felt like the opposite of a light-bearing present when Martha let me know that our prayer meeting together would have several other church leaders who might be able to give support. Boy was she wrong in picking the people and thinking that ten was a small number! At least a church friend went in with me while I plastered a polite, obedient smile on my face. The Congregationalists in the group had no idea what to do with my story or me. I hated being in the antiseptic assemblage answering their questions. I have always been very transparent and honest, so I didn't feel insensitivity from the church people even when they asked about intimate issues like "Did you experience child abuse? What kind?" It was irritating playing the role of a wounded orphan going to yet another group of grown-ups who felt that they needed to know the events in my life.

I felt powerless and like I didn't have a choice, so I told them, "Feel free to ask me anything. I'll provide information in any way I can. I know my harsh life is confusing, sad, and a great deal to take in—I know, I lived it. Until my early twenties, I had moved twenty-plus times, so I'm not great at relationships, and there's been lots of abuse and neglect and going without, many hard times, but that's not representative of who I am. I just need guidance on getting squared away."

So onward scrutinized these medieval monks, probing my delicate parts, examining if I was being honest and authentic.

My sleep deprivation over the past months and nervousness around the church elders apparently made me look confused, powerless, flighty, and in need of good therapy—which was true. However, I was actively in therapy, trying to sleep without disruption, had been praying to Jesus (no longer for healing but for protection), and making great efforts to be the overachiever I knew I could be. Martha explained to the group what I had said on our phone call. I wished that church people were adept at hiding their inexperience, fear, and disapprobation better. I wished I could love myself.

The music ministry leader said she wanted me to know I was a beloved child of God. I appreciated her and her genuineness. The elderly, reformed alcoholic beside her wanted me to know that I was searching for all the wrong things in all the wrong places. Before getting up and leaving the room in frustration, he made statements without context that I couldn't understand. For example, "Read your Bible. Jesus is the answer." Apparently, sympathy and heartfelt concern weren't nearly as effective as a verbal slap to the head. He just didn't want to be there any more than I did, and it showed in his loud voice and angry hoot-owl face. Maybe he thought I had a spiritual virus that he would catch if he stayed. Either way, that man's behavior felt like truthful reprimands painfully laid on me. I wanted trying to conform to the church to hurt less, but I didn't know how.

Words are better when expressed with love and compassion, but my experience was that both were hard to find. When the elderly Congregationalist scolded me in the middle of that group and left, I could understand that he was unprepared for the drama and complexities of my experience. I could understand how he—having mentioned during prayer meetings how he was delivered from alcoholism—knew the answer to everything in life was Jesus. However, without explaining how that could be or what that truly meant, I wasn't feeling related to but like I was being scrutinized and rejected for something I didn't yet understand.

Today I am grateful for the learning opportunity despite the burden and shame I then felt. My mistakes and the reactions of just a small number of people to the situation in which I found myself tangled made me feel naked and attacked. I felt the way a person who identifies as gay might feel when they are told that homosexuality is not allowed. Though it must be said, the gay person can feel like the sin defines who he or she is as a person. The reactions that others have to the drama and complexities of practicing homosexuality can feel to gay people like they are not allowed in Christianity. Maybe now I can explain to those who have sinful inclinations that they are not their sin, that ways to fight back exist, what sin is and how complex a subject it is, and that there is so much more to people's identities than the mistakes they make and who they feel and think they are.

After the man left the meeting, two ladies, who embodied my

childhood image of what a true lady is (so authentically feminine as if without fear of people using that against them), came to my aid. They were mothers with grown children who had walked away from the Lord, so they knew heartache and probably felt the burden of guilt that so many godly mamas feel for their precious lost lambs. I love the way one pointed out a verse, "Take heed lest he fall" (1 Corinthians 10:12 KJV). She explained to me that it came to her as I was talking about how I never in a million years thought that I, such a logical person, would fall into the new age trap. She didn't label me but understood that I had tried to use logic as a safety measure but ended up making it a false god. This beautiful lady trusted the Lord and focused on comprehending who I was trying to be, not who and where I was. She was so "in Christ" that I am still learning from her simple reference to a Bible verse. Praise God for her!

The two women prayed for me after pulling out the book of Ephesians' armor of God references. It meant a lot to me that these mothers would take time out of their lives, nursing my wounds with gentle voices that prayed compassionate prayers to a Savior they knew. The people remaining in the group prayed as well, but I must have needed some loving, godly reparenting since I was still sapped from having to rehash the last several months of my chaotic life to them. The moment I realized how drained I was, the dizziness—I assumed from my antidepressant—started subtly growing. When the prayer was authentic, vertigo kicked in, and I knew it wasn't the medication but demonic. I tried to alert Martha with a tug on her coat, but she ignored me. I just wanted her to know that the dizziness was returning and that they were coming. I couldn't rely on her to fix the situation. She was just a person.

I looked around the room to fixate on an object and pictured Jesus dragging his cross and beaten so hard, for me, that he didn't look human. I was focusing on that passage of Scripture and feeling the faith, the genuine belief in biblical truth. It worked and I started feeling less dizzy. I told the group I thought I might throw up. I was embarrassed and hoping not to vomit; my face couldn't have burned any redder. I was oversensitive, so truly my humiliation at sitting in that circle is on me and not them. I even understand why Martha thought I was distracted and inappropriately medicated. Not only did she pray for me, but she also had one of the ladies, a nurse, affirm that the antidepressant made people feel like they were "crawling out of their skin" and that I should rethink taking it with my psychologist. The group gave me their honest efforts. While the situation wasn't ideal, I am so blessed that Martha didn't shirk her Christian or pastoral duties to help me because I received intimate corporate prayer for the first time in my life.

Chapter 14

The Cleanup After the Storm

Draw near to God, and he will draw near to you.

—James 4:8 ESV

Two weeks later, Dad had a stroke. He didn't get better as expected and started dying that Wednesday. Gramma Marie (Dad's mom) had left a voicemail. She never called me, but here she was now telling me about the stroke, leaving a quick little guilt trip to remind me, "He is your father."

I had no idea what that meant. Did that mean I should visit? I'd never disowned anyone before. So many conflicting emotions triggered, rooted from family dysfunction, neglect, and Dad's lifestyle. My siblings encouraged me to decide what to do for myself and, remembering all the enabling that occurred, I chose to maintain boundaries until Becky urgently called, saying Dad was dying. The three hour drive to the hospital left me alone with my busy, guilt-filled thoughts. It's hard to honor principles while feeling love and regret for a father. At the ICU, I reconnected briefly with my paternal relatives, recognizing both warmth and codependency which made me conclude that true love requires boundaries and guarding my heart.

Meditating on that and finding ways to apply that to my life would have been good at that moment. I groan inwardly now because it is so crystal clear that I was in the wrong, but I mentioned to Gramma Marie that I could try energy healing on my dad, and she thought it was a great idea. I understand why I frustrated that hoot owl–looking Congregationalist man. Like a dog, I returned to my vomit!

I walked into Dad's room, and his body looked so small. It was so unreal until I saw his comatose face. He looked awful: sallow face, hair unwashed and limply clinging to his skull like a yarmulke. The thick hoses didn't only puff up Dad's chest with air; they caused him to gasp for breaths in forté volumes. It reminded me of the famous Ingmar Bergman film *Cries and Whispers* showing a cancerous woman dying in bed. Her gasping was equivalent to Dad's. I remembered a comment about how audience members needed to leave the cinema when the movie debuted because that scene was too real and disturbing. Now I understood.

I stayed in the room and moved closer to Dad, principle forgotten. Except for corralling my niece and nephew and dictating to my sister that she needed to get her husband out of the car and involved in watching their kids so the ICU nurses would stop scolding us, I did nothing other than focus on Dad. We remained in that state of purgatory for hours. I suppose a sense of commitment is what made that possible since I was running on nothing but tea and grits from that morning and entering day two of my stay like that.

In between this time, a group of us talked to Dad, and I made a stupid, nervous joke that slipped out of my mouth before I could catch it. Someone gave me a gelatin cup and a granola bar to placate my stomach. I could actually eat it despite the odors emitted by Dad's comatose body shutting down. The stench of belly button, several-days-old bad breath, hospital hallways, and an elderly person's home blended together. I interacted with this rancid rainbow of smells more than I did with family outside Dad's room. I spoke to Dad like he was a friend interested in my life and not my dad. When I caught myself, I stopped. It wasn't who he was, and we didn't have that relationship. He didn't need to know about trying to wrangle energy healing.

Dad had become an old timer before time even caught up. Dying was what he planned for since at least his forties. He often made comments like his desire to buy a small house or buy us four-wheelers near his death as an inheritance. In the moment, I couldn't see that Dad was finally, at age fifty-three, getting what he wanted.

Desperately trying to help using energy healing, I said my quiet, bastardized prayer to Jesus to keep me safe and to work through me so I could alleviate the trauma in Dad's head. Praying to Jesus while doing reiki is still wrong, as I discovered. A massive blood clot on his brain bulged out the side of his head and slowly moved around his skull. I held my hand above his head to guide the energy healing, hoping the golf-ball-sized clot would stop. Stupid, desperate girl! I hoped there would be healing and that it was of God. I felt the prickling sensation that indicated receiving energy from his pain in my hands. I could also feel something on my arm a little. I was still naïve to think, *Maybe Jesus sends comfort through me and my energy healing*, but I got dizzy and the tingles started. I needed to get real and to do what I knew for sure. I focused on the soldier that I was; someone from my platoon was wounded and needed me. I put my hand directly on Dad's blood clot despite the wrenching in my stomach and stroked his hair with my other hand.

From time to time, supernatural things touched me, causing tingles and brushing over my arm with what felt like long hairs. I knew it wasn't my hair or anyone else's. I was standing near my unconscious father, talking to him and keeping my hand over the blood clot that still moved around his head. I played with fire, but I wasn't asinine, just dim-witted: dim in hope and exhausted to the point of heart palpitations and dehydration. I ignored this routine with the demons pestering me and focused on my dad's body, which was failing further. His gasping breaths worsened with the now-removed life support tubes. More decrepit bodily smells and tears escaping his closed eyes kept coming. The odd energy pulses continued, but I focused on my comrade, my fellow life soldier, and remained in the trench with him.

That's when I knew and felt with such intensity that there was no hope. This must have been the final criteria for my own mind going into shock and my stomach clenching without end. That shock didn't break for around thirty days, when I would feel warm, almost hot fluid on the right side of my head. I would reach up to touch whatever it was, but nothing was there. That's when I would realize, *I must have been in shock. This whole time I worked and lived, but I was in shock.* It would be an entire year before my stomach would return to complete normalcy, so damaged was it by watching my dad struggle. However, the stomach clenching would return if I pictured Dad in the hospital or thought of him in great detail.

At this moment at Dad's side, not only was I empty inside, I felt hope disappear like vapors in cold, biting wind. When all four of us kids were at his bedside, we talked to him. His final hours would have us letting him know that it was okay if he needed to die.

Miah's little family of three and I checked into a motel to rest. I read from my Bible and settled into bed with it. My brother held his three-week-old baby girl (Aubergine), and she looked like a panther lounging in a jungle tree with one paw dangling and the other outstretched. We got the final call that Dad died around 12:30 a.m. I don't remember the exact time, only baby Aubergine's little hand doing swimmies as if she was still in the womb and slowly paddling with her hand. It's funny which moments and details imprint on us when our lives are on pause. How odd life can be disrupted so easily and you just have to accept it: I permanently lost my long absent father. Because his life of lack wove through a bleak culture, maybe it wasn't I who lost him that night but he who lost me.

The funeral couldn't take place for another six days, so I went home. The attacks were strong, but at least they were fewer in frequency. Still, conjuring healing energy for my dad with this ridiculous and dangerous new age practice had added fuel to a fire that the church and I had been trying to dowse. Unfortunately, the church didn't believe in Christian healing or deliverance and couldn't give me a replacement for the occult. Because they were ill equipped to handle a messy case like me, they couldn't protect me, and it wasn't a church where people felt like family, so isolation was still problematic.

The first night home, I planned on sleeping, but I knew by the night before with all paranormal activity and the lucid dreams brought on through the last energy healing that it would be tough. I only needed some peace that night so I could sleep, just a little. For more than two hours I tried sleeping, praying then sleeping, calling Mom and praying, but the demons that pursued me were at my heel. I was weary, but I found no rest (Lamentations 5:5) until I went to spend the night at my former boyfriend's apartment.

Chapter 15
Recycling Foolishness

*You who are trying to be justified by
the law have been alienated from Christ;
you have fallen away from grace.*

—Galatians 5:4 NIV

Having just lost my father (and any hope that he would have a healthy, fatherly relationship with me) and with demons bothering me, I thought that I had no better source of comfort than Andrew. When I was alone, I was afraid, and that fear was leaving me exposed. That's when I called him and told Andrew the situation.

But I didn't belong in Andrew's apartment, and I could feel the awkwardness of the situation even through my fatigue and shell shock. Andrew's best friend and roommate was like a sister to him, and I loved seeing her, but I was interrupting their lives—the lives I wasn't a part of anymore. But I felt stuck, so I summed up what happened with Dad's stroke and the occult attacks, then spent the night.

Trying to sleep on the couch in such humid weather gave way to sleeping on the floor in Andrew's room. The fan was good enough, and I slept through the night. Hardwood floors couldn't compete with exhaustion. Andrew was offended that I wouldn't sleep beside him in bed, but

I had already entered into an unintentional romantic relationship with him once and had to shut off who I was as a person just to continue in that relationship. Being emergency fallbacks for one another did not mean I had to compromise myself again. I had demons trying to do that to me; I couldn't let myself suffer anymore that night! The second and final night that I returned to Andrew's place, I reluctantly slept beside him, but the amount of sleep wasn't enough and blankets and pillows were not enough separation. I'm so awkward!

One valuable lesson I took from the new age world, other than "do not get involved with it," pertained to archetypes. Andrew and I discussed how he had a vampire archetype: He had been a regular person until he was attacked. He had a sad story that garnered true sympathy for him. He existed in agony with a very addictive personality, finding solace in cigarettes and alcohol. Andrew came most alive and fully functioning at night, and because of what he was—a wounded victim—he had sharp fangs. He was so friendly but quick verbal barbs would shoot out of him without control.

While fitfully sleeping next to Andrew, it did not escape me that the hyena-like demons had left me alone for the second night in a row. I discerned that hyenas tended not to invade a bigger predator's den and that I had a bigger problem to handle when around Andrew because he had his own demons. I could feel it.

I don't mean to imply Andrew was a danger to people. Until I found him professional help, he was just as lost in life as I was. I was going to him for guidance and not the Lord, despite attending church, because even though Andrew was no different than any other addict, I had a personal relationship with him. He was real.

The next morning when we woke up, he leaned on me blatantly. I turned my head away, explaining, "I'm not here for anything other than sleep and spending time with a friend." He was irritated, but I pushed, "We weren't ever supposed to be together. I should have stuck with what I knew and trusted myself in the first place. You know we make better friends. We're too wounded."

He agreed, and we moved on to breakfast and more details of the spiritual battles happening.

This is how we spoke to each other: aware we were two lost sheep simply trying to survive. We couldn't honestly fault each other for how we were. After all, we could see in each other that we would have turned out like anybody else if we hadn't been exposed to extended periods of pain. We could wish each other well and acknowledge that we were trying to live better than what we knew. It was odd but honest. This awareness allowed us to trust each other when we shared wisdom and insight learned from surviving abuse. We drew from a deep truth that spiritual people notice and Bible readers refer to as something that Christ breathed into us from the very beginning of humankind's creation.

In that embarrassing situation with Andrew, God reconstituted into goodness what the Enemy intended for evil. When my church got back to me and prayed for me, a few weeks had passed since my dad's death. I didn't need to be at Andrew's after more prayer, but I did have a discussion with him. We revisited the vampire archetype idea.

"Andrew, do you think a predator is a good example of a vampire archetype?"

He thought about it as we fleshed out the profile. I repainted the scenario of the nights at his apartment after Dad's death.

"Yeah, you were going through a lot," he replied. "You were harassed by the spirits, dealing with your dad was emotional, and you come from bad stock."

I continued filling in more of my perspective on the recent time with Andrew. "You can see how it would be a low blow to be hit on by a friend who had no regard for my distressed state because he had lascivious intentions. When you woke up after that second night, you were no different than a vampire or . . ." I let the silence sink in.

This point is what allowed Andrew to see that he needed professional help, and he let me set him up with a local female therapist. Though we are to avoid bad situations, we can trust that God is in control and that he will redeem even the worst situations.

A Tatterdemalion's Testimony

❧

After making rough plans to attend Dad's funeral, Miah and I decided to split the cost of a hotel room with two queen-sized beds at a fancy hotel we frequently drove past as kids, the Senator. It had a whole spa! We grew up with Mom telling us that when she worked there as a cleaning lady, it was so expensive that she could only afford the rolls at the restaurant, even when she was pregnant with Becky. Surprised when my brother told me the amount that seemed affordable, I loved the idea. The pool area had a hot tub and a lavender-scented steam room. Spending time with my brother and being grown-ups was fresh sunshine. With the funeral just around the corner, we could only play at adulting later.

While seeing Miah was great, everything was so disorganized with the funeral planning. I assumed it would be like other funeral experiences, but this one was organized by my family. We were sent to the wrong funeral home until Carol called us and reoriented us to the correct place where we needed to choose a coffin for Dad. While I wanted cremation, some pushed for a casket, revealing that Dad left no plans or funds for burial despite claiming for years that costs would be covered. Though the funeral expenses only totaled $8,000, my mentally ill, low income sister was the only one who offered to pay the expenses. To protect her, I reluctantly agreed to pay. My hopes rested on selling Dad's expensive, new bass boat and possible life insurance to cover costs. The next few days blurred by with the cousin who took over in the ICU handling arrangements and paperwork in exchange for Dad's truck. I didn't have a say, of course, but it was hard feeling so excluded when eulogies were delivered without my input and seeing how disorganized and avoidant of reality the family still was. Being thrust into responsibility while navigating grief and financial chaos opened me up for wrestling with duty, injustice, and a desire to break the cycle of neglect found in my family.

That night after Dad's funeral, the demons came back. I had finished reading one of the Psalms and felt tingles in my left leg, the sign of demonic happenings. I had been off the antidepressant that caused this side effect, so I wasn't fooled into thinking that was starting up.

Immediately, I shooed the pests away with a Jesus-named rebuke and focused on feeling confident that Christ's blood was covering me, like the church recommended.

I stifled embarrassment, but I felt like such a failure. Miah, Ashli, and baby Aubergine were asleep only a few feet away. I was used to sleeping alone, well, okay—I was used to living alone and sleeping with demons harassing me. Sharing demonic experiences, showing just exactly what I had gotten myself into, was not how the night was supposed to go! Was I going to have to start pacing the room, praying and reading the Bible out loud, waking my family and explaining, "Oh, sorry! Did the demons and I wake you? We still tussle a little. You remember us talking about this over the phone, right? Yeah, just return to bed. This is normal for me." Awkward!

The spirits left, and I prayed quietly but aloud. I disliked praying out loud because then spirits could hear what I prayed for and how I felt. I hated the idea of anyone but God knowing my thoughts and using them to hurt me in some way. I had such poor self-esteem and had gone through so much trauma. I only wanted a little peace and a few hours of sleep and maybe I could eat slightly more for breakfast so my stomach could heal. I put my head on my pillow, ready for sleep, though still praying—until I felt and saw the demonic shapes across the room on my brother's side. This time they tried something new besides going after me. They went after my brother, but so did I.

Chapter 16

Accountability: A Call of Duty

However, I consider my life worth nothing to me; my only aim is to finish the race and complete the task the Lord Jesus has given me—the task of testifying to the good news of God's grace.

—Acts 20:24 NIV

WHEN WE WERE in our teens, Miah had told me that he used to get bullied during the elementary school bus ride. I had no idea. I could only remember a small incident when a kid his age had been mean to him once on the playground and I had defended Miah. The mean boy's sister, my classmate, came over assuming I was targeting her brother. Not only was I wounded by the assumption and her retort to leave the kids alone, I also did not make everything better by protecting my brother or by clearing up the misunderstanding. Instead, I had stormed off with hot tears pouring down my face, my value destroyed because I felt like such a failure and loser.

Though frustrating, this memory is important for two reasons. One: It seared into my brain a pronounced shame that I did not protect my beloved, hurting brother when he needed me. Two: I knew from as early on as elementary school that I was "too sensitive for this world."

Seemingly small moments can have big impacts. The world provided me with repeated blows that left me calloused over the years, but the importance of protecting my brother: that never changed. It's an honor and a healthy burden to be an older sister.

Years later, staying in the Senator for my dad's funeral in August 2010, I felt the same older sister pull and drive to look out for my brother to compensate for that lost opportunity. The man in my life who I knew and loved and was proud to call my brother lay captured by something hurting him, and it wouldn't let him go. I went from resting and praying in bed to feeling leg tingles and seeing a spirit flash over to the bed where Miah, Ashli, and the baby slept. The demonic spirit in the hotel room went fast and low, so I couldn't see if it was under the bed, near the dog cage, or by the table. I sat up with a start, looking for activity, when there was movement on the other bed. My brother started moaning and moving around to the point his wife woke up. She looked around and asked what was happening. Ashli was excellent to be around, such a considerate person. With the newborn sleeping between her and my brother, she reproved him.

"Babe, you're moving around." She looked at me. "I don't want him to wake the baby." She made some adjustments around herself and the baby and leaned over to my brother, now groaning outright and thrashing at something.

One of us said sympathetically that he must be having a nightmare because he had been through so much. But after saying that and both of us having sensitivities to the supernatural world, we sensed that something was very wrong.

He was fighting something in his sleep, and she didn't know what to do. Ashli tried shaking Miah's arm to wake him up again, but when it didn't work, she turned to me and said, "I don't want him to suffer, but I don't know what to do."

Right at that moment, Miah started whimpering loudly and in rapid succession. "Sofuk. Sofuk. Sofuk."

I was at his side instantly and jostling him—still unconscious. Then I heard my Little Scruffa, my little Mighty Mouse, start to cry. I didn't care what Ashli would think of me. I needed Jesus, and nothing else was working. The strong, Bapti-costal Southerner inside my broken body rose up inside me. I leaned into my brother with my right hand on him and said with all the authority I had, "In Jesus's name, wake up!"

He did. He woke up as if nothing had happened.

While Miah was rousing in those first few seconds, Ashli and I saw the same event occur, but we both have different perspectives on what was happening. I watched a fuzzy one-inch white orb rise from my brother's head area, then float over in the direction of his feet. Up and out of the room, it just disappeared. I turned my head to my brother, asking him if he was okay. Miah remembered nothing at all! Even when we told him what happened, to him, he had just been sleeping.

I said, "I had to wake you up in Jesus's name. Nothing else worked!"

Ashli followed up, "Yeah, I saw a black light get chased out of the room by a white light."

"You saw it too?" I asked her. I mean, I remember seeing her watch the scene out of my peripheral vision, but the thought hadn't taken root because there had been no time. I wasn't accustomed to the luxury of validation. It was so nice to have and helpful in recounting events to my brother and, later, family. I love that about both my sister and sister-in-law. They are excellent for this support.

The rest of the night went okay for our group. We got our bearings, and Ashli and I whispered back and forth until she fell asleep. I was in shambles though. *God, help. I don't know what to do.* I spoke to God like that. It might have even been out loud. Sitting there in bed, holding the paperback Bible clasped between my hands, I was hurting for others, upset that I had opened doors to the demonic supernatural world that I could not close. I was unsure of many things.

I looked down at the Bible for some reason, and it opened itself up like a teacher opening a book in class and pointing to my reading assignment. The title of the book within the Bible was Habakkuk. *Ok, I'm supposed to read this and I'm going to.* Halfway through the book and a quarter past several face contortions, I questioned reading this bizarre and scary book, written by a minor prophet in the Old Testament. *God, you want me to read this?! This is terrifying!* Sigh. *Read it anyway. It's very short; there's no excuse.* And it was personally made clear that God was answering me.

When I finished, I took a deep breath. I told God that I could see why he wanted me to read the book because of the prophet Habakkuk but not the violent attacks part. I asked God to give me understanding, and I read the book again, fleshing out what I hoped God was telling me. *So I'm like Habakkuk asking for rescuing. There are bad people attacking Habakkuk and other innocent people. However, God's going to overpower this injustice by directing evil people to the bad guys?* This was not comforting.

This is like in Jurassic Park *when the blonde girl and her brother are fleeing from the velociraptors. The kids are running, hiding, scared. The velociraptors are terrifying brutes, so the kids are desperate and in need. Out of nowhere, a* Tyrannosaurus rex *comes onto the scene, the most dominant foe that existed. He stuns with the presence of his power. The* T. rex *represents the evil people in Habakkuk who will defeat the bad guys. However, it would be bone-chilling to think that this is a victory worth staying around and watching because eventually the* T. rex *will win the fight and turn to the victims, now in even worse trouble.* I imagined a close-up of the evil *T. rex* eye on me, and an icy metal rod of pure fear shot through me.

Observing this fear gave me a visual of how in control God is of every situation and an immense respect for fear. I would come back to it many times in the following years and every time I studied Habakkuk. Unsettled in the moment, though, I could do nothing but trust that I was on the right path. "What I'm going to get out of this, Lord, is that God is immense! He will handle the Assyrian versus Chaldean/Babylonian attack described without getting involved. He is orchestrating everything without even getting his hands dirty." With that, I slept.

While driving back to Massachusetts, I had a moment where I started to grieve. My brother called me not even two minutes into that pain to ask me if everything was all right. My sister was on the other line, as he assumed that she was the one having an emergency. It was odd; we siblings were sensing something wrong, so we were checking on each other. We didn't know what to make of this except that we were so sensitive and concerned for one another at this painful time that we were more in tune with one another. It was nice. We told each other, "Be careful and call if you need anything. You know the drill."

The pastor from the Congregational church returned from the five-week vacation and suggested that he, Martha, and I meet. He told me that I should eliminate anything new age and un-Christian because those "things have a way of creeping up" into life. After an inventory of what I had, he was right. The energy ball I wanted from a science store hadn't been available, so my brother-in-law had gotten me one with a Buddha holding it. It was a morbidly obese and gross Buddha too! Yet there it was, a centerpiece on my kitchen table. I found a group of things including a CD of angel music that promised healing. I had bought it years ago, but it felt wrong because halfway through the hypnotizing music was a voice asking angels for healing and idolizing them. What I did not trash, I ended up giving away; I just had to get rid of everything in any way possible now. I was purging myself of anything that could act as a stumbling block. I was committed.

The pastor laughed over some of the things I gave away. He knew I loved crystals and rocks before my time in the occult and expected that I could handle normal gems in the future, but he could tell that I valued these things and that I felt better about giving them away instead of trashing them. He told me that when he had felt the presence of Christ, it had changed him instantly and he had been born again. However, he hadn't thrown away the drugs he had on him. He had given them to a friend because he didn't want them to go to waste. I felt like that because I grew up low income and money seemed to be an idol for me. I could reason that crystals used for healing by me should be given away and not trashed because someone else wouldn't be going through the same things I was and could just enjoy a lapis lazuli and rose quartz necklace. I ignored my reasoning since it had clearly been broken for some time now and listened to the pastor.

I asked, "Why did this happen if I'm a Christian?" I said, "I *think* I'm a Christian, although I'm open to your guidance, and I've had powerful and miraculous moments with God, but I've never had that big moment like you have had where some dramatic presence changes you. What does that mean?"

The pastor was a Southerner transplanted into cold Massachusetts and had such an easy way about him so the conversation went well. He had me pray the sinner's prayer and I was open to it, but I explained that there was no change in me because I prayed it in earnestness pretty much every year since age three or four, which was also about the time I asked God for patience, hoping that whatever patience was, God would have enough time to give it to me when I needed it as an adult.

Martha had been listening and said uncomfortably but as delicately as she could, "This might not be the right church for you."

Though now I think differently, I was ticked off she said that. I thought that she was supposed to help and have answers. Really though, I was just oversensitive to her difficulty relating to me and I couldn't see beyond how "churchy" and fluent in Christianese she was, so I couldn't relate to her either.

By March 2011, the spiritual attacks had dimmed massively, and I left the Congregational church for an Assemblies of God church. However, I still attended some of the Bible studies associated with the Congregational church where I could learn more about biblical financial planning and study J. Vernon McGee's *Thru the Bible* series—in particular, Habakkuk.

I left the Congregational church completely when some dopey guy old enough to be my dad made a pass at me. A recent divorcee who I showed compassion to clearly did not remember the multiple times that I was a church friend and supported him. He acted like he wanted friendship only to weasel into something more. A much older church friend was interested in him, so I wasn't expecting him to have sexual feelings for me. I invited him to join us in the Easter Chorus, and he felt I needed to know that I'm "sexy with a sense of humor."

Not knowing what to say, I replied, "I'm going to take that as a no that you will not be joining us."

With my childhood traumas, this kind of random behavior made it easy for me to hit the roof of shame because I had just enough church experiences at such a young age to think that all church attenders were good and loving and that someone my father's age wouldn't want to have sex with me. I didn't mind befriending someone without social skills, and I didn't leave the church in a huff. It was his lack of respect for age limitations and him ignoring my obvious blinking neon lights pointing to my boundaries. I've learned to be blunt. I say, "I'm not available for that kind of relationship, but I wish you well." Pretty clear.

So, the betrayal of a church friendship from someone who had taken the time to get to know me—and me knowing this man consciously ignored a pure and innocent friendship where I included him in groups and pulled him out of his shell to join us in trying to do life together even though pain existed everywhere—was a huge hurt. There was no love. And what was it about churchgoers and perversity? I didn't have boundaries for people in the church yet nor had I truly experienced a Christian conversion (though that was still unknown to me). But just before this, Uncle Chris, a long-lost former uncle (one of Aunt Rona's ex-husbands), had propositioned me for sex after telling me how involved he was in church.

Chris popped up on Facebook, and I responded that I hoped all was well in his life since I had last seen him in grade school. He's the same uncle who brought us three kids to see *The Little Mermaid*. He complained that his wife spent all his money and his daughter spoke about sex in front of his younger kids despite being routine churchgoers.

I apologized he had to go through that. What else could I say? It had been decades.

He then offered to take me on a romantic getaway to Okinawa and offered to pay my way for everything.

I was floored and felt disappointed and powerless. In his mind, I was still a kid and somehow also a sex object.

When I told Andrew, he laughed at how absurd and trashy the situation was. "You come from bad stock."

I explained that this uncle wasn't even genetically related, but it didn't matter. I knew what Andrew meant. Did I really have to deal with this now? Story of my life: perverts. Guess we found my Achilles' heel.

I deleted and blocked Uncle Chris and told my sister to be careful since she saw him online too. I couldn't deal with perversion here and from someone at church because I kept thinking that church should be different. Boundaries and sexual harassment education–type talks were only things I heard at work, never in churches. My vulgar stepdads were all churchgoers; Mark even got a certificate to marry people in the church, and he let it be known what he thought of my body. I guess I'm a slow learner. Church just didn't feel like a safe haven.

I sent an email to Martha letting her know I was uncomfortable remaining in the church and three years there was enough. I thought maybe I just needed a change and I'd taken bigger hits from creepy men, so I moved on. It concerned me that I experienced many church men failing at serving or protecting in the church. Women pulled up the slack. I wasn't seeing unity or a community spirit yet. There's no shame in admitting that we need help using our voices, and I was hoping for help at the next church.

At the Assemblies of God church, just down the road from where I lived in Gloucester, I recognized a transient from my food bank days. Just like then, he stared at me the whole time. I learned he was a heroin addict and often homeless, but that didn't stop him from telling me to come home with him. It's hard dealing with this, and it has happened at just about every church I've attended within the first month. It doesn't matter how much effort I put into my appearance or not. I don't know if these undesirable men are just unable to find anyone so they desperately go to church looking for a lady, but it's an off-putting welcome committee. The drug addicts and mentally damaged men are scary because you don't know what they'll do to you. A friendly ask on a date is fine; the persistent chase when I've said, "No, thank you. I'm not available for that," is not. *Do I really have to reiterate how unavailable I am? Aren't we in church for something bigger than this?*

Relationships deserve so much more respect than getting tossed to anyone who will enter into one. Someone who is extremely lonely and dismal might bypass solid mental help and a healthy life, but I didn't want them to invade my personal space. I sought health too, after all. It didn't seem like I was in a place where I'd find sacred friendships or even common ones. The AG church helped maintain my church experiences, and when the heroin guy wasn't around, I could plug in, but I wasn't comfortable in my religion or mature in life. Church politics and culture confused me, and it didn't feel like home.

At least exposure to unwanted advances and conflicts teaches us how to recognize the signs before they happen. Probably because of my childhood, I particularly hated sexual harassment, but I knew genuine friendliness could attract attention from people who don't understand what their misplaced affections were doing to me or the other people around them. However, I've been seeing others deal with this in work, school, and churches for years, so I can proudly say that I handle this commendably now. Having to lean on "church people" and to face the demonic world in spite of boundary breaches forced my skin to get thicker. I've learned to deflect, self-advocate, and work seamlessly with a bunch of male engineers and even perverse characters who have not worked with a woman (or at least successfully) before, and I've come away unmarked. Eventually becoming a Christian helped me delve into these issues deeper, and I thank God that I've been able to accomplish this.

I gave the Assemblies of God church a year. If anything demonic came up, as it did from time to time, I acted on what Martha and other Christian leaders thought: As we draw closer to God, Satan gets nervous. When it seems that Satan is trying to draw us back into a spirit of fear and apprehension, tell it to leave in the name of Jesus Christ. Consistency and drawing on the Lord for strength are vital. Ask God for his help, safety, and closeness. Eventually, Satan will quit, but he can still sense fearfulness. He will try to break trust in God and to lead God's sheep astray. Personal prayer, not succumbing to isolation, reading God's Word, and leaning on him are the action steps.

Back at the time of my father's stroke, the boss at my marketing job had written me up for taking three days off for my father's death and funeral. He had wanted payback on the documentation I sent to human resources on his lack of qualifications in his job and why there was a 100 percent attrition rate. I hadn't learned to pick my battles and naively thought the business might care about what was occurring. I needed to stop being a justice seeker. Then when I took a vacation at Thanksgiving during my year at the Assemblies of God church, the boss had the new supervisor write me up for "more mistakes that were made during the four days off." The reasoning for the firing was that when I had been out, a lot of mistakes were made. One cannot fight back at a place like that. A subordinate's role is to make the boss look good, even when he is not.

It was a painful time and I had to wear a brave face, but I got through it. Was this so different from getting rejected for a permanent job after outworking a temporary job's duties? No, but creating job security for me meant being indispensable to the boss until he was admonished if I was out or meant being able to quantify my work and my own value. ADD makes pacing yourself and your workload hard because office work is innately boring, so pressure from deadlines and complex strategy means stimuli that I want to start sooner than later. Depression makes proving that both your work and you are worthwhile problematic because your energy levels are sapped and your brain says, *There's no point in selling your efforts because you're probably going to encounter the same old hurtful end point, and you don't matter that much anyway.*

"I'm not just spinning my wheels. I accomplish a lot" is not enough for bosses who oversee work but don't know the minutia of what you do. Been there, done that. I couldn't stand unsteady employment. Exploring where I belonged and what I should be doing was limited as I had no one to support or guide me, and I didn't understand how to change this. I just understood that I was hurting and needed help. My life held eclectic experiences and people, and I was doing my best to navigate it.

Chapter 17
Choosing True North

> *There was a man of the Pharisee sect, Nicodemus, a prominent leader among the Jews. Late one night he visited Jesus and said, "Rabbi, we all know you're a teacher straight from God. No one could do all the God-pointing, God-revealing acts you do if God weren't in on it." Jesus said, "You're absolutely right. Take it from me: Unless a person is born from above, it's not possible to see what I'm pointing to—to God's kingdom."*
>
> —John 3:1–3 MSG

IT'S HARD TO know what to do with yourself once you are delivered out of the hands of demons but are not yet a true Christian, someone with an awareness and personal connection to Jesus's spirit. I pretty much slipped back into the life I had before the occult world became mine. I had to be careful not to lose myself. Slipping into nothingness makes it too easy to vanish from the world because no one notices a nothing. I've never wanted to be blank though. There were no boundary lines that way. Recycled paper had already been thought on, and I needed that messy structure to push against. Blankness is like nothing, and being nothing is the devil's last-ditch effort to keep us thinking, *This is all there will ever be for ME.*

But what if this isn't true? I have to at least try. With insomnia and living in Gloucester—where nightlife is pretty much bar hopping or hanging around with townies whose families all know each other and grew up together—I felt like a blow in, what locals called the nontownies. I didn't belong, but the rent was affordable. I walked at all hours to a local beach or a drugstore because it was the only light shining through the night. I wondered if I could get to a point someday when I would have a place always open but maybe a place full of hope for other lost people. It's easier for a girl to dream of helping others than it is for her to help herself.

I hated living in a state of ennui. If stoicism was my childhood archenemy, ennui was its adult form. It is so hard to beat because it tag teams with depression. Sometimes I just wanted to disappear. I thought of ways that this could happen, but I had some ties that just couldn't be unbound. For example, I had hope that my mother would climb out of a proverbial pit, meaning stop conforming to her husbands, find her own identity, and lead a healthy life so I wouldn't have to worry about her.

Hope also came from my nephew and niece. When my nephew (Aaron) was born, charred remains of my life fell away, showing little green shoots of life budding up that I thought had died years before. It's undeniable that Aaron's birth brought a desecrated part of me to life and no less deniable that when my niece (Zoe) was born, that growth continued, and I wanted life. This wouldn't stop suicidal daydreams from luring me, but it helped grow hope and resistance to my cursed existence. Love was transforming the burdens in my life. Children, even those still moving around in the womb, are miraculous and bring immense blessings. While my mother's lifestyle dragged at me, my kids lessened my load. And now that I could stop fighting the occult, I could try to fight the depression chewing at me.

I wished for blessings of my own but felt the insecurity of living paycheck to paycheck and in debt. I still had school loan and car debt to pay, and my cheap computers were as fickle as my jobs, always clunking out on me with spotty internet access at best (another reason to spend so much time at libraries: free internet access). It's not like I could stay connected to the world that way, and unreliable technology made it hard to have phone interviews or do work assignments from home.

After four years of talk therapy, I was all talked out. My ever-changing insurance would no longer cover the sessions anyway, and medication was pointless. We couldn't find a good fit. The one antidepressant that worked for a while wore off, and I was not responsive to any ADHD medication. I couldn't see the point of continuing on in this area of life (therapy and medication) nor could I remember why I should care anyway. The days of caring were long gone just like my working and short-term memory.

The heaviness of the world physically pressed me to the point where my gait became too slow to match someone else's average pace. Depression has very visible symptoms. Sometimes this still happens, but at least now I am not dwarfed by the enormity of the pressing.

My mom emailed me asking how I was doing one day, and instead of calling her, I emailed her. I stopped initiating phone calls with family members to see who would stay in contact. No one asked me to be the point of contact for the family anyway. Since those spirit issues, getting fired from that disappointing job, and Dad's death, my love of self-help and striving were long gone too. I couldn't sense the difference between morning, afternoon, or evening. I had and would have strong trauma-related issues that made self-management grueling. It was as if the moment I let go of having a real and good dad, job, and life, I let go of a bunch of other good things too. Feeling unworthy and losing hope makes showering, shaving, and brushing teeth arduous and time consuming. Simply getting out of bed or off the floor long enough to wrestle with thoughts about grooming was the real accomplishment.

My thoughts from that time went something like this: *I can save money by not wasting necessities and personal, precious care on my plain old self. The soaps and razors cost money and have value; I don't.* I couldn't imagine anyone buying me for a price unless it was for sexual use. *No one buys people in a good way—for noble purposes*. I hadn't read the Bible story of Hosea who buys back his wife. I thought no one would want me for pure reasons, and you certainly can't just love someone for no good reason. For me, love always came at a price.

When the job losses, spiritual attacks, and Dad's death hit deep woundings, it was the straw that broke the camel's back. *Hopelessness* and *letting go too much* were my terms for my drifting away, but doctors referred to this just as trauma and PTSD. Because of this trauma, I had been so lost in life that navigating a typical gym was confounding. Gym equipment was no longer toys. No matter what, I couldn't get my bearings, so I was lost in a grown-up playground. A former blessing didn't make any sense and new surroundings and grocery stores baffled me, but God meets us where he sets us, doesn't he?

Hebrews 6:3 (NLT) says, "And so, God willing, we will move forward to further understanding." Through officially committing myself to church and flooding Bible studies with my intense personhood, I moved forward. I desperately needed these groups and this knowledge. I guess inconsistent church attendance when I was younger planted some biblical seeds, but I didn't know nearly as much about the Bible as I thought. There was an overwhelming number of biblical truths and ideas for biblical living that I needed to know, and fast, because I had inadvertently wandered into the devil's backyard. I had to physically and spiritually fight to get away and wanted to keep myself away from this dark side of the world.

Chapter 18

So Now What?

> *"How can anyone," said Nicodemus, "be born who has already been born and grown up? You can't re-enter your mother's womb and be born again. What are you saying with this 'born-from-above' talk?"*
>
> —John 3:4 MSG

ANY HOPE AND faith I had in life had faded and what was happening to me wasn't making sense to me, so I couldn't help myself, the only person I really trusted. Was my body reacting to lack of job security, the fear of not being able to pay my bills as an adult, grieving Dad, struggling with mental issues, and living with the back and neck pain? Did I just have a recurring mental fracture that existed from childhood- and young-adult trauma? No matter what I did, I didn't have answers and I couldn't analyze my dreams for answers because I didn't have them anymore. They just stopped during this period. I was almost at rock bottom, not realizing that Jesus is the Rock of Salvation and that I needed to fall a little more so I could land on him.

Mom started getting concerned. She emailed me again asking how I was, and this was my brutally honest response:

Why tell you my status? You can't help. When I was nineteen and dangling from a towel holder and sink saying, "Mom I can't hold up my own body weight. I think I'm paralyzed!" you didn't get an ambulance or even take me to the ER. That was an obvious, in your face, situation and you didn't do anything but say you didn't know what it was and walk off.

When I was 12 and said, "Mom I'm feeling sad like a cloak of depression, maybe from life issues, is overlapping the other cloak of depression that has landed on me, maybe from becoming a teen . . ." I was taken to a doctor who said I was fine, but I didn't get good help and I probably wasn't ready for help either. I just want to belong; I wanted a home and hugs. Why talk to you about things now. There's no one between me and God that can help, so I'm out of luck.

Go help Miah find some workable solutions to his hernia. He has to keep poking it in. I'm finding that my own brother is a cracked crystal, he's struggling in life. He's pulling away from the family. We're losing him.

Go support Becky. I've learned the problem with Inattentive ADD means that I am very visual and I absorb people and the world like a sponge. People with Inattentive ADD are like living brains. That is a gift and a curse. I think it's made me a too sensitive piece of technology that has cracks and is broken. The problem is me. You can't help.

Eventually, I would read Scripture that explained that it was for my benefit that I suffered such anguish in life; God kept my soul from falling into the pit of nothingness and has since forgiven all my sins. I had moments of comfort during still dark times and moments that were like streams in the desert. Yes, I had fallen into the occult, but now I had to run to the Lord, who had always been with me even when I didn't know it was him helping me, for safety. It was through seeking the Lord with something akin to innocence, truth, and abandon that allowed me to experience security, which put the pain and fear in my life at ease long enough to hear what my sorrow had been speaking.

The sweet voice of sadness tells us exactly what we need to hear if we listen to it. Listening to the language of sadness coupled with properly reading God's Word (reading the Bible and meditating on the reading) doesn't simply allow us to relate to the Bible's internal contents. It allows the Holy Spirit to translate *our* internal contents (the sorrow and brokenness of our own life) into how God is molding us. That honest and unobstructed view of the truth is a throbbing and thick pain, but it's so temporary. It's so life-giving that when we watch this self-transformation, we start to feel the divide between who we are as a soul and spirit versus who we are as a person with an earthly body; the earthly body interacts with the world like we are no different from it. But Christians are different from the world, aren't we?

A new insight starts to develop that grows tremendously when one becomes a Christian. Every moment of the salvation journey is precious—milestones and experiences, events and insights. However, I'm referring to when we learn our identity (who we are as Christians and what that means) when we have the strength to go deeper in our faith. It's when we examine and/or discover why we are allowed our specific burdens that we learn to die to ourselves. This is how we know that we are always in process, always being saved by the Lord. My ability to explain is cruder than I would like, but I ask that the Lord illuminate or at least translate what I am trying to write because I have experienced this form of insight. Leaning into life pain leads to peace and healing in the various fractures and chambers (if you will) that structure our lives. Picture a complex video game when you finally conquer a level. While the end of that level plays the celebration, the screen shows you the entrance of the following level that you had no idea even existed, then you get the massive overview of what is yet to come.

That is what I saw weeks before I started writing this and wondering what to do with myself now that I'm not on a two-year mission and not a brand-new Christian. However, literally trusting the Lord and leaning into my pain seems to have upgraded me to a higher quality, better sadness that gives me hope in completing this next stage of my spiritual journey. For example, trusting the Lord as I would trust a husband to provide a paycheck in time of need brought spiritual restoration. Money just appeared. Trusting the Lord to look out for me led to protection. Prompting from the Holy Spirit to repeatedly read Job prepared me for when I would discover my family had lied about my father's estate having no money until five years after his death and it was all spent. I leaned into the pain and realized that family and neighbors manipulated and deceived Miah and me, but God warned me then (through the book of Job) and told me exactly what to do.

My now adult nephew calls this *leveling up*. I suppose the comparison would be easier to understand if I compared it to table salt. Cheap table salt doesn't taste good when you sprinkle it in your coffee or hot chocolate. If you want the really good, to-die-for gourmet cappuccino latte foam experience, you have to use the kosher or pink Himalayan salt. The right salt makes the difference. Staying with what you know is like the table salt; it works most of the time. Dealing with sadness, like using fancy salt, surprisingly leads to something so much better.

As a person living by the law of the flesh, could I leave behind my go-to behaviors of pain (physical and emotional), bitterness (toward hypocrites, entitlement, and people who had grace unearned), and distrust (of those who had power over me)? I tried not to be, but I was trying through my own efforts and swearing by the sacred idol of self-protection. What would have happened if there had been some consumable insight at this or previous times in my life? What if someone had said,

> Sarah, you are not simply a body. You are a soul within a body in the most literal and physical sense. Remember the movie *Men in Black*? There's the morgue scene where there's the little alien who dies after saying, "Orion's b-b-b." That little guy is an alien, and our souls are aliens to the world because when we become Christians, we are given God's pure righteousness. That righteousness is called, in the Bible, an *alien righteousness*

because the world cannot understand God and his perfect way because the world is in sin, which is why we call it a *fallen world* in Christianese. Back to the little alien: His body blends in with the world (the Bible calls human bodies *earthen vessels* and some translations even say *jars of clay*), but Christians should be in the world but not of it, and they must control their bodies but not alone. They get support from the mother ship.

Now, I suppose I could be far more intellectual and mention that I was living to preserve my ego and thus harming my true self, the self that God intended humans to be before the great fall. But I would have taken any mentorship or quality discipleship that existed. However, 2011 came and went and nothing like mentor or discipleship programs were even remotely available within a twenty-five-mile radius of my home—I checked religiously and desperately. Throughout my professional work, mentorships were always mentioned as being necessary for career growth—and mentorships and spiritual leadership by therapists and self-help gurus—but I didn't see any people able to start life coaching anyone unless they were paid therapists. What successful people would have time anyway? I wasn't sure how to find this. In fact, my intensive search and the lack of services available are very likely why God himself thought that I needed help.

Now, I'm blessed that God didn't give up on me. I had pursued the new age world until it pursued me with a vengeance. It was only then that I would give Christianity a shot. It shot back with the most ultimate light in the most life-giving and life-teaching way. At the end of October 2012, I would become a real Christian, giving up everything God would take, including control over how I lived. I would ask for him in every way I could get him. I would have courage and a beginner's level of trust for the Lord. Just a few days later, I'd also have an eight-foot-tall vibrating column of energy standing before me: a translucent angel. It would point to a Christian role model, one who cleared the path for others and unintentionally showed me how to grow new levels of perseverance, character, hope, and trust. Then, I had no idea there was something more to him, that learning from him would change my life as a mentor. Further unexpected and still more startling is why and how he would be woven into my journey.

Chapter 19
Bible Covers with Clichés

Jesus said, "You're not listening. Let me say it again. Unless a person submits to this original creation—the 'wind-hovering-over-the-water' creation, the invisible moving the visible, a baptism into a new life—it's not possible to enter God's kingdom. When you look at a baby, it's just that: a body you can look at and touch. But the person who takes shape within is formed by something you can't see and touch—the Spirit—and becomes a living spirit."

—John 3:5–6 MSG

AT THE END of October 2012, just two months before the Sandy Hook tragedy, I started a customer service job at a call center/warehouse that sold Christian items. In the gift shop, there was a faux-leather Bible cover with football texture labeled New Found Lamb. It was only twenty-five cents, so I bought it on a whim, thinking that I would eventually buy a Bible for it and pass it onto my nephew or something.

The money I made at this place was the lowest I had ever received since working at a McDonald's when I was sixteen years old, but I was trying to surround myself with Christian things and hoped I could apply for other positions once I got in. I really hoped to find holiness. It wouldn't be so bad: a decent atmosphere in a place where a job is just a job, right? All I had to do was work my personality and knowledge of books and be a good church girl. No mischief, no justice-seeking heroics, and no fooling with the supernatural. Just blend in and do my job.

With no eye for time clocks, my behind was put in the hot seat my first week out of training when I was a few minutes late for clocking in. The manager I was assigned to was so acerbic and superior that she actually told my coworkers that they were stupid and ripped into them even when they were in tears. I would hear complaints and try to arm people for self-advocating during breaks, but many of the people in that call center were prone to self-blame. The manager was especially hard on really tender people. She reminded me of Gramma Peggy with a cold, queen complex.

Looking back, I wish that I had been a strong Christian with protective eagle's wings for my coworkers. There were non-Bible-reading Catholics who worshiped Mary and the Roman Catholic saints and who thought purgatory was in the Bible. No one had ever invited them to a non-Catholic church. Naturally, no one stood up for them to the manager or the other two women who were the three to look out for either. I tried to learn the politics fast, but I didn't yet understand the differences between denominations, let alone churchianity.

What I saw and heard wasn't holiness but lost people. There were people raised Catholic thinking that they were not necessarily welcomed in a Protestant church based on how the boss and the other two catty women acted. My heart bled for these relatable people and their feelings, even though I was never Catholic. It seemed like most of us just wanted to belong but didn't know the rules of religion and denomination (churchianity). I was surprised to learn that some coworkers also felt like they didn't belong in churches at all and just attending a Sunday service would have resulted in awkwardness, shame, and (if they were raised Catholic) feeling inferior. I couldn't believe they felt the same way I did! I thought I was alone in this. One of the women, desperate for this temp-to-hopefully-permanent job to work out so she could quit working at a liquor store, attended the church of the Salvation Army and extended an invitation to two of the Catholics in our group. I hope my ex-coworkers went with her and learned that they mattered.

I was learning how people really were once they got outside the church building. I learned that places that call themselves Christian are no different from church buildings; they are full of both real and false Christians and those on the journey to becoming Christian but aren't there yet. You can only know them by their fruit and discernment.

The manager made snide comments to me. I deflected or ignored her comments. She used nasty verbal barbs like my second stepdad, Mark, so I avoided her, focusing on the work. A sweet woman (Stacey) approached me and a coworker at lunch. We each had wanted to know if the other had been involved in the commotion we'd heard the manager make earlier.

"Sorry to butt in," Stacey said. "I wasn't trying to overhear your conversation. I wanted you to know that she did the same thing to me when I started. I used to drive home in tears for months until I was made permanent. She would tell me that I was worthless. My husband is disabled but not able to collect yet, and I had lost my job as a teacher, so this is the only income my family of three has. Her demeanor may get better once you are permanently hired. She doesn't talk to me anymore. So maybe she tries to see who is really committed."

It was sweet validation that I was not the problem, especially when I struggled with time management (thank you, inattentive ADHD!) and with being in a corporate and Christian environment where I felt I did not belong. Stacey's kindness was honey to my tart pomegranate personality, and I used that for encouragement to keep going. The manager was probably no different from the people found in church buildings: somehow damaged and looking to receive healing, love, belonging, and camaraderie. It appeared like she even provided some of these things to a few of her peers.

I'm glad I met the scathing manager. She might have had a broken heart, but her caustic remarks bit into my competitive side, which would prove to light a fire that had been shut up in my bones. The fire would start whipping out of me with the woman's assumptions: "You're lying to customers. There's no way you can read that many books and recommend them. You're making things up to sell more."

My quizzical thoughts would pop out, "Why would I do that? I don't get a commission or anything, and I don't even know these people to want to impress them."

There was no response, and I would walk away trying to have a balanced perspective. I was someone who theorized and said things like, "Maybe this is why something is happening," and I used symbolic language and not everyone synthesizes information that way. This manager was very literal, so I needed to deal with being someone who knew better around someone who did not. If she couldn't see things from my perspective and misunderstood how I spoke, I should be careful and use an elbow's grease worth of effort on self-correcting.

However, the unmistakable truth that I had a real bully on my hands who was hurting people in a job where she was allowed too much freedom made me want to do something. When the fire in my bones raged, my plan to just do my job with no monkey business started to singe.

I wanted the manager to see that she was wrong about everything and I wasn't going to let her take control of me. I wasn't intimidated even at my worst moment. Far greater things than a miserable, self-titled "Methodist with the faith of a child" had attacked me in the past. She had nothing on the recent demons or the bullies from junior high. I read more, I listened to more audiobooks, and I confided in God that I wanted to not simply improve my already good sell record of $8–13 per order but that I wanted to hit the mark of $300 to be the most successful worker despite my surroundings. I knew I could do it.

I also used my first month on the job to watch my environment as if in a foreign country. I liked to know why people do what they do so I could connect them to what they should be doing. Whether it's being a mascot (something I enjoy) and playing with kids who need to have some fun, mentoring jobless people (I've spent lots of time fixing resumes, telling them where and how to search), picking the right tools for a team to use (profiling is a strength of mine), or how materials should be used, I have an energetic marketing type of mind. Add this to working with fellow readers, and I helped them find exactly what they wanted and needed. Put this mix in a call center, though, and my call time, even streamlined, was more like that of a product specialist—I wouldn't stop until the job was done, and I certainly wouldn't just upsell. I was supposed to learn to handle people better so my time on the phones was shorter.

It was weird that a place having Christian in its business title didn't focus more on the human touch that could have been present in a department dealing with customer service. I was seeing a church system used to organize and help people who follow the Way (Christianity)—good. Personal and interactive relationships between people existed—good. It didn't seem like people knew they were connected to each other somehow, despite being only acquaintances or strangers, a connectedness that I would read about in Christian books and in the Bible. This family feeling, a sense of belonging, I would have to find from somewhere else. I couldn't just walk into a Christian place or church environment and expect a safe haven or retreat. I kept hoping for a heavenly experience, though.

When I wasn't working, I was in God's Word and getting exposure to his teaching through online church sermons and small group Bible studies. God created seeds of knowledge that I did not know I was lacking. He was interesting and delicate; the Lord was smooth and soft. There's that spot near a man's temple about an inch below it that fits the same description. No matter how coarse the facial hair, that spot is so soft and tender to touch. The Lord was smooth and simple like that during this time. This period was a respite but not yet a comfort. *I wonder how I can get that comfort? Missionaries have those amazing stories with miraculous things happening. Old Testament people looked up into the sky and spoke with God out loud! I wonder what that would look like. What if I walked with God the way Enoch did?* My mind kept coming back to this longing.

The Bible says Enoch really did walk with God—like, physically walked with him on a road. This wasn't just symbolic language but a literal walk because the passage in Genesis 5:24 reads as if Enoch and God were walking along a road and lost track of time. As if they went too far beyond Enoch's home, so God said, "Well, you've come this far. You may as well walk a little further and come to my house. I have snacks." *Wouldn't it be cool if we could walk with God the way Enoch did? What if the church people who told me this could no longer happen were wrong and people really could still walk with God like that? What if I could?* I pictured looking up at an expansive sky with powerful clouds, thick with color. In the middle of the clouds would be a brilliant light shining down but a softness to the light for my human eyes. I could walk with this and know that God was walking with me. Every now and then, I could look down at where I was stepping and notice the feet next to mine.

Meditating on God's Word allowed me to become fertile soil that held the seeds of knowledge the Lord was giving me. Though I still thought I was a Christian, some part of me understood little by little that something in my life was missing. I was chewing on this frustration so it would stop gnawing at me. Driving home one night, I was in my safe place (Matthew 6:5–6), me and the protective shield of my car around me. I prayed a vulnerable and personal prayer, like others I've prayed before, but the feelings in this talk with God were different. I was well aware that anyone else hearing this talk would see my weaknesses. Any spirits would have insight on how to better attack me since I was speaking out loud, admitting to God that I had become worth far too little. I sounded frustrated, passionate, and simple.

> God, I'm tired of working so hard for everything just to have it taken away. No matter how smart or hard I work, the company will still go under or I'll get laid off. No matter how much exercising or pool time I do, my body still hurts. I pay off bills, but then I wind up owing again because of things beyond my control! I admit I want to be "spoiled" like those people who have a healthy work/life balance and take time off work to recuperate. When they are tired, their spouses say, "You should spend a

three-day weekend at a conference and getting a massage." I really want to be one of those people who can refuse a job because they aren't desperate for it.

I give up. I can't do this anymore. The storms are over, and I'm still hanging on, but there's no reason to anymore. Everyone is gone, and I'm still refusing to give up, but there's no reason for me to hang onto anything anymore. I can't do this on my own! I have a terrible life, and I'm living like an orphan. No one has ever taken good care of me, and Dad's not even alive anymore. I've tried other things and nothing is working, so I'm trying to do more with you, God. Nothing else matters. I want you to be my father and mother. I want you to take care of me. Be the father I never had. Take care of me, fix me—I am nothing, I need help! Be my everything. I want to walk with you the way Enoch did. If he can walk with you, then I want to too. Ugh! It's not fair—Enoch walked with you for three hundred years. I don't have that time!

It would be almost a month before I realized and discovered that this was my sinner's prayer.

My body continued on, confessing, "I don't want to break the rules and I know I'm not supposed to challenge you, but Jacob wrestled you in the desert. I don't want you to condemn me, but I don't know what else to do and I don't know about this religious stuff. There's no male church elder to come to you for me like the church people say. I have to come to you myself. I want to walk with you now, and I want even more than what Enoch had. To compensate for lost time, I want to know you so well that I know you as the Father, as the Son, and as the Holy Ghost! I want the closeness a mother has with her children, not the distance she has with strangers."

This is why I became a Christian. I was done. I confessed that I needed the Lord. I surrendered to him when he gave me the gift of repentance.

I had prayed similar prayers before, but this moment was different: There was trust in a way I'd not had it before. I thought of those wiggly bridges on playgrounds. There are small wooden planks that run parallel to one another with about one foot of space between them. Chains on both ends hold up the planks and a solid panel of wood underneath allows kids who slip off the planks to step onto that flat wood bridge just below. In order to get across, you look down at first to assess the situation. Then you have to look ahead at the planks and to the end of the bridge to keep your balance as the other planks start to move. This is how you cross, but because you can't look down at where your feet are and where they will be in one second, you are actually exercising trust.

For me, though, I felt like I was taking a step using faith. I knew I was taking a step, but I couldn't tell if the step was one inch below or one foot below. *Am I nervous, afraid? What is this feeling?* I wondered. It was the feeling that comes with the start of an adventure. It was excitement that threatened to bubble over the surface in the midst of the to-do list of life. It was the exhilaration that was somewhat scary; I didn't want to get my hopes up in vain. I wasn't sure I liked feeling such elation I couldn't control. I hadn't planned any of this and was not yet consciously aware that I was asking God to have a personal relationship with me. I was just talking to God in the raw and intimate way I had done during the week after "the world went quiet"—a time that taught me to believe in his existence, to feel married to God's existence.

I'm still not sure if the Word became flesh within me at that moment and I was born again at that time or if my conversion only counts a couple of days later when there was a visible sign. I don't think it matters. I only know that I wanted authenticity and to return to the ways of the original and early church, honoring the Father, using the Holy Spirit without neglect, and remembering Jesus the Christ, trusting God as a *real* person. I was on that quest. Maybe after becoming a Christian in the moment, the Holy Spirit was germinating tiny born-again seeds that sprouted and became mature enough to see during the most excellent phone call that I have ever had.

Chapter 20

Miracle Call

*You will seek me and find me when
you seek me with all your heart.*

—Jeremiah 29:13 NIV

A FEW DAYS AFTER the confession in my car, I was at work on a typical phone call. A woman was asking to buy books for a mission across the globe when I felt a presence above my right side and watched it descend, resting at desk level right before me. It didn't produce heat and I didn't feel incredible love as some people say, but it had my attention nonetheless! The woman told me what she was looking for, so I suggested a book on discount and it was an upsell. She loved the idea, and to my surprise, she ordered $324 worth. Whoa—a steady presence had just descended in front of me and I was upselling the $300 goal that I set! This was so delightful because it was a sign that God cared about the goal I set for myself. Then everything pivoted 180 degrees, and the sign became so much more for me.

In less than a blink of an eye, I felt like I was on a soccer field during a game and the pressure was on! In the vision, an official was gesturing for me to move to the forward position. *I'm a fullback*, I thought. *I don't have the endurance for forward.* I was suddenly in forward position without my body even moving, and the game was back in motion before my brain even had a chance to process what was going on both in the game and outside of this daydream, which I will just refer to as a vision. Two things were happening at once: the literal action of the phone call and the symbolic vision of the call.

The woman talking had been ready to complete the order, but for some unexplainable reason, she started to question her decision. "Maybe I shouldn't do this after all."

Uh-oh! I could feel deep inside that this order needed to happen. When I say the pressure was on, I mean it. This felt like a high-intensity, stress-filled moment, and I needed to use everything I had in me to succeed. I couldn't manipulate this woman, no matter how desperate I got because I knew that would be cheating, but I had to do something. I asked the woman what gave her pause.

"Shipping something like this would be expensive and, well, the post office might mess up . . ." *Shipping cost? She doesn't have to pay that, especially if she's giving to charity!*

When she finished mentioning the postal issue, I had to hold back my excitement. I am a fast talker and a very passionate individual despite my imperfect life. When children, animals, or good news abound, so do I!

"Well, you don't have to pay for shipping on this order since it's over $100," I said. "You have to ask for it, and I think that's what you just did! We won't use the regular post office either. You have options."

She was pleasantly surprised and thanked me for helping her navigate packing and tracking code information. I went through the rest of the motions of completing an order and let her know to take her time in getting her payment information. Inside my body, I was freaking out like a sea cucumber spilling out its nasty little guts!

Simultaneously, the soccer game was still going and I was on the move! From the moment the game went back into motion, it was my responsibility to move that ball, and we were making progress. I kept the ball close and moved into the bodies around me. Pushing into them was my response when I played soccer as a kid. I'm not squeamish about touching at all, and this movement was great for protecting the ball from extended legs. I used my feminine body and its attributes with no shame. Running past one person and up to another slow runner, I hip checked one with an exaggerated step to the left and shouldered the other on my right, knocking him and her off balance and giving me space. A tangle of outstretched legs made wild kicks, but my balance was solid and my weight grounded. I had confidence while running and kicking through shins and past thighs. I forced a couple of bodies out of the way and kept moving. I have never been good at juking, but I was on a mission. Our Maker had called his sheep by name and I answered! I zigzagged between solid, unmoving frames and pulled to the center of the goal line. Instinctively turning my head to the right, I didn't look for the coach. He was outside the field.

I needed the team captain, the one who was both player and coach on the field, the one who knew what it was like to be in my position. I looked for the one who saw my every move, the one who was seeing my thoughts at that moment before I even consciously knew them. I had turned my head without even meaning to because I was about to feel doubt and unworthiness, but the team captain was there looking right at me and holding me accountable. His look and very presence gave me truth in my very core and through every atom that made up my body. I was spurred on. Eager-to-please sheep that I was, I did what I knew he wanted before my mind had a chance to even catch up.

Turning my face from the man representing the Son and back to the game, only a second had passed by me. Like lightning, I lunged forward with my left leg, shifted my body and connected with the ball steady, straight ahead. I had an "in the zone" moment; I knew the ball was going into the net, but I could feel the hype, nerves and the anticip—

The woman returned to the phone with her payment, and we verified all necessary information. The woman had everything she needed. I copied her confirmation number myself and let her know that I would also be keeping an eye on the books for her. There was no way I would let this slip through my fingers. I added some free Christian booklets that the mission might appreciate and submitted the order. The lovely woman and I were so gracious to one another and praising the Lord. We hung up after expressing our mutual hope that this gift would be God blessed.

Back on the soccer field with leg muscles engaged, I slam kicked that soccer ball so hard, I blessed the mess right out of it. The goalie missed the ball as it went straight into the goal's net. Score!

I breathed and hung up the phone. I felt the presence rise from my desk, and then it left. I sat back and breathed again, exhaling an incredulous little almost laugh.

I didn't have a name for what had just happened, but it was miraculous. It was so much more sophisticated and strategic than any other miraculous moment than I had ever had. It changed the way I view strategies and left me in awe. I never expected a threefold miracle let alone one so amazing where I could actually be involved. I performed the final half of the miracle. Me! God let me be involved and . . . I was . . . and I did it. This was crazy (or in Christianese: I was awestruck and delighted in the Lord!). There was a difference between the Father and the Son. God let me know that. He showed me because I asked. I got to do that despite being a female in the church.

Like many born again, I couldn't shut up about it; though initially, I held this private and personal moment for myself. But this intimate exchange between God and me was uncontainable. I had to tell someone. Paradox aside, I kept replaying the moment until I needed bodily rest. Furrowed brows and guttural moan-like sounds were the best "words" I had for my experience. *How could any of this be, and how could it just happen, then stop as if it was a common event?* There was the daily bustle around me, but inside I had been completely changed! The spirit of Jesus pulled me out of darkness. *What can one do after such a profound yet simple experience like this? How do you live and feel after watching Jesus lay your death in its grave while you face an expanse of freedom?*

After a couple months, I gained some amount of control—enough to focus on why I scored a goal. There was something about the action that felt like a sub-layer. If performing in a game (symbolically) and upselling the books (literally) represented one interactive miracle that made me feel amazing and was precious to me (meeting the $300 goal), then what was scoring the goal all about?

As I thought about this, the forgotten, quiet part of my heart felt light shining on it. When I played soccer in junior high, I had never vocalized my desire to score a goal to anyone—or at least anyone who gave an indication of listening to me, the middle child of five. I was always a fullback. The one time I played forward in a game, I got as far as the goal but needed someone else to take the shot. I could manipulate the other players up to the goal line, but there was only that one time and my shot would have been blocked. The only reason I was in the offensive position that day was that I vocalized to the coach how all the girls in the game were grouping around each other, forgetting the ball, but I saw and could fix things. After that play, everything went back to where I felt I belonged: in the background supporting my team and defending it, not advancing. That is the way it was. I didn't notice that a hidden part of me wanted more, but God did.

I couldn't believe this. The realization of what this experience meant was dawning on me. *Wait*, I thought. *Was God looking that far back into my past, remembering my potential, and giving me a shot? Did he think about that time when I was twelve and I wanted to be a halfback more often but I didn't have the dexterity or energy? Food pantry food for a family of seven can only get you so far, and I spent time reading not jogging or practicing. Maybe if I had a dad or one of those stepdads that did fatherly things with their children, I'd have confidence or maybe even we'd practice together making the ball go into the goal instead of just getting the ball away from the goalie through trial and error. I would have had direction. Like so many people in my generation, I didn't have a good father figure, and I didn't have the Lord then, but I have him now and he helped me score this goal!*

Now, to even think about getting to score the goal, I needed a few months. Why a few months? Well, I needed time because my mind was blown friggin' away by my conversion. Whoops, I mean, I found myself awed by the Lord's gracious presence. (Insert any other Christianese that I have forgotten.) Anyhow, I'm very passionate and innately fight stoicism (since that was an old enemy of my childhood). I also welcome a little

ADHD-friendly pandemonium. Thus, I prefer a few things happening immediately, so while processing the miraculous $300 upsell, I couldn't focus on the details.

Gratitude for my newfound relationship (when I became a genuine Christian) with the Trinity had me reaching out to him, talking to him, looking for his physical body only to remember that he didn't have one. My hands formed a bodily shape in the air when explaining to people that God was transactional and interactive like a real person. The Trinity was life changing, and I let him know it without regard! I let God know that I was available for everything I asked of him during my confession in the car. I also wanted to know what more he could show or teach me.

Chapter 21

DVDs and Celebrities, Not Scrolls and Camels?

Beloved, do not believe every spirit, but test the spirits, whether they are of God; because many false prophets have gone out into the world.

—1 John 4:1 NKJV

A COUPLE OF DAYS passed on my authentic conversion experience. It was early November 2012, and I still preferred not to pray out loud about things intimate to me.

After my transformation, I was spiritually born again. However, this was in the spirit, so I still held fear in my physical body. I felt like I needed to maintain vigilance so I wasn't fooled and victimized again by demons/fallen angels. My lifelong interest in angels had been completely demolished since I had been violated by angels; I couldn't accept the fact yet that those were fallen angels. I was so guarded, still wounded, and my life was still very hard pressed. But when God shined his light on me and called me his own, I had so much wonder and joy!

Not even a week after what I started referring to as "playing soccer with Jesus," something radical happened. I was still on cloud nine and could not keep my mind off my relationship with God. *He was a God from whom I had wandered in my youth, but he is the last God I will ever know!* But I am silly and I got so lighthearted with God. My internal dialogue is always on the go, so I kept making similes and metaphors about my relationship with God, allowing my mind to keep exploring this. As the metaphors mixed in my rapid brain, I took a fifteen-minute break from my desk at work.

Setting the timer on my watch, I moved from my desk toward a few conjoined bookcases about twenty-five feet away that served as a reference library. Almost in front of the library center, I reflected upon another miraculous moment when God had parted the sunset clouds over to display the word *hola* and compared it to my new conversion experience with the Lord. They were two amazing moments where I felt connected to God the Father and the Son. I jokingly pretended to be a self-righteous snob and said to God (not out loud): *Don't worry, Holy Spirit. Now that I'm walking with the Father and the Son, I won't forget about you.*

Instantly, I felt a magnetism very gently pulling me. When you pull two magnets apart and flip one over, you can feel a gentle force between the two magnets. There's nothing visible there, but you can feel it. This is pretty similar to what I felt. I looked over to my left, from where the magnetism was exuding, and stepped toward a clear, vibrating column of energy that extended from the floor through the ceiling, or at least that is my impression since I could not see through the actual ceiling. I was in an ordinary, no-frills-at-all call center with the removable tile ceilings that you find in public schools. When I touched the column of energy with my right hand, the energy was still there as I expected, but I could put my hand through the transparent energy waves without them affecting my hand. I wrapped my arms around the energy pillar, and it wasn't much bigger than a person.

Could this be energy from an enormous printer or from some IT server? Where is the plug? There is an outlet giving off energy somewhere. I didn't only look at the carpet, at the wall behind the vibrations, and the room behind that same wall. I actually walked around the column of energy, even though it was see through and touched everything. I wasn't sure what it was doing there, but I started thinking, *Hmmm*. Something unexplainable was happening, and I wanted it explained. I watched my behavior looking for a logical explanation while my brain started connecting words like *energy, vibrating, movement, mysterious,* and *supernatural.* The truth was all that mattered to me. I needed to face my distrust, which is truly fear with a coat of armor, and to face what I knew this was. Something in me clicked into place though I couldn't acknowledge it right away. I was willing to call this thing energy. That was all. I narrowed my eyes, and with a cold distrust, I scrutinized . . . it.

Finally, it dawned on me that I was sensing more than an eight-foot-tall column of pulsating energy and started seeing a humanlike shape in the transparent form in front of me. *It's so tall!* I shook my head to clear my thoughts and to stay on guard. My poor little body had encountered a great deal during the spiritual warfare of my past. It wasn't going to let me go so easily. My eyes narrowed again, and I looked away quickly, then back. It was still there. I looked around the call center: No one else was looking. In fact, the place was oddly quiet and sparse. No one else was taking their scheduled break for some reason.

I looked back at the vibrating column of energy. *That's what I can see, and factually, that is all that there is to it.* It was still there. I took three angled steps to my left and peered over the demi-cubicle at one of my coworkers. He didn't look up from his computer even though I was staring at him, two feet taller than the cubicle, and right in front of him. *Okay, no way. He should be feeling this too. He's right next to me!* I went to another cubicle where an associate was listening to a customer on his headset. He looked at me quickly, then went back to the conversation like everything was normal. I made a facial expression that said *Umm hello?!* and gestured, but I got nothing from him.

I walked back to the vibrating column of energy. Clearly, I wasn't going to get any validation, but I needed something so I could let down my guard and trust this thing. After all, I wanted to know what was happening and *it was so tall!* I felt so much reverence for this *really, extremely, tall . . . angel.* There, I thought it deliberately. I admitted it. I certainly wasn't going to say anything out loud to it, especially not now! My spirit was warring with my flesh big time.

I did not want angels in my life any more than an angry, elderly curmudgeon wants young whippersnappers on his lawn. My occult experience made me feel like all angels were predators and I was prey. My flesh knew what this object was immediately and started responding before I actually figured this out. My flesh wasn't over the hurt of the past, and I was going to need divine intervention to change that. Though it was a prejudice, I was still feeling fear. I felt this inside me, but I also felt this: *I will not back down.* I made my resolve; I felt the strength this gave me, and with my hands on my hips, I faced the angel so tall that I knew it extended beyond the ceiling.

It was an enormous, powerful, and respectable sentry. Though I couldn't exactly see details, I knew it was human shaped enough to have a head and the outline of eyes. When painters have to draw wind, they can paint a clear gloss over the scenery. It's not the easiest thing to see, and it provides the outlining needed to represent wind. This is what the soldier of God looked like, though I wasn't certain it was of God yet. As I really looked, I felt respect and honor for what I would compare to an accomplished, captivating Marine. I looked it over. It didn't budge and neither did I. My watch indicated that ten minutes had passed. I had spent about eight minutes looking around and touching this vibrating column of energy (it took well over a year and a half for me to start referring to it as an angel). I softened some when I looked up and felt awe over how tall the angel was. I cannot repeat it enough. This wasn't an enemy angel luring me in with its beauty. This angel was a soldier of God doing its job, and it was a messenger that deserved not to be shot down with fear and distrust.

Oh! Angels are messengers of the Lord, and they come bearing messages. The angel's duty finally dawned on me. I spent all that time trying to do the smart thing regarding the angel, but finally, my part in the experience emerged. I straightened myself up and looked around feeling like I was only two feet tall and wearing a diaper that failed to cover up my mental infancy! *In case the angel is not of God, I won't speak to it out loud.*

I could attest that only God could read thoughts for the most part, so I put on my best poker face and said, in my head, "Do you have a message for me?"

Unaware that the angel had arms, I was surprised to see its left arm unbend and point! *God must have told it! But I still don't trust it completely. It has an arm—whoa! Don't stare; that's rude. You're not supposed to focus on the arm but the thing it's pointing to. I don't trust it. The other angels could direct my hands to things . . .* Thinking I was smart, I decided that I would allow one final test. People had always said, "God doesn't take away your free will. He lets you choose." I decided to hold my hand over the stack of books where it pointed to see if this general of great stature was of God or not. If anything closed around my hand, it would be the Enemy and I would rebuke it.

It was hard to see where the angel's arm ended, so I had to go by touch only. Like a blind woman, I put my hands up to the middle of the vibrating arm that extended to my right and walked my hands palm by palm until I reached the stack of library materials, all the while feeling conflicting emotions of distrust, openness, amazement, stubbornness, and unpreparedness. My hands were awkward against the angel, but I remembered my determination and spent the next two whole minutes with my right hand hovered over the stack that had a DVD on the top and my left hand back on my hip. I was afraid that I looked like I was doing the Hitler salute, but I stuck with the plan anyway. Even when my coworker (the one who attended the church of the Salvation Army and wanted to work at a Christian company instead of a liquor store) walked by, I stood there.

Wait! I was about to get my validation though I no longer needed it. As she was walking by, my sister in Christ looked at me standing in the middle of the aisle looking absurd, then she looked at the angel like it was a real person in the flesh—only she looked at it like it was nothing extraordinary! God was clearly teaching me when this came into my head, *She can't see beyond the veil. She saw without seeing.* I pictured a veil, even clearer than the angel, between the woman and angel. She would not get past the curtain because something was there. She stopped, seemed to look through it, but it was a divider.

I asked her later, "When you saw me standing with my arm outstretched like this [I showed her], and you looked across from me, do you remember that?"

She said she did and that she had been on her way to the ladies' room and noticed me but that she didn't think anything of it at the time.

That made sense. God's thoughts echoed with me. She saw me and it but not really. She saw without seeing. Pharisees had opportunities to throw stones at Jesus, but they didn't because God put a veil between Jesus and them. Interestingly, I told the woman this full story and her role in it a few months later. She still remembered and corroborated the event, but she could not access what she saw. But then, I was the silly lady confused by a sacred encounter with an angel.

This is ridiculous! I picked up the DVD and looked at the angel. Nothing in its body language changed, and I only felt the vibrating hand on the one movie. *Did I do this right? How do I know how many of these materials to take?* I felt beneath the DVD—no vibrations. The only thing that the angel touched was the DVD. *Do angels point to DVDs? That sounds gimmicky and nutty.* I looked at the image of a man on the movie and went to put the documentary back but didn't set it down. The angel didn't say or do anything except the arm was no longer extended. I had trouble keeping my focus on the DVD and not the angel. I finally trusted it enough to let it do its job, and I realized that I had encountered an angel like "holy" people had in history. I was so touched. God sent an angel.

I was mentally nudged to not focus on the angel but where it was pointing. I looked at the movie case again. There was a young man I recognized from another book cover, a motivational speaker and athlete. I looked back at the angel. I turned back to face the media shelf and committed my attention to the movie. I saw that it was a football guy, Tim Tebow, who looked like he could be my brother (that friendly, boy-next-door look), and there was a small title that wasn't worth even a thought at the time. I didn't know what to do with the DVD, and so much was happening in such a short time, so thoughts were speeding past each other and overlapping.

Forgetting that God could read my thoughts, I said to myself (still not out loud), "I already have a brother. I don't need another one." I didn't understand. I remember turning my head to the right, but I didn't see anyone standing there or hear anything but my jumbled thoughts. I said in my mind again, "I have a whole brother and a half. I don't need another one," and shrugged.

My thoughts held phrases about *two years learning from him*, and I was dismayed at enrolling in anything for two whole years until I could receive whatever God was giving me. If he was giving me gifts, I wanted them instantly! As a newborn born-again, I struggled with what the Lord wanted me to discern. I wasn't sure at all if the two years popped into my own head because it was my own thinking or if God sent angels to answer my questions. Blessedly, God made this clearer a few times and even warned me when there were only six months left of the two-year pilgrimage on which I was about to embark. I called it a *mission* or *pilgrimage* even though I was not physically going on a pilgrimage but rather staying put and simply learning from this footballer from afar.

I was willing to do whatever the Lord wanted, but his ways of growing and developing me required spiritual maturity and profound perspicacity. I looked at the DVD again and figured maybe this footballer needed a friend or a coworker. I envisioned a future where one of those "funny coincidences" would happen when you are thinking of friends or family and you get mail from them, then a topic concerning them is on the radio, then you get a phone call from them. I assumed that I would have a pen-pal type relationship with this potential friend. We could work together and email back and forth. I mentally moved on. My time was up. The angel was still standing there but nothing else happened, so I returned to my desk, checking over my shoulder a few times. It waited for me to leave. When leaving for the night, I returned to the scene in front of the library and nothing supernatural was there at all. *It's not the place that is holy but the encounter.*

I nodded my head, acknowledging the advice that just so happened to pop into my brain. I still thought all my intelligence was my own and didn't realize how much of it was God speaking into me. My pride was preventing me from realizing how involved in my life God actually was. But for now, I had a movie to watch.

Chapter 22

Goodness

But when the Holy Spirit controls our lives he will produce this kind of fruit in us: love, joy, peace, patience, kindness, goodness, faithfulness, gentleness and self-control; and here there is no conflict with Jewish laws.

—Galatians 5:22–23 TLB

WHEN I GOT home, my mind churned through the experience. Who wants to watch a movie when you stood across from an angel of God only hours earlier? I was a complete wreck, just undone and psyching myself up even more. I wandered around my apartment on autopilot, replaying the events and pretending that many people had also seen the encounter. I shook them and explained how huge this was and what it meant. The human body was simply not made to hold in any heavenly experience! Despite my giddiness, there was a solemnity to God sending me an angel. Even in retrospect, I think of the angelic encounter not as it was but what it represented in my life.

Picture an exceptional networking event or reunion where you know many people and organizations and it's a great time. You actually get to see, interact with, and laugh with mentors. The topics and resources are all familiar to you, and you're allowed to eat and drink everything because the catering follows your diet. The craziest part is that you are allowed in the presence of the Lord without exploding or going blind! You know he would be attentive and make good eye contact. Anyway, I was so pleased to know that the only genuinely loving Father that I had known (and who had been real and there for me my whole life!) would metaphorically meet me at this event. He did this simply to address how much I wanted to be in union with him. My father knew I needed guidance and relationship.

He may as well have said, "To get started and make the progress you want, you're going to need counsel. I want to do so much more than tell you about having an interactive relationship with me. A visual will help you to remember what you need to learn. I know your working memory and short-term memory are still healing, but everyone needs examples and models. Therefore, don't take this as insufficient on your part. In fact, I'm giving you a gift that means as much to me as you do. There he is, right there. That's Tim Tebow—you've heard of him. I highly recommend him to you, and I take this very seriously."

I wish I did more than shrug and say, "Umm, okay," to the mission on which the God of the universe was sending me, but if I told it any other way, then this story would be fiction. God didn't need fictional inspiration anyway. He had been doing crazy, phenomenal things for me since my conversion.

I have since asked God to send a message of thanks to the angel I shunned, explaining and apologizing for my frigid behavior. No joke—I manned up and deliberately gave the soldier of God the professional respect owed to a being that could have shirked its duties or terrified me but chose otherwise. I even look forward to working with it in heaven when I am big and powerful and the angel is lesser. The goal: being as professional and courteous with the sentry as it was with me; there will probably be saluting and a firm handshake. Regardless, I hope to return the favor to show our God how much his work and everything he does means to me. The trick for me would be to understand and try my hardest to continually revisit why God sent me a leader and how that would affect my relationship with the Trinity. My relationships hadn't involved denial of self or a step toward *metanoia* (repentance and realizing who I am in Christ), just neglect. Now was a chance to change that.

Quite frankly, I could see exactly why God pointed out such a role model to me. I've never really had a loving dad, but I do have a brother not even two years younger who served as the man in my life. We were closest to each other when we were both in high school and competed in the same sports and shared some classes. With the emotional calluses God was about to remove from me, I needed to find comfort in a brother.

With the plans he was going to reveal, I thought for the longest time and with absolute certainty that I would run from the "too much" that God might expect me to do. In fact, for well over a year into the two-year mission, I fought the urge to run. I decided to stop trying to run right after another Old Testament book about intimacy, Hosea, was illuminated to me by God. Hosea tells the story of the prophet whose relationship with his fickle wife represents God's relationship with his people. However, the Lord put me at ease so I would not run from the pain of God's pure love, and he used the tender, loving man from the DVD. God sent me my own Hosea figure. The Lord selflessly thought of whom I would sincerely accept as a friend, would respect as a mature brother in Christ, and someone with whom I would be truly comfortable because I was going to be spending plenty of time learning from him. But back to the documentary.

I couldn't delay any longer. The DVD was in the player and the documentary *Everything in Between* started playing. The moment Tim Tebow's face appeared on screen, I knew exactly what I was supposed to see. "He's got goodness," I exclaimed out loud in a one-sided conversation with God. He had my full attention. I hadn't yet memorized the fruit of the Spirit, and even after I did, I flew past it in recitation, not connecting it to the heart knowledge that I personally had with goodness. Pausing the movie, I thought for a while.

Goodness probably has layers to it the way C. S. Lewis says that love does. There is the acquaintance (*storge*), friendship (*philia*), erotic (*eros*), and unconditional (*agape*) loves. The goodness that surprised me in the documentary was obvious enough that I didn't need to meet Tim Tebow to see that he had it. It wouldn't be a storge, philia, or eros type of goodness but something rarer. It's worth coveting for those who don't have it and worth sacrificing to keep predators from detecting or touching it. I hadn't even consciously looked for it in others but have known to keep my attention on this hallowed item. It hid internally and safely guarded the way only a five-year-old survivor can hide her most special things, where no one thinks to look. The closest synonym is innocence as in purity and not naiveté. The meaning still gets lost in translation because God gives it to us to take care of it and because it's of God: Nothing can take it away, but many will try.

Resuming the video, I noticed that Tim is like my brother with normal, simple, passionate behavior and tremendous commitment to hard work. He must struggle with wanting to earn something the way I do, but he had what looked like a healthy balance of knowing how to be successful in the world while succeeding in the faith. The way he mastered his body, making it his slave, was different from the times when I did this. I did this the worldly way and ended up massively injured. He did this the godly way, respecting and caring for his physical body. I think part of what helped him was having a nurturing and protective father and mother. However, I saw a team of people investing in him and looking out for his best interests. I was definitely surprised and happy for him and interested in people who look out for each other like this. I had a felt need for mentoring, life coaching, and being discipled because I was such a mess and the farthest I had gotten, at this point, wasn't enough—clearly why my loving God intervened.

Every few weeks for the subsequent two years, I pictured a basket I had woven in summer camp (paid for by scholarship money; thank you, donors). More important than wetting the reeds was working the strands together bit by bit and simultaneously so the structure would not fail. It was difficult, but once the challenge was over, I had a basket that lasted for more than twenty years. I knew weaving it was a metaphor for maintaining a healthy life, but when I became an adult and life dominated me, I couldn't be bothered to weave a basket. Baskets had about as much functional value as my own self. Watching Tim Tebow's life, I wondered if now it was time to start basket weaving again.

I thought living healthy must be part of character building. Having character sounded important, but I had to spend time learning what character looks like and how it is defined. Unfortunately, the more I learned about character, the more I learned that I didn't have it. "Lord," I said. "I want to have good character. I know I'm always looking for hope, but I want better character too."

[Note: A year after asking for this, I was walking through a gym when this moment popped into my mind with a might that made my head jerk. *Your perseverance is growing.* Yes, I realized that it was! I had always thought that I was pretty good at persevering because even when I became frustrated with myself, I didn't quit. If God was going to give me a more sophisticated layer, I certainly wasn't going to stop him. Then I remembered the verse from the apostle Paul: "Suffering develops perseverance, and perseverance produces character, and character produces hope" (Romans 5:4 NCB). Well, I had been asking God to increase my hope and character, so wahoo! I didn't know he would actually do it. Why didn't he say anything before? This was so exciting!]

I still loved overcoming barriers and getting around obstacles, but Tim Tebow is healthier and more spiritually mature, so I got to observe in the documentary and eventually in other media an older brother (he's been a Christian longer than me, so he's an older brother in Christ) fighting the good fight and doing it so well. Watching him was fun because it took me back to high school and college: jogging with friends through the woods and time hitting the weight room. I saw the Rocky Balboa influence in Tim and loved everything about the documentary including the soundtrack. It was helpful to discover a broad-minded adult, a Christian who knew what the world had to offer but wasn't isolated from it.

Watching the documentary also made me see someone relentless who loved people, and I wished that if I were ever buried in rubble or lost in the wilderness that I could have him on my rescue team. *I bet that's a person who would not rest until he found me. Hmmm, time to live like someone who's worthy of finding.*

Fertility in a Christian's life comes from splashing Christ's blood on the living canvas that is our spirit until the image forming is that of perfect purity and conformity with Christ. With my whole Christian life ahead of me and Tim Tebow apparently guiding me, I dipped myself in the blood of Christ and started painting.

Chapter 23

Letting Hope Change Me

*It is the glory of God to conceal things,
but the glory of kings is to search things out.*

—Proverbs 25:2 ESV

TIM TEBOW BECAME my Google search of choice. I wanted to learn more. But for all I knew, I would have to protect myself from him to avoid his judgment and rejection. I was a Christian living by the flesh still and not by the Spirit. I didn't know how to stop this. I only knew that my guard was up, even with someone so kindhearted and relatable as my new brother in Christ.

For honesty's sake and to take this further where it belongs, I have to say that having this opinion of him was more than the Spirit generally warring with the flesh. I also had PTSD and trust issues that were getting in the way. My flesh still had layers of sin on it that housed my real self beneath it. I was prideful and too protective of myself. When I read news about Tim Tebow, I liked him very much, but I also had my doubts about his genuineness. When I examined my thoughts and feelings, could I like and appreciate him as a spiritual guide without having the Lord address my cynical attitude? A tiny part of me wanted to shake Tebow's pedestal to see how firmly he was on it. I loved his relatability and connected to it, but my flesh (behavior and attitude) was still natural. It is only natural for me, after enduring the kind of abuse and neglect I had, to wonder if someone is as genuine as is supposed. I even wondered at times if he could be a false convert like I had been. I excused this suspiciousness: "Thinking like this will prevent anyone from taking advantage of and disappointing me." However, Tebow was not disappointing to me, not a single time.

With no inkling that he was on a two-year journey leading a younger sister in Christ, my distant friend never let down either me or our triune God! *How could he fail with the Spirit indwelling within him? Of course he is an authentic Christian.* Regardless, I had so much to learn.

I spent the first five months of the pilgrimage researching and observing. I found a plethora of helpful information on Tim's behavior and character. I surmised that God wanted me to compare the ups and downs of his career with mine. He handled the criticism and the lack of understanding in such a more polished way. Bad moments didn't keep him down because he wasn't desperate or defined by those moments. Often, I was busy living life and didn't have him on my mind when news pertaining to Tim would come to me and teach me another life lesson like this.

Oddly, big moments—such as concluding that I needed adult baptism—would come up and I would get an email or mailing from Tim's charitable foundation. I chalked it up as coincidence because he was a household name at that time, but when godly insight struck me in a profound way and there was also direct mail from his organization, I took it as God motivating me to keep following Tim's faith walk. It's hard to know the difference between happenstance and divine intervention when you have a dream or premonition that comes true.

Who dreams of receiving junk mail and fundraising appeals? Well, I did, and I would have something in the mail the following day. Strangers would walk by me talking about Tim Tebow. It was odd because I still lived in Massachusetts, where any sports celebrity discussed was usually Tom Brady. I was surprised every time these godly coincidences happened. But then, I did ask for the relationship that God had with Enoch, and it's possible God was giving me a taste of what he had with

Enoch. Enoch knew certain things about the future and so named his son Methuselah, which means "when he dies, it shall be sent," which refers to the great flood coming (Henry, Matthew. *Matthew Henry's Commentary on the Whole Bible*. "Genesis 5" (concise/online edition), BibleHub/Bible Gateway. Accessed August 11, 2025.) I just don't have an explanation.

What didn't make any sense and is still a little perplexing is my change in lower back pain since my conversion. It was always there, but I either had a flare-up or I didn't. Some flare-ups were far worse than others, but the pain didn't come and go depending on the minute. My flare-ups had lasted for days and weeks even with epidurals, but since my born-again experience, I could estimate that my overall lower back healed about ten percent. Almost two and a half years after my conversion, I had an MRI on my lower back. The three herniated discs were now just two and they didn't show herniations but bulges instead. I didn't attribute this to my salvation as the doctor went over the report, but one can wonder . . .

So back in the timeframe of these first five months of my genuine conversion, I unexpectedly had an additional phenomenon. It's like God gave me healings as gifts in addition to allowing me the gift of salvation. Testing out the ten percent decrease in pain, I actually overstrained my back. One slight twist in my chair and I could feel a flare-up start right there at work. Mortifying! Bending over like Quasimodo, taking baby steps, or draping oneself over furniture is so awkward.

I had prepped for a moment like this and waddled into a private hallway for a break. Afraid to go too far, I stayed up on the third floor of the call center and walked into another hallway or kitchenette where there were counters or cubicles for support. Instinctively heading for the usual deserted areas, I rested in a dark alcove as the pain lessened enough for me to stand. Well, sort of stand. I lose an inch and a half in height when my back seizes up and the positioning makes my gut stick out. So in between the sweat-inducing, painful efforts, I had the pleasure of looking fatter.

This doesn't happen usually at a job. I'm so careful! The flare-up returned and departed a couple of times, so I leaned or sat for a few minutes, dumbfounded at this change. New to the faith, I wondered if God would heal this back pain as I hobbled into the lobby. Careful not to put too much pressure on my thighs, I made sure my knee cap wouldn't dislocate again. The last thing I needed was another meniscus tear.

Resting against the lobby wall, I silently prayed, "God, you are handing me my pride. I'm scared, but you can take this pain away." Nothing happened. "Hmmm, do you want me to wrestle you in the desert?"

Nothing happened, so I clung to the Holy Spirit and asked him out loud to bless me. "Lord God, I KNOW you can do this. Give me your strength! Take this pain away. Just thirty seconds, that's all I want. Thirty seconds so I can get through that door and to the railings."

In the blink of an eye, the flare-up had lessened! I spent two seconds stunned, then I moved fast. Making it to the heavy corporate door, throwing my weight up over the lever handle, I got through the door. At the mezzanine, I hung my upper body weight over the third floor's stairwell rail and made for the stairs. Almost two flights down, the thirty seconds were up. The metal rail was my crutch again. Everything was back to normal. I had a flare-up, but I could now see that Christian healing was possible.

Not wanting to wait on the Lord to send another angel, I tried to learn as much about Christianity as I could. Living with the Holy Ghost, I had more success than before my conversion, and I picked up knowledge about Christian integrity on my own. Watching online clips was really helpful for learning about character and understanding what odd Bible phrases meant. Online sermons from Mark Driscoll of Mars Hill Church explained that "gird your loins" was God's way of telling us to "put on your cup" to protect delicate parts from inward-bound hardships. That made so much more sense. The only thing I had known to do with a loin was to marinate it or ice it after pulling it.

I couldn't wait to hear more of this from Tim Tebow's motivational speeches. With his natural passion and raw enthusiasm, I figured my spiritual brother and I could start a spiritual bonfire! I wished there were more one-on-one videos with him just sharing because I would have bet that would be a massive strong suit for him too, but I was happy to see his realism in whatever form possible. I had no spiritual fruit yet, and I saw that he had plenty. I wanted to bear fruit too. I was way behind him there and needed to start playing catch-up. I wanted to be the next in line to him so I could be of good character too, so I kept plugging away and further developing.

⁂

Carrying through to the beginning of 2013, bad spirits still had infrequent access to me. Their return felt too soon, and I wished for a permanent way for them to stop. I plainly handled them the way that worked: feeling faith in Christ and rebuking them in Jesus's name. Sometimes standing your ground is the only action you can take. This was at the time that my landlord's wife passed away and an incredible evil presence was waiting for me in my home.

I would make habitual quick scans of the one-bedroom apartment—okay, the large studio that I had sectioned off to look like an apartment—but never turned up anything. My place was an in-law sectioned-off apartment, tucked in the back of a four-story home in a safe neighborhood. The only time I ever locked the doors was when I was in the apartment. I was the most valuable item I owned, so my system worked. But just in case, I would often scan the bedroom, then check the laundry room and behind the bathroom door for anything suspicious. In eight years of living in Gloucester, an evil presence had never been waiting for me until after my landlord's wife died.

I was going to watch a movie before bed, but when I walked through the living room, I saw a man's shape standing in the dark laundry closet that connected with my landlord's basement. I walked past it, into the bedroom entry without stopping, but my mind was jumping into action. I presumed that my landlord—a non-Christian Catholic (he attended for tradition only) who openly prayed to saints of the past and his deceased wife—was "opening doors" that I would have to show him to close, and evil spirits could prey on the vulnerable mourners so with recent deaths, it appeared to me like this was the source.

The poor landlord was the negligent driver in the car accident that killed his wife. I shook my head, sighing. Little things like lights flickering had him thinking that his wife was communicating with him, so I knew he was hurting but that his vulnerabilities could cause trouble. I had just escaped new ageism and its slow burn to demonic attacks. Now I had a wounded guy who wouldn't consider Christianity ("It's not for me," he would say) and my experiences since he lived in perception and not in truth.

I didn't want to have to deal with another spiritual battle when I was still so weak. However, I had to protect myself while also working with the landlord to help him. Like I had been duped, he was struggling, and it hurt to see him suffering. It would be the Holy Spirit's job to refresh me if I became worn down by frustration. I made a mental note to work with the landlord and looked back at the demon in the laundry closet.

I felt like a weary old woman from the ghetto dealing with an old problem dressed new. He radiated a forceful evil that actually stopped me from rolling my eyes and snapping at him as I rebuked him in Jesus's name. I prayed about the situation and felt the faith. Then, keeping as much distance from him as I could, I swung the closet door closed and went to bed. I could still feel the evil lurking there, but this wasn't my first encounter with evil and "a thousand shall fall at thy side . . . but it shall not come nigh thee" (Psalm 91:7 KJV). I slept safely within the invisible bubble that I picture when reading Psalm 91.

God was doing amazing things in my life, and I remembered the book of Habakkuk. I fell asleep thinking about God handling battles without ever having to get his hands dirty . . . and I envisioned the dinosaurs from *Jurassic Park* symbolizing the evil destroyers in Habakkuk.

Only some months had passed since I played soccer with Jesus and started the two-year pilgrimage. But I was young and in love with the Lord. We do silly things when lovestruck! Part of my worship was telling the Lord that I still couldn't believe that he had revealed himself in my life. I was still undone and barely recovered from my conversion and angel encounter. I asked God to do another amazing thing so I could be amazed by and connected to him again. "You are more than enough. Blow my mind, Lord," I prayed aloud. "But in a small way. I can't take much more!" I quickly added.

See, I at least learned from my Bible reading and these Spirit-led experiences: God is really, really big and his clothes fill a temple. God won't hurt me but what's small to him is still really, really big for me. I became distracted, and this request became forgotten like the New Found Lamb Bible cover purchased that October. That item, worth mere pennies, lay somewhere in my apartment near a fake pearl necklace that I had fashioned into a cross.

Chapter 24

Growing Thicker Skin

*The purpose of life is not to be happy.
It is to be useful, to be honorable, to be
compassionate, and to have it make some
difference that you have lived and lived well.*

—Leo Rosten

I was learning how to interact with church people, but I had questions. *If I had been a false convert, others could be too, right?* I found myself suddenly surrounded by people who called themselves Christians, but I met many who didn't act like it (didn't believe in biblical living like abstaining from sex outside of marriage and avoiding habitual drunkenness, were anti-traditional marriage, and pro-abortion, etc.) in various church organizations. I focused on my own behavior, trying to change myself.

The Assemblies of God church I still attended was speaking in tongues during church services, and that was surprising. The apostle Paul says right smack in the Bible not to do that (unless there's an interpretation; see 1 Corinthians 14:5). But I didn't know about the interpretation part and only had many warnings from other church people about only bad churches doing this. How is a young Christian supposed to battle fear between denominations? I didn't want to be a church hopper, so I tried to stay anyway.

The heroin addict who stared at me increased his efforts to engage with me, and it scared me. He kept asking where I lived and how often I was alone. I didn't want to be in a church group where I had to cope with that. Staring, not such a big deal. If all you know is darkness or stoic living, fill your eyes with light and stare at someone who motivates you. But this guy was crossing a line. Living walking distance from the church, I felt like it would be too easy for the guy to follow me, and attending a nonbiblically anchored church scared me too.

While searching for a new church, I watched fascinating clips from YouTube evangelist Ray Comfort. While it was helpful to learn his methods of evangelism, my spiritual nascence was showing when I wondered increasingly if anyone was a Christian. How can you know with certainty if someone has good fruit or bad fruit, especially if you are mere acquaintances? I, myself, was now a legitimate Christian, but I had no fruit. *Hmmm, guess I have to keep feeling around in the dark.*

I left the Assemblies of God church and started going to a seventy-person Bible church. I spent the next two years attending even though it still wasn't the right fit. I parked my butt in a pew, giving it my best shot. I had also started attending a Messianic fellowship group that was developing, and I came across a missionary. An ex–drug addict turned Jewish scholar, he was masculine, clever, Spirit led, and a smoking-hot babe who had bountiful spiritual fruits and experienced many signs, miracles, and wonders that changed other peoples' lives and his own all the time. He inspired me to lean into the Holy Spirit more. My favorite lesson was praying during the offering since I usually gave online. When my small Bible church would take offerings two and three times in one session, I kept from audibly groaning and rolling my eyes by hunching over and praying. It was okay to retreat in the Spirit instead of feeling pressured to give when I couldn't.

Like a diapered infant, I rewatched my big brother in Christ, Tim Tebow, in his documentary many times and picked up more cues on navigating Christianity. When I rolled and crawled after him, I saw him acting like a grown-up version of my nephew, loving and having a servant's heart. Aaron has always been so caring and good with babies. At a playground when he was in elementary school, Aaron saw a little boy trying to get into a swing. Unable to boost the boy up without the swing moving, Aaron got down on his hands and knees in the sharp wood chips. The little boy took a step on my nephew's back and turned into the swing.

Maybe selflessness wasn't popular in the secular world, but I was learning through people like my nephew and Tim's walk that it's emptying the ego and a gift of love from Christ.

I developed only the mildest form of diaper rash in my spiritual infancy, but it was still irritating. Someone made a comment about orphans that chafed my little white Christian behind. I could relate to the orphan archetype as we were parentless for a period and I didn't have healthy parents. It simply hurt to hear the label used repeatedly instead of *kids* or *children*.

God moved in my life and my aunt Cilla coincidentally contacted me around this time to apologize for referring to me and my siblings as "the abused kids" when she was a young adult. I didn't feel she owed this apology nor had I realized this was a wound I even had. Cilla apologized out of the blue and said that it had been what she heard and repeated. She continued, "I remember introducing you kids like that to someone. It's a weird and wrong thing to do."

I thought about this for a second. *Whatever*. Heart-to-heart discussions belong in the heart though and not the head, don't they? And in my heart, I could feel something. I thanked my aunt for this unexpected healing. "Actually, that means a lot to me and I didn't even know [that hurt] was there. I really appreciate that because I guess it mattered somewhere in the recesses of my brain."

I still floundered socially in church settings. One day, just as church was ending, I was excited that my personal prayer time in the church sanctuary could start. I could have all that sacred space practically to myself, and the lines leading downstairs to the coffee and snack area would lessen. Only two minutes into prayer time, a soft-bellied, several days unshowered, and calloused older guy grabbed my shoulder. "I've been watching you through the service," he said.

There's a great conversation starter! My mind was still in prayer mode, really prepping myself to connect better with the Lord and using my fingers to keep track of my main point. So how could I notice much around me?

The interrupter advised that he rarely attended church because he was so successful at running his own business but that he interrupted me because he believed that I needed spiritual guidance. He thought I looked lonely and nervous. I let him know that I was fine and in the middle of a prayer and turned back. The rusty-haired man said that he was from Georgia and that he thought I was new at the church too. I said no and explained that I had actually been attending that church for over one year and that I attended every Sunday, both morning and night, so if I needed anything, I knew where to go.

Captain Bothersome spoke on. One of the church elders smirked, like he knew what was coming. He watched while everyone else left the sanctuary. When the line was ending and the lights dimmed, the elder seemed to decide that coffee hour would be more entertaining. He stopped watching us, and I was alone with the annoying man upstairs. I held in my frustration at the lack of chivalry. I just didn't want someone flirting with me without my consent. The guy wanted me to know that if I needed a shoulder to cry on, he was available and that God had blessed him substantially. So awkward, and he was much older than me, not what I liked to experience. I love single people coming together when they are consensually joining and on equal footing, not a boy in a man's body who doesn't know what's offensive. I did not like being in a now dark room with a strange man who I'd never seen at that church, and I felt cornered and on the defense.

I waved him off, trying to go, saying, "I'm not interested." Why won't these boundary violators settle for a friendship, which is so precious and valuable? Why won't the church push the gift of male and female *friendship*? This is tough to tackle at a church because when I have had to get firm, out-of-touch church people have said, "That's not very Christian! What's the harm? Age doesn't matter."

When did "I don't want to, and I don't even know you" become an insufficient answer to a persistent man's "Why not?" If churches are filled with mental illness and abuse survivors, shouldn't harassment not be tolerated (not babying grown adults but protecting them), and shouldn't more Christian organizations rely on filling church positions with intelligent individuals able to combat unwanted behavior?

The man preceded to tell me that he was more spiritual than religious, and he seemed stable enough. Having an ADHD moment, my mind wandered from whatever he was saying, and I—presuming that no one I came across was actually born again—assumed that his soul needed saving. I asked, "Hey, do you know what *repentance* means?" I defined it for him and told him how to become a Christian.

The lonely man took my desire to introduce him to Jesus for romantic interest and went in for what he thought was the hook: "I lay tile, professionally. People like the way I do it and I take my time, so I always get work. I've got some equipment in my truck. I'm the real deal."

Crickets chirped in my brain. I was so confused. I tried to ignore my frustration and focus on leading him to the Lord instead of just making an escape, and he was, I guess, trying to prove he was worthy of a date. He reminded me of a much older guy who had recently asked me out because he could only date women in their twenties or thirties because women his own age were "bitter." I wasn't looking to be a young, trophy girlfriend to that guy or this one in the church. But I didn't know what to do, so I froze.

"I lay brick too." The laborer interrupted my at least twenty-second lack of expression and confusion, no doubt to sweeten the enticement.

What did that mean? Is that a colloquialism? Is there something appealing about how a person lays down tile? Was he using the word lay *hinting at carnal pleasures? He wouldn't act with unmitigated brass in a church, would he? How does Tim Tebow handle personal intrusions? Oh, that's right. He travels with someone who helps him!* I made a plan to connect within the church more so I wouldn't feel like a sitting duck.

I congratulated the man on having a successful tile-laying job and let him know that it was only natural for Georgian men to struggle socially in Massachusetts specifically. I've seen them struggle with the coldness of the people and treated as hicks and the weather isn't for everyone. Then, I walked off still not very friendly and very guarded, for coffee hour. He followed me everywhere, even to the bathroom, waiting just outside.

The pastor, giving me a look when he saw the guy following me whenever I got up, did not make me any happier. The pastor's wife was thirteen years his junior, and he understood that the church was a great place for lonely people to no longer be lonely. This is true, but it felt like we were in the middle of nowhere and we all had to take what we could get. I grew up with this philosophy. It drives me bonkers when people think that we live in the 1800s and that the Pony Express mail service should arrange marriages.

The man asked a woman he knew if I was single, and she came to me and said that she knew someone who liked me. I was ticked off then, not liking forty- and fifty-year-olds playing teenage romance games with me even though I was "old enough" at age thirty. I told the woman I was very much not interested, and then I lied and said that I was dating someone.

Yep, that is right. I was a coward, though old enough to know better. I felt sick of men and wondered why, from the beginning, Adam hadn't stepped up and prevented Eve from eating the forbidden fruit in the first place. Where on earth was that man when Eve was talking with Satan? It sounds like he wasn't too far away to do something. Wasn't he in biting distance of the fruit?

I stopped dating in my mid-twenties because I knew I was meant for so much more than the three relationships I'd had. I was so broken I couldn't heal myself. I needed to remain single, try a little more therapy, and continue on my godly two-year assignment, learning to be a genuine Christian. I was just going to ignore these men and duck away from them because I didn't know what else to do.

In the same period, another guy started in. He looked like he was actually pregnant and had the largest amount of ear hair I had ever seen.

He asked me if I was single, and I had just walked through the church door! "Hi, nice to meet you. I'm a single man. Are you single?"

I was so taken aback that I didn't even know what to say. He was rubbing his pregnant-looking belly, and I lied, "I'm dating someone." He was kind after that, and we did end up appreciating one another from a distance as two Christians. When he started showing signs of interest again, I was staunch in my behavior and pulled the "I'm not single" line. I just scared easy.

Frankly, I think having lady parts makes things a little harder. Sweatshirts, pants, and no makeup cannot hide that women lovely up any scene. Trauma makes unwanted attention more painful than it has to be, and I just felt like I was desired as an object instead of worthy of love.

God was about to get involved with me again, and he was going to rip off the biggest scab I didn't realize I still had. He allured me into the only wilderness in my area, the forest near my home, not to force anything on me but to invigorate my spirit. He spoke tenderly to me until I wanted to understand more. He was then silent. I started searching for him and his answers. When I was thoroughly lost and confused, he freed me from my sin-crusted façade. Baptized in my own tears, the pain hit with full force, but then I started to feel life.

Chapter 25
Hosea and Gomer

Brothers and sisters, continue to think about what is good and worthy of praise. Think about what is true and honorable and right and pure and beautiful and respected.

—Philippians 4:8 ERV

FLIPPING THROUGH MY Bible restlessly, I had the thoughts of an immature Christian. *Legalism isn't so bad; it keeps us on the right path. What exactly does* fruit *mean? I don't want to street preach at all, but am I going to have to do that? I thought women weren't allowed to be pastors because then they are ruling over men, but I'm supposed to street preach and evangelize according to pastors on YouTube and my churches? Why on earth is it said that women would be "ruling over men" but no one ever refers to male leadership as "ruling over" anyone?*

Closing my Bible, I said aloud, "God, help! I don't know what to think. Is Billy Graham really a Christian? How am I supposed to know? Everybody says they're a Christian in the US. What does this have to do with my pilgrimage, and how do I distinguish my thoughts from divine thoughts?" For the second time since my dad's death, the closed Bible between my hands opened itself directly to an Old Testament book. This time, it wasn't Habakkuk and it wasn't scary but still confusing. Having only read most of the New Testament, I was not prepared for the book of Hosea.

As with Habakkuk, I knew instinctively to read the whole book and did so more than once. The story sounded distant and meant nothing to me. Having never studied it and never understood any reference to Hosea or Gomer, I was reading a book about a prophet who married a messed-up wife so Israel could have a visual when Hosea warned them that God would punish them. Ancient Israel had idols, causing chaos and drama to ensue. I didn't know what to do with this and was fundamentalist enough to know not to write myself into the story but Spirit-filled enough to appreciate that the hand of God was at work . . . somehow.

I would have to learn the history so I could read the book in historical context, but I knew I needed further help to understand the lesson gifted to me. I planned my library trip while I whined to God, "What am I supposed to know, God? I like the first two chapters, but this is boring to me, and I don't know what this has to do with being a Christian or learning from Tebow." I thought briefly, *There is a man named Hosea and a woman named Gomer. Tebow is a man, so he could represent the prophet, and I am a woman, so I could be the prostitute. No way! I don't want to be a prostitute. Come on, God, that doesn't make any sense! Hosea and Gomer's relationship is somewhat interesting, but . . . this relationship is the point of the book, isn't it?*

Isn't it so much easier for a woman to picture herself as a dirty person instead of a prophet? We feel worthless so easily. Because of child abuse, I chose the puritan role of a good girl as a way to fight back from becoming the opposite. I needed to protect myself when there was no fight left in me by being a person obviously uninterested in lascivious behavior. The opposite role would be a Lolita or a harlot. While that's a natural role for someone else to take to appease the people around her, it wasn't for me.

So was God not being literal but symbolic with me? Various Christians told me alternative ways to read the Bible, but God is not confined to any denomination. Maybe he would lead the way I read too? I would lead my owning thinking though. I was a smart cookie; my Head

Start teacher even said so. I honestly had the opinion that because I was good, because I had been born again, and because I understood both good girl and harlot roles as survival mechanisms, this was probably why God revealed the book of Hosea to me. This was why funny coincidences continued causing me to return to Hosea. Those women's studies classes from UMASS Amherst were kicking in, and I was going to help myself. After all, how unacceptable was it for a modern woman to immediately assume she played the harlot?

I thought that I needed to be strong because if I was weak, God couldn't use or be strong through me. Very wrong thinking, but I didn't know that yet. I uttered some internal swears and called Mom looking for guidance since I still didn't trust church people enough to go to them. Mom was familiar. "Dammit Mom, I don't want to be the harlot!" I laughed off my confusion and frustration after telling her what was happening. "No matter what I discover, another reference where I'm the floozy comes up. Does God call people names?"

We were giddy that God was speaking to me and showing me the Way, albeit displeased with the visual. However, my humor had degenerated like the discs in my back, and God had not yet shown me how to refine my speech. Conversion does not magically make us perfect people with perfect ways, but it does start perfecting, saving, and sanctifying us beyond the born-again perfecting through Christ, which allows God to give us mercy. At least, I think that's how that works. I knew I sounded immature, but Mom still entertained my company. We prayed that God would continue to clean me the way Aslan cleaned Eustace in *Voyage of the Dawn Treader*. However God wanted to work was both fine and praised by me!

Within the next few days, I decided that maybe God was simply letting me know that I was symbolically like Hosea and that maybe Tim Tebow was struggling like a symbolic prostitute and could use my help. A terrible and embarrassing guess. I had so much confusion about what God was doing. I felt blind and dumb. I was so unsure of myself and my recent experiences that I doubted everything. My spiritual life had completely changed, so I wasn't sure what normal tools and understandings applied. Maybe common sense and confidence would be bad because I would be using pride and not trusting the Lord. *How am I supposed to know anything, God? I don't understand.* I wanted to, but I had so much to learn.

I learned a little about Hosea's Israel and thought about the role of prophet. *Was that me somehow?* Missionaries are like modern-day prophets, not in the Old Testament way but warning people that we all need a Savior, so I lightly considered the notion. Some church friends said I would be a prophetess (which sounded hokey) while others said nothing at all. To recharge my batteries, I went for a walk in the woods one afternoon.

Walking through the woods, my reflections on God's plan for my mission were rippling in my brain while I kept walking into things. Slapped in the face with a branch and tripping over rocks, I got mad, stopped meditating, and decided that I had this Hosea thing all wrong, but I wouldn't think on it anymore until God told me in plain English. My spiritual maturity was so small that I paid little attention to God's unchanging, heavy-as-an-anvil ways. When he isn't clear with us, we can rest assured that he is unchanging and will guide us without relying on the fickle finger of fate or a frustrated blonde with bugs in her hair and twigs in her clothes.

Rereading Hosea over the next few weeks, I told God that I wanted to know what he was trying to tell me. Francine River's book *Redeeming Love* arrived, and it made the relationship between Hosea and Gomer so much easier to understand. It was a moving story. I treasured how humane the book was with redemption and hope within it. However, I never became promiscuous, and I couldn't exactly flesh out the skeleton of the whole story of Hosea. God's relationship with Israel at least made more sense, but my heart needed more molding.

Chapter 26

Two Unexpected Revelations

*But if from there you seek the Lord your
God, you will find him if you seek him with
all your heart and with all your soul.*

—Deuteronomy 4:29 NIV

I STARTED FIXATING ON what the Holy Spirit was trying to tell me. July and August 2013 marked the point of my pilgrimage that had evolved from a time of research and observation to a mission with an inherent deadline. *God wants me to interact with him and for me to pursue him as he pursues me.*

Early one evening, my efforts at finding answers frustrated, I set aside my ponderings on the book of Hosea. I surrendered. *I'm doing what you want: Bible reading with earnestness, asking you to give me a desire to be in the Word and to give me understanding, getting involved with the church, plugging into the community, learning from Tebow . . . My attitude is changing. Isn't that right? What do you want me to know, and what do you want me to do? I submit whatever it will take, but what am I supposed to do with this Hosea stuff and my Spirit-led experiences?*

The Scripture in Hosea was illuminated with such clarity that my head jerked with the intense inspiration, and I wondered:

How is a prostitute made? What ingredients do you combine to create the recipe for a harlot?

Strippers and hookers usually grew up with sexual abuse.

If you take child abuse, add poverty, then top it off with the hopelessness of despair, you can create a prostitute.

When I reflected on this dialogue between the divine and myself, it wasn't a soliloquy or lecture. The Holy Spirit was educating me and letting me ask, or rather, think questions and additional comments in return.

This would apply to people who are not actually prostitutes too. Anyone with this background could slip into this prostitute archetype because it's so natural.

Ever quick on the draw, I realized that this formula for the prostitute model applied to me. Forgetting that I was addressing the God of the universe, I replied with gruffness, *Gee thanks!* I thought longer. *That hurts.*

God had just taught me that he viewed me as Gomer, the seriously frustrating woman who Hosea should not have married if he was in his rational mind. I didn't for a second regard how the book of Hosea explained that God felt about Gomer. *At least I understand why she was that way, and it makes sense*, I thought to myself. *I still have character flaws and I'm learning how not to have them, so there is evidence that I'm the harlot.* I thought the first revelation was powerful, but the one that was about to occur was shocking.

That means I was wrong about Tebow playing a role in this Hosea story. He's a spiritual role model, and God is the prophet who I need to appreciate more. I guess that part was obvious.

A deliberate and inspired thought from the Holy Spirit replied, "Gomer is a gift."

When God spoke, my mind went silent. The Lord gripped my worldly, sin-stained shell. I pictured Hosea loving Gomer no matter what she did. His love showed best and deepest when she needed him most despite her inability to free herself to receive him. He would need to pay a high and unnecessary price for Gomer's liberty. I started to understand.

The Lord's teaching was so tender and precious. His Holy Spirit continued and ended with one final sentence that hit my exterior so hard that I felt the crack in my shell form deep and long. "You are the gift."

The shell had grown into me so the pull of the shell away from myself caused both emotional and physical anguish. It wasn't anguish alone but a grievous torment! Praise God that the Holy Spirit was with me and that we were in a trusting relationship or the pain, which I know now was a deceptive relationship with my own humanity, could have fooled me. My own flesh had lived in that armor of sin for so long that it went from a perceived protector to a disgraceful encasing that caused my descent into complete submission—and I was pining for it!

Though I ignored this in the moment, the gravity of and deep appreciation of this wisdom was crucial in interpreting the Enemy's plan: Tire my resistance beyond submission while pressing me lower and lower from the land of the living. Because of the Word planted and growing within me, and because of my God-breathed spiritual awareness, and not doubt because of prayers from invisible Christians and their powerful prayers, my flesh could let go. Waiting for me in a low pit, where only the crucified Christ was, the Lord reunited with me, the Gomer he called a gift. What evil meant for harm, God meant for good.

I slid the Bible away from tears that would flood Noah's ark. The more understanding I gained, the more my emotions grew. With the hull of my old flesh gone, an astronomical thud and intense pain in my chest remained. Was my own heart taken from me and given to this story between Hosea and Gomer or the other way around? There are Bible words about this: "I will give you a new heart, and I will put a new spirit within you. I will remove the heart of stone from your body and give you a heart of flesh" (Ezekiel 36:26 NET). Israel's identity transfused into my blood, forming me into the story. *Oh, Israel purchased for a price! What this means!* Scripture was illuminated in the most moving, living, and vibrant way. The accuracy and meaning of this drama were painful! "For the word of God is alive and active. Sharper than any double-edged sword, it penetrates even to dividing soul and spirit, joints and marrow; it judges the thoughts and attitudes of the heart" (Hebrews 4:12 NIV).

It is hard to know how much time passed. The floor was still hard, the lights were still on, and the radio was off. My setting was the same though I was not. The worst of dying to self was over and the journey had advanced. However, let me ask, is it peculiar that the comparison to a prostitute was far easier to accept and far less painful than the comparison to a gift? I deeply wondered why I felt more comfortable with the harlot role. My family, the Trinity, tenderly ministered to my smarting skin. They reassured and steeled me for the removal of the next layer. Still exposed was the hardest, most solid part of my undershell. I had to trust the pain, which only felt natural as an ex-athlete and someone neglected and abused. It hurt still, but surprisingly, it was less painful. I trusted that this process would improve, so I made no attempt to resist. Once an adventure takes you this far, why turn back? Something special was transpiring. Like a child, I held onto the Lord and let it come.

With the initial shock and stupefaction of God's teaching moment and ministrations, I started connecting his pronouncement with the black-and-white story I had been studying. Part of what I was asking about was, *What am I supposed to do now? If I am Gomer, then do I get a loving husband? Why do I feel my heart opening to love now? Gomer is a gift to Hosea, who represents God. Praise you, God, for loving me, but this hurts!* How could I *not* stop in awe at this concept to which I was exposed? I worshipped into the side of the couch and on the carpet which I was still lying on, but it was genuine. My worship was instantly halted when a racing thought ignored the direction my mind had taken and sideswiped my worship to be front and center. *I could be a gift to people. I could experience sacred love. I could have a healthy marriage, a sacred covenant.*

My weird mind pictured the two dogs Old Dan and Little Ann in *Where the Red Fern Grows* loving each other unto death. Could I be in a romantic relationship one day where I was loved until the end? *No!* I didn't picture a godly loving couple; I hadn't seen many of those. I pictured animals! I got spooked like a horse and started bucking. *No, I'm single.* With the removal of my sin-bearing outer skin, I was running back to my old identity. I could not have been more aghast.

I don't do relationships. My people know this. I do not date. That is not for me; that's something you do once you're in a relationship. I only date people

I know, and I don't do that now . . . I didn't like where I thought God was going with this, but why would I get so upset if I thought these thoughts were coming from me?

I was absolutely horrified at the very idea of being in a God-given relationship, now without my outer skin and with my shell smashed to bits, where I would have to trust God and have faith. I protested, "I don't know about this! I, I, well, I'm not available for anything." *That is pretty serious stuff. Way too much. I don't do all that!* My anxious protests turned on a dime. *I'm a prostitute.* My sad admittance and whimper held little hope. I hurt God and that knowledge hurt me.

The moment I pictured myself receiving abiding love, I bolted and truly played the part of Gomer. I'm sorry for that. I wanted to be in control and to negotiate. *I'll partner with someone and be a friend.* In my multitude of thoughts, I could recognize that I had value and things to offer, but I had not ever realistically considered myself as a special, intimate, or sacred gift before now.

No matter how many times my eyebrows raised in shock, God's healing love gave me a worth I had never known. There's no way I had earned a position of one of God's saints or anyone's sister in Christ. *Is it okay to accept what God is teaching me? God, you want me to literally accept and feel this lesson without a chattering, busy mind? This is how I am to sit with these ideas, to heal and to understand these feelings and the power of your love, right?*

The sensory overload was too much, and I started crying again. You know, one of those bawling moments when there's snot, tears, and sobs and your head is throbbing and emotions are pulsating so deep, you assume that every leaky part of your body must be running. Did I shower away the swollen face? I didn't think I could muster it. I only remember going to sleep several hours early that night, after I had dragged my heavy body to my bed and burrowed under the covers the forgotten way I used to when I was a little girl just taken from Mom's custody in threadbare, hand-me-down pajamas and whispering tears to the night that "I miss my mom."

Chapter 27
Playing Christian Dress-Up

*Then Job replied to the Lord:
"I know that you can do anything,
and no one can stop you.
You asked, 'Who is this that questions
my wisdom with such ignorance?'
It is I—and I was talking about
things I knew nothing about,
things far too wonderful for me.
You said, 'Listen and I will speak!
I have some questions for you,
and you must answer them.'
I had only heard about you before,
but now I have seen you with my own eyes.
I take back everything I said,
and I sit in dust and ashes to show my repentance."*

—Job 42:1–6 NLT

"**L**ORD, HELP ME to want what you want. You know I want security since I have so little of it. The same goes for my family. We need so much help and work. I will keep learning, but I don't know how to help anyone else, and I feel pressured to already be this holy person like Mother Teresa and an evangelist, but I'm not." At least I was getting much more comfortable praying aloud; it was progress.

Within a few weeks' time, my next layer of old self melted away, and things went better this time. It felt good. I felt like I had inside information beyond what non-Christians had, now I knew God who was truth, even though I had trouble knowing how to live. Why wasn't everyone else in my church enraptured with God? *Maybe they're afraid of being Spirit-filled,* I thought. *I'll just focus on rousing them with the Bible.* In small groups, I would share my passion only to get a mixed reaction. After all, not everyone was a new believer like me and still in the honeymoon phase of their relationship with the Lord.

So young in the faith, I had no idea the different opinions each denomination had about each other nor did I know that Pentecostal doctrine can draw criticisms from other Christians in the same way Catholic and Orthodox doctrines do. I wish someone had explained that to me because I loved several parts in Romans 5–8. In small study groups, I would get excited (which coupled with untreatable ADHD means physically and verbally) and say, "Do you see what is happening here?"

I would point out a play-by-play of Paul's behavior. God simply blew my mind with his strategic, miraculous ways. I was on fire for Christ! And Paul! And Romans 5–8! Some of the group would then start slowly engaging in the discussion without passion, and others would head to the snack section. Meanwhile, I was realizing for the first time the bold claims that Paul was making. "Do you know what this means?" I would ask.

Only a couple of people did. "God is powerful and loves us," "We need to put on Christ and act like Christians," and "We can't earn our way to heaven," they would say. Then there was silence, like even after the end of chapter 8, just before chapter 9 starts . . . crickets.

"That's it?" I would ask and look around. I might have been the youngest one there, but there were women who could run circles around me. "No one sees how intense this is? We are slaves to Christ!" My fist was a gavel against my hand. " 'If God is for us, who can be against us?' This is real and the apostle Paul means it. He's not just a saint; he's a leader rallying the troops so they understand what power they have attained through the structure of godly slavery."

I didn't know this was weird talk. I mean, I'm weird and do weird things all the time, so I should know that people are going to find me confusing and weird. I should have followed up with the part about God setting us free and even talked about how we only get free will through getting bought by Christ's blood and God setting us free too. I love that God would give focus and tender correction to someone in the wrong. This meant so much to me. Saint Paul's words repeatedly moved me.

"Paul is crazy exciting, and he's obviously the first charismatic example in the New Testament. The man practically invented Pentecostalism! Okay, no, he didn't, that was all the Lord. But look at how zealous he is for the Lord through verses 36–39. Paul sounds like a man in a pub yelling over the crowd about his favorite sports team! He defends what he loves, not afraid to name names or list his team's trials. He's in the moment, feeling in his body that 'we are victorious.' His faith is the kind that moves mountains, and Paul even goes on to explain with a lack of sobriety that he is 'convinced that neither death nor life' will get in the way. Height and depth will not serve as obstacles! Who but someone intoxicated would wonder and speak this? Then Paul balances just before the tipping point, declaring that 'nothing created' will triumph over those of us 'who are in Christ Jesus our Lord.' " Yes, there was a plethora of body language, but I remained in my seat at least.

With awkward shuffling, church leaders started busying themselves with other things. At least some of the old men, who were military vets, were on my side. We have always bonded well, what with being a little shell-shocked and banged up. I didn't understand that the group leaders found this to be charismatic and Pentecostal teaching and not what they believed. Some lay people in the church noticed the awkwardness too, and we had no idea what to make of our church. Eventually, I figured the problem out: I was scary.

In a small-group sermon, the pastor brought up a story of warning. Two Pentecostals were invited to the church. However, when their Pentecostalism was discovered, they were told that they were still welcomed, but they could not speak in tongues. "That's not Christian." Therefore, I guess the two never bothered entering my current church. What I had thought was me sharing my experiences of how passionate I found Scripture was almost like bringing up Christian Science, Jehovah's Witnesses, and Mormonism to this group. Because I have been outspoken, I did this several times in a very thorough and passionate manner for several months. So much for being all things to all men. I humiliated myself in public and was just as confused on whether or not God still allowed baptism in the Holy Spirit and healing and what I was allowed to believe.

There I was moving so fanatically fast through this world of Christianity with no one to disciple me or protect me from myself. But I loved it, I still love it, and I wouldn't change much because my Father has taught me to love myself more. Embarrassing experiences allowed me to get frustrated and vent my unmet needs to a Christian friend (Doug, who I call a modern-day John the Baptist) who ended up leading me to a New Testament theology group that changed me in profound ways. Also, God wasn't neglectful. The more time I spent marinating in his presence, the more alive I felt. I admit that I was a loose cannon who God recently had purchased for half price from the occult, but at least I was turbocharged with the passion of the Christ. Someone should have hollered, "Clear downrange. New born-again coming!"

I confess that on at least two occasions, I physically and verbally animated scenes from Romans 8 (in front of adult churchgoers), what the apostle Paul would have done if he was in a pub evangelizing (aka "drunk in the Spirit"). I demonstrated how he would have reveled in awe at our Lord and Savior as Paul rode his donkey home after winning (maybe playing soccer with Jesus?) at "all these things" (Romans 8:37) and everything with the Most High. "The mighty God, who controls the sun, the moon, and stars—even the thunder and lightning," I stated, in case someone needed reminding. In a friendly small group, I would wonder aloud, "Maybe Paul would be drunk off of the Holy Spirit [see my childhood Pentecostal experience?] and fall off his ass as he rode home, high on the life of the Second/Last Adam. Imagine his last thoughts of the night. He must've looked into a big, beautiful night and appreciated what our God created in the blink an eye!" I'm so weird and needed more maturing.

Well, okay, I did also marvel at the happenings at the base of Mount Sinai in Exodus 32. One night, a small fellowship group gathered where most of the people showed up for the snacks. Not me. I hiked my sweet little patootie from half an hour away. Instead of realizing that church people don't always study the Bible, sometimes they just gather and call it fellowshipping, I joined and kept bringing up Exodus. The leader wasn't sure what to do with me, so I tried to engage her in conversation and included anyone who would listen.

"I just read about Moses in Exodus. I can't believe this happened! There was an ancient sex riot right there in the middle of the wilderness because Moses, the guy who parted the Red Sea, took too long talkin' to God! Can you believe that? I meditated on this because I want to visualize everything in Scripture, so it's like I was really there. We have to learn from this stuff!" I paused.

Crickets sounded in the room, except for an older friend of mine across the small circle we were in. She had fallen asleep until I started animatedly talking. She stopped slouching, closed her mouth, and wiped the drool from her chin. When she straightened herself, the rickety chair cracked. While the leader's husband went off to find a new chair, she sighed and called for a break. The pastries were ready. Some of us remained in the circle and so did my passion for this explosive discovery in Exodus.

"And I learned the golden calf was a young male bull. It connects to fertility symbols and sacrificing the best. So people were willing to make this important sacrifice to someone other than God! Can you imagine yourself in that situation, especially after you've had manna from heaven and walked with Moses, who conversed with God? This shows an influence by ancient Sumer and Egypt and knowing about their sexual festivals, all because the Israelites were impatient. It sounds extreme, but I'm not wrong, am I?"

My bored friend nodded and edged her way to the snack table. She always had a sweet tooth and ignored my ramblings. Two others gestured in deep thought, being considerate while I stumbled on.

I asked, "Weren't the Israelites technically like our version of a church? Like, a big religious group?"

The remnant thought about this, and someone laughed in agreement.

"So this would be no different than a modern church event with people mounting a golden bull and having an orgy in the church pews. Unbelievable!"

The Bible study ended earlier than usual, once the pastries and tea were gone. My inappropriateness embarrassed me, but it's like trying to stop a freight train. Some of us will never wax eloquent, but at least we're authentic soldiers making camp where the Spirit leads.

Chapter 28

The Word Small Redefined as "Un-Friggin'-Believable"

So we are no longer to be children, tossed back and forth by waves and carried about by every wind of teaching by the trickery of people who craftily carry out their deceitful schemes.

—Ephesians 4:14 NET

GOD MADE WATCHING the documentary with Tebow again give my Christian walk a steadier rhythm. I busied myself with defining Christian living and modesty and what everyone thought it could mean. I never expected for women's clothing and especially women's behavior to be such sensitive subjects within the ecclesiastical world. It was still difficult trying to distinguish the authentic, biblical church from religious people and when I should focus on this. Christian attire and roles played, even without regional or cultural consideration, could have its own board game. I was finding that modesty and women's roles were such sensitive and complex subjects, and it made little sense to this brand-new, born-again bride of Christ. Sometimes the good news was forgotten by people, and how one dresses can be like stepping on a landmine because you're either not modest enough and therefore a "liberal" or too modest and therefore a "legalist living by the law." I tried to avoid pitfalls and focused on Galatians 3:28: "There is no longer Jew or Gentile, slave or free, male and female. For you are all one in Christ Jesus" (NLT).

I even heard a wonderful, solid Christian teacher comment about women wearing provocative clothing to attract other husbands' attention. This godly woman doesn't let her fame get to her and she stays out of the limelight, living in the country despite how polished and beloved she is. Even she succumbed to painting modern women with a broad brush. It's just a human foible that we all make. However, the off-the-cuff remark from a household name made me realize that if a church leader brings it up in the middle of a sermon or serious presentation, it's a hot topic, so I better be intentional with how I dress!

I had thoughts like: *How can we know what a woman's intentions are especially in a church? What about those women who have no social graces and wear tight bandeau dresses because no one has lovingly and gently explained appropriateness? What about thoroughly educating women and men on how visual people will recall certain body parts in the future and lust after or compare themselves to certain attire and exposed bodies? Anyone raised with television shows and store magazines will be influenced with what the media and the culture deem appropriate.*

I couldn't keep my attention on things that seemed irrelevant. If God wanted me to do something, I would do it, and I would try to go to God with concerns and consider if I was causing someone to stumble. If someone's clothes are extreme, people can always mimic the Amish and avert their eyes. Thinking that was it, I realized that there was a Christian perspective on everything. Learning about rope and camels going through needles was a whole lot easier!

My choices regarding my appearance seemed to be:

Option 1: Present your best self: Dress up with a full face of pretty makeup like a celebrity starlet.

Option 2: Show up in sweats and flannels like a college student with honesty and realness.

My best natural self had just died. When I surrendered to God, I had let go of the control I was exerting for executive function and memory. I still carried the bloody show in my hands to remember the birth of my new life. Is it too snarky to envision dressing up as Lazarus coming forth and making that my version of Christian apparel? Navigating through churchianity was possible, but between how much I was sprinting through anything Christian and then dealing with church rules, I started to need help from other Christians to learn what was permissible and still possible for me. I'd have to start trusting people more. I care deeply about the ecclesiastical world, and I have learned so much from high church rites, sacraments, and customs. However, the churchianity, or Pharisee-like politics, must be tamed and harnessed, and I could only do that with help. In addition, I needed to keep following Tebow's life lessons for pacing and experience. It's not like I had to actually face him or anything.

The first edition NET Bible I had recently discovered was spectacular. Comparing various translations both word-for-word and thought-for-thought is a great practice, but I wanted to get the purest Bible translation I could possibly find, and the NET Bible looked like that might be the best one. The NET Bible I used at work cost more than $100 because it epitomized class! The leather was top grain, and there were scholarly notes based on the Hebrew, Koine Greek, and Aramaic languages. It wasn't even a revised Bible but went straight to the original sources. I wanted one! Testing out the "ask and you shall receive" idea, I asked God for an NET Bible.

One afternoon, I went to the work store and found a bunch of free books, including an NET Bible. I was upstairs and back in my seat when I remembered asking God for a NET Bible. This free copy was the compact size and premium bonded leather, which meant the leather wasn't as soft as the enormous one and maps couldn't fit in this more portable-size Bible. However, I loved it, and it would act less as a trophy and more as a tool from which to study. I hadn't quite moved away from Bible worship yet. Whoops!

I was so silly and so excited at my cute little nugget of ancient wisdom that I bit into the top left corner of the book. Was it my unique way of showing God that I was aggressive, young, and mentally off? Was I excited and looking forward to wrestling with God and his Word, and thus starting the match? Am I just a very passionate biter who must keep beef jerky and other leathery goods in stock to keep from harming polite company and precious objects? *Meh, life is boring without harmless weirdoes, so what?* The marks of my top two front teeth on the back cover and three bottom front teeth on the front from pancake flipping the Bible were certainly evidence that I planned to keep it.

Bringing the Bible home, I set it with my ever-growing collection of books. I try to increase space in my small one-bedroom apartment by having no more than twenty-five books— no, wait, twenty-five books not including yearbooks or magazines—no, no: fifty-ish books—well, perhaps eighty-five books not including audiobooks, Bibles, yearbooks or magazines or literary anthologies and art books. The realistic number is around one hundred unread books, and the rest are books that I must keep. Of the one hundred, the goal is to read them and immediately donate them because I have several library cards in various regions and I'm constantly at the libraries. This is also why I liked the NET Bible. Books give us access to the world! I had another ancient text to add to my collection.

A few weeks went by and my temp job came to an end. I still told people about my playing soccer with Jesus moment and that a "vibrating column of energy stood in front of me, pointing to a DVD of Tim Tebow." Many people received these stories and most were amazed, but all were confused as to what these divine occurrences meant. It took a long time to realize that being set apart and loved were very different than being special because of something that I had done, earned, or been noticed for being. Praise God that most of us don't have cameras trained on us from late childhood to adulthood, navigating through puberty to our hot and cold careers! Life was hard enough as it was; peering eyes and public scrutiny would have been too much for baby Gomer. I couldn't even keep my mind on learning from Tebow's lessons. I got distracted by my career. Apparently, I was too focused and in need of a wakeup call.

At 7:00 p.m. on a Sunday, I was not observing a Sabbath but applying for jobs. Stretched out on the side room floor, I churned out cover letters and resumes like butter. My system was so fluid that I could keep going through LinkedIn and finish within twenty minutes! My attention shifted a little, and a few very steady thoughts popped into my head. They were of the theme: *Tebow and I have been in similar situations regarding our careers. Praying for him would be refreshing. That's a good idea.* Without hearing any of this out loud and without regard for my actions at the time, I turned my head halfway through these thoughts and nodded my head at their conclusion. I said a quick little prayer, the usual, and felt good. Immediately, I snatched back my borrowed attention, not wondering why or how it moved in the first place and went back to job searching.

The following afternoon, I got home and hopped onto the computer, standing at the kitchen spice bar and enjoying the warm air coming into the apartment. A few hours later, my sister called while I distractedly danced through the wonders of the internet. We chatted and complained about Mondays until she gave me the reason for her call.

"I know this probably isn't news to you. You probably already know, and you did think months ago that it would happen, but since you weren't sure . . . it was in today's newspaper. I thought I better call you and share the news about Tim Tebow signing with the New England Patriots and whatnot."

"Wait! What?" I had no idea what she was talking about and stopped what I was doing to give her my full attention.

"Yeah, on the radio they mentioned it too. It's pretty groovy."

The Holy Spirit must have been working the previous Sunday night and I was oblivious yet again.

"Since you keep on top of this stuff now, I figured I would be telling you something you already knew."

I did try to stay in the know on Tim Tebow news and to support his charity, and I would share that with others. I guess I had been slacking.

Flabbergasted, I started to realize that I knew what she was referencing. "I had no idea that this was in the news, but I knew this. This is crazy; you are not going to believe this!" The veil in my mind lifted suddenly, and I pictured the night before.

"Last night, I was writing a cover letter when out of nowhere I had these thoughts about Tebow and how we are on similar spotty career paths. I actually turned my head automatically, as if someone was to my left telling me this even though these thoughts were just in my head and not out loud. No one was in the room and I didn't feel anything, but it was like when you are in a high school classroom and someone leans over a row of desks to tell you what time after school you're supposed to meet for practice. I actually nodded my head in acknowledgment after an angel said, 'It will be announced Monday that Tim Tebow is joining the New England Patriots,' then I turned back to the computer and finished writing the cover letter like nothing weird happened!"

My sister was so excited for me. "That's awesome! I just knew I had to call you and share this with you."

The Holy Spirit was my reminder that I was on a pilgrimage and that Tebow was instrumental in showing me the way.

The Holy Spirit moves like lightning and simply blows me away. How can such a powerful, proud, loving, Trinitarian God be so considerate to remind me that my attention and prayers needed realignment? Yes, job searching mattered, but I asked God for a Christian mentor and he gave me one in Tim Tebow. I needed to harness my focus and keep learning from him so I could be better. He certainly had my attention now! I combed through news stories about Tebow and wondered how he had so much time to do so much. I felt like any time I came across what should have been underbrush and obstacles on my pilgrimage, he had trampled that area already, making it easier for whoever would follow him someday. I wondered, *How could such a strong, casual, sweet man be so considerate, making my walk so much easier than I expected? Is he just a man after God's own heart, or can I become someone who also does such good things? Is there hope for me?*

The pearl cross that had been my mother's necklace lay nestled into the spine of the Holman Christian Standard Bible at my bedside. The faux-leather Bible cover sat on the floor with other Christian resources and presents I had yet to give away. I love gift giving. The NET Bible that was utterly cute and bodacious was front and center. For some strange reason, thoughts of the faux-leather Bible cover, the plastic pearl necklace cross, and my NET Bible kept crossing my mind, each item braiding together. Who pays attention to thoughts like these?

Another week went by and then I started to daydream about the Bible cover and the Bible I liked so much, along with the necklace turned cross—they all belonged together. After a few days, the daydreaming returned, and I started to wonder why the three items belonged together. The NET Bible was a gift from God; the cover I had bought before I was even a Christian, but it was the perfect size for the Bible. *That could be a coincidence.*

The cross was my attempt at salvaging my mother's necklace. She wore that necklace when she married her second husband, and I loved it. I grew up thinking those shiny faux pearls were as beautiful and heavenly as the pearly white gates that I heard about. As an adult, my mom had told me she didn't like it and only kept it out of sentimentality. I had made sure to let her know that I would gladly receive it if she felt the need to discard the highly sentimental necklace that sent me into celestial reveries every time I saw it. The Thanksgiving after my father died, the little 'uns and some of us adults had been doing crafts at an enormous table when I was stunned to see the white tubular and round beads mixed in with several others. I would know them anywhere. When questioned and reprimanded, my mother said that she had forgotten that I liked the necklace and had ripped it apart for the kids. Besides, I had her other necklace and she thought I liked that one.

"I liked them both! You said you would save this for me. It has no value; they're just plastic beads. These were the beads you wore in Georgia."

She didn't understand that the two necklaces were my inner child's connection to the first family, homes, and life I knew as a child. The necklaces connected me to a time when I thought that my mother was a loving, attentive safe haven. A bunch of children sleeping in a puppy pile, wandering half naked, and covered in clay dug up from the roads had been an intimate community. Never quite healing from a neck injury that affected her memory, Mom had tossed the beads aside without thinking. Lucky for me, the beads weren't attractive to anyone else and that is how I got them back. I even made sure that all the kids knew how important I thought the beads were when I exchanged my nicest ones for them. No one felt manipulated, and I had gotten all the beads, fashioning them into a cross held together with flexible copper wire.

What is the connection? This could be in my head because of some latent desire to go on some Old Testament prophetic journey. I saw something about fans getting to watch the N.E. Patriots practice for free at their stadium. With that, I blew off the thought of giving Tebow a gift. I was acting like one of those weird Christians who think everything is of God even when it's not. That must be what was happening. *Could be pesky demons trying to throw me off my pilgrimage too.* I didn't need that or my own inexperienced mind thinking that God still sent regular, nonspecial people like me to do holy things. I kept getting the impression God wanted me to gift something to Tebow, but I wasn't a missionary so I didn't go on missions like to Africa or something and surely going to Gillette Stadium would be weird. It didn't occur to me that using this same thinking would have me doubting the born-again experience that showed me I was an authentic Christian and the vibrating column of energy that pointed to the Tebow documentary.

I donated the faux-leather Bible cover even after I saw that it fit the NET Bible and considered, *What if this has something to do with me asking God to blow my mind in a small way?*

Chapter 29

"You Have to Go to Him Because He Won't Come to You"

> *I can pray this because his divine power has bestowed on us everything necessary for life and godliness through the rich knowledge of the one who called us by his own glory and excellence.*
>
> —2 Peter 1:3 NET

Several days later, I had another vision even though the book cover was gone. In it, I was clutching my mother's pearl necklace cross and bringing the NET Bible to Gillette stadium. *No one does this stuff!* I'd tested out the scenario with a church leader, and he'd said, "God doesn't tell people to do things anymore. People have a desire to go to foreign missions to help people and might feel an urge but . . ."

I tried again. "Would he give us dreams and speak to us giving urges to go somewhere and do godly or normal, simple things?"

I was told then what I was told just before writing this memoir: "Be careful."

I tried to tell myself that these fantasies were in my head and nothing more. I mocked my Poe-like internal ramblings. *What's next, a raven perching above me quoting, "Nevermore!"*

The visions were persisting but not nagging, and they were the same. All my Bible reading was not wasted, despite not having a theological teacher yet or a charismatic guide to grow my spiritual life. I needed more help than what my current church could offer, so I reached out to online ministries after trying to talk with my current church's pastor. There had to be more than the Bible-thumping command: "Read your Bible. The answers are there. The Bible makes it clear."

Some of the greatest minds studied and really digested the Bible throughout their lives while still feeling like they didn't have all the answers. That encouraged me to keep going, and the curt Bible thumpers helped me to see how I had been acting like them and worshipping the Bible at times instead of focusing on the God who inspired and was described in it. The leather binding on a Bible didn't make it any holier than the one dressed as a mass-market paperback. I wanted to be biblically anchored while Spirit-led like Abraham, the apostle Paul, and Enoch even more! *I have no idea what to do, God, help! What am I supposed to do? Is this my mind, or is it you? I want to be Spirit-led by you and only you in Jesus's name! I can do all things through Christ who strengthens me, but are you strengthening me? What if I'm wrong and I screw up? I live near the ocean and a big fish could swallow me like Jonah.* I have an attitude problem.

Not knowing God's nature and how he would not just toss me to a fish or punish me for acting like the sheep that I was, I brainstormed ways to get help. I was certainly not accustomed to going to a bunch of much older men to get their counsel on intimate things, but the Bible mentions going to elders. I wasn't comfortable with these random guys since we had no relationship. I wasn't comfortable with them because some were uncomfortable with me because I was a much younger female. Some were very set in their ways, and others were really behind the times, very out of touch, so did I really have to go to them? Some were offensive while others very active in the church, and one would actually go overseas to aid in missions.

However, all were anti-intellectual unless it involved apologetics, so it seemed like they were insulting how I thought and me as a female for wanting to know context on their decisions on what Scripture meant. They were uncomfortable with a great many denominations and leaned on the importance of "righteous judgment." Well, okay, but using this section of the Bible to correct other denominations didn't do anything for me. Congregationalists were not very different from the Baptists/nondenominationalists, and isn't the goal of leading the church to grow us into thinking for ourselves so our faith is strong when testing time comes along? I struggled with going to these elders for direction for days. *But I have to be here and try to make this church work as the church leadership advised, right? Otherwise, I'm "abandoning" the church. If they're not leading me anywhere, then I must be doing something wrong.*

I spoke with some of the men unfruitfully. Some didn't understand why a female would deliver a Bible to a man. I said I was comfortable doing such since I had just started working alongside engineers at a company that never hired women. I was learning that navigating a sea of testosterone wasn't hard for me but was hard for men both in businesses and churches.

The female theologian at the church told me to get permission to complete my godly mission from the men or I'd be out of alignment with Scripture. I wondered for a second why I couldn't go to her. If she was knowledgeable and had biblical intellect, why couldn't she help? If people entrusted her with their kids as an AWANA leader, couldn't I? I realized that just because someone's got a degree in theology doesn't mean they like discipling people or wrestling with the Holy Spirit. If everyone is rigidly dogmatic and thinks that being close minded is a way to protect from Satan, they won't hear what is being said to them and they will be too afraid to have an adventure, knowing and trusting that the Most High will always be there for them. Sigh.

Getting permission from my church would be like going to HR to report harassment at work. You have to have some tangible versions of proof and witnesses. So much work has to be done on the victim's part, and it's embarrassing. It's better to stand up to creeps or just leave and find a better environment. Unfortunately, I still had a survivor mindset and thought I needed to fight through the confusion and wrong fit. It wasn't smart of me to stay at a church that didn't believe the Holy Spirit still worked and led people because this was a Spirit-led event I was considering. The Holy Spirit was constantly molding me for what was to come and giving me the freedom to challenge what people were telling me, but I didn't know how to execute on that yet.

Because of my disappointment with the current church, I had been trying a few online women's ministries and some local ones on the North Shore of Massachusetts. Some of their events were not as fun as the men's events, though. At those, I'd make friends with the men, and they would describe the pig roast the men had had and describe the pulled pork smoking technique so I at least got to *feel* welcomed there. They'd let me know the men only talks the pastor gave them. They were so excited to share with their sister in Christ because they felt so special! I didn't have the heart to tell these guys that the talks could be found online or that if they wanted someone to look them in the eye and passionately tell them to "act like a man and grow a pair. That is your job," then they could have come to me. I loved this blue-collar joking and getting to know Christian men that were like brothers. They revived my spirit. My appreciation for "as iron sharpens iron, so one person sharpens another" (Proverbs 27:17 NIV) grew. One male friend in particular counseled me to follow the Holy Spirit, no matter what the church leadership said. He also told me it was okay to think about other churches. With that, he wished me luck at the upcoming women's conference since he had just come back from the male version.

I tried the Christian women's conference—a direct offshoot of the men's—with my family, hoping to help with their conversions. I adore conferences, but it was such a disaster that so many church groups did not return including my own. On top of the logistical issues and all the offerings taken, we were asked to give money to support the men's conference because it was "more important to evangelize men as studies show." Sigh. Even the married women felt the sting.

Despite the proximity to Boston, some of the ministries and groups were so antiquated and boring it harkened back to when I joined the Girl Scouts at age twelve. We spent several weeks coloring Disney photos while the boys learned how to put raw eggs on a stick, cooking them over a campfire. They even got to build shelters in the woods. Without summer camps, I wouldn't have learned to excel at archery and gain wilderness survival skills. The activities allowed for my gender were unfulfilling, and I didn't want faith to be like that too.

After the conference, I had another vision. I gathered the Bible and the necklace cross together and sat on the couch alone in the living room with my wonderings. The pearls were beautiful against the black leather cover and the stark contrast made my heart beat deeper with the two gifts. One gift came from my mother when I was too young to know that she was an illusion of love and that she couldn't be everything I needed her to be. The other gift came from my Everything when I learned he is the reality of unconditional love. He is everything that I never wanted for my pitiful self. He is what I never knew could bring such security and trustworthiness.

Sitting on the couch with this meditation, I implored God, "What am I supposed to do? Do you really want me to bring this to Tebow?"

In response to my prayer, God instantly cleared my mind of any thoughts in a way I have certainly had not experienced in my entire life. In my head and not aloud, I heard very deliberately, "You have to go to him because he won't come to you."

That was my Moses clay tablets moment. This moment was unlike anything else. There was no dropped veil, no scurrying ant-like thoughts, and no confusing what God wanted me to do! Needing to commemorate this moment, I grabbed the nearest pen and paper and wrote down the words "You have to go to him because he won't come to you." These precious words came from the Savior, the savior of humankind. They were from our personal Savior, who we can know intimately like a real person if we will just leave the world behind.

I sat with the moment as is typical for anyone after sweet, elusive occasions like this, especially after born-again, supernatural occurrences. I called my family. They knew of the various supernatural things that had been popping up left and right, but the medium to larger moments like this were more exciting and remarkable.

On the phone call, my mom and sister freaked out together. The Holy Spirit of Jesus was moving in my life! My brother thought that these godly moments were neat but used my recounts as springboards for jokes. Brothers take the edges off, don't they? They make any adventure crazier, faster, and way smoother.

❦

I put the Bible in a crimson box with a little note explaining to the opener that God apparently wanted Tim Tebow to have this. Done. I wish I could say that I was confident and obedient, but I wasn't. I thought that no matter what God did or said, I had to seek counsel with the church. So I emailed a conservative women's online ministry that the Congregational and Baptist women dubbed "safe."

The ministry focused on unlearning lies that the Enemy creates for women and how biblical living will set them free. I started there. Weeding through the email advice they sent back, I started hurting. The advice was to "find a brother in Christ who you can trust to deliver the Bible for you." *Ask a male Christian to drive two hours out of his way for a mission that had nothing to do with him because he won't be tempted by or tempt a fellow Christian man?* This ministry might only serve fearful women or those hiding behind religion. Most of all, I thought, *God didn't tell someone else to do this. People in the Bible were always doing the opposite of what God wanted and they screwed up so bad Jesus himself had to come down and get scourged and die!* My mission was an honor, and these women were unwittingly taking it from me. The thought made me claustrophobic. It's like I was back in Daddy John's Army gunny sack, upside down and packed in tight as he whirled me around the room until he felt like stopping.

God told me to go on this mission, and I wanted to do what he asked. When I played soccer with Jesus, I got to perform the final half of the miracle. I got to be a part of something awesome. Not interacting or receiving what the Lord teaches is depleting and awful. You know that feeling when you have a crush on someone and they stand you up? Isn't that what the Lord feels when we don't show up for him? When your flight is delayed and your husband is waiting for you, don't you have tunnel vision of landing on that tarmac and being with the one you love? We're supposed to run to the Lord. When your kids are only a phone call away, but reception is blocked, isn't that denied emotional touch stifling? *Maybe I better call the Lord myself. He's been waiting . . .*

God was at work in my life, and I resolved to remember that. Deep down I might feel like the lowliest of women, but my kind lived throughout Old and New Testament Scripture accomplishing dramatic feats. *A slave to Christ means what it says. I really have no choice or freedom but to do God's will because now we're unified. He's always right, and he's a sure thing, not a bet.* After emailing back the ministry ("Thank you, but I need to follow the Lord"), I went to work finding out when I could deliver the Bible and move on.

Chapter 30

Too Much Love for Gomer

But be doers of the word, and not hearers only, deceiving yourselves.

—James 1:22 ESV

"God was not created. He always was, is, and will be. He is I Am, and he exists outside of time and space." I heard this when I was a kid memorizing Bible verses in AWANA. There's a problem with only memorizing verses though. A sense other than seeing, hearing, etc., is needed for such complex concepts. I could only picture gray matter, then God speaking the universe into existence. However, gray and matter are things, so God existed before that, right? I gave up trying to understand and could empathize with atheists and agnostics when someone says this to them without any supporting direction. Even then, this required focusing, meditating on God's Word because the very existence of God is vast! *Wouldn't it be nice to have someone explain this, maybe an example?* I got more than a simple example and sandwiched between it was a field trip to Gillette Stadium in July/August 2013.

In the land of action and bumper-to-bumper traffic, I was nervous and unsettled at my lack of details regarding this Bible mission. I did not want to follow the Lord's prompting. I kept dragging my feet and showed up on time instead of very early as I had planned. Arriving early would give me the choice of dropping off the Bible then or after the practice if there were no earlier opportunity. I had invited some friends to watch practice, but no one wanted to go since it wasn't a real game. Even before I got out of the car, I sat in the parking lot, remembering when I directed traffic at that same spot during college. However, I wasn't there for reminiscing.

Checking for the one-millionth time that the Bible was in the little box and that my mother's necklace was right handy for me to clench or give away, I traced the teeth marks in the top left corner of the NET Bible. I felt foolish for putting them there in the first place. *I'm sure no one will notice, but why on earth does Tebow need a Bible? Can't he buy one?* I exhaled. *I don't know what he's going to do with this, but I hope he appreciates it!* My heart softened. *Maybe someone in his charity needs it.*

I shook with nerves so much more now, parked outside of the stadium. *I am actually going to do this!* When I pictured handing off the package, the shakes were held at bay and became minor convulsion. It felt like exposure therapy. Tebow still felt like an older brother figure to me, but following God and trusting still scared me immensely. The soldier in me started walking.

I was surprised when I internally made the excuse to look through the gift shop . . . and the top of the plaza. The unruly part of me blamed ADHD, and I rationalized why I should walk in the opposite direction of everyone else. *I should take a little tour so I know the area. Maybe another angel will pop up and point at something inside.* Almost wandering into the catering area, I scolded myself with *Get your butt in the elevator. You're not VIP; you don't know anyone in these executive offices. Start walking!*

Leaving the building, I continued in the same direction, not realizing that the area was fenced off and that the room with Tebow and his teammates was a mere twenty yards away. A security guard sat by and two college-age people were talking, and they would probably stop me from walking in—except I looked so benign and my experience from working with event control people was that if I walked by them with purpose and authority, they wouldn't stop me. But I'm not a party-crashing, sneak-in type, and I had no reason to go in there. *God, you wouldn't have me doing this, would you? This is too absurd!*

Returning to my sense, I walked around to the practice field. Walking to the grassy field close to the practice area, my minor convulsions went from cold shivers in legato to deeper and staccato. It took thirty seconds of strong focusing to kick this. I marveled at my body feeling fear; it was exposure therapy after all. Afterward, I wondered if this had been part of God's plan. Did he need me seeing how wounded my poor little body was and that, without realizing it, I had downplayed the trauma in my life as so many victims do? I wanted to test this theory.

Sitting on the grass, I felt no different than when I took a hot air balloon ride as a young adult. The ride had been so gentle and smooth that I hadn't even noticed when we had lifted off. After checking the sky and the billowing balloon material, I looked out across the field and realized I was at least thirty feet off the ground and lifting fast! My hands tightened automatically around the baskets. The connective ropes and my body started shivering with an automatic response that every mammal displays when afraid. Mentally, the ride was so cool. Physically, my whole body was tight despite my attempt at willing myself to relax. It took all my effort to pry my hands off the rope and onto the basket. The nervous shaking had never quite stopped, but I had calmed it down so no one had noticed any twitching. After all, I'm not afraid of heights at all. *This body is so silly. It's just nerves.*

When Tebow was just a couple hundred feet away, I played self-therapist: *Press into this fear and face it.* So I did. I let myself go, and I was Gomer unaccustomed to what Hosea represented in my life. My teeth were actually chattering, and the trembling had quickly turned to minor convulsions again. Some glanced at me, and I rubbed my arms as if I was cold and pretended to fish in my bag for a coat in the summer heat. Calming myself, I waited until Tebow got closer and let myself simply feel again. Yep, there were the shakes, so what was it? *It's too much love,* I answered back to myself. *Too much love.*

My brother, Miah, would display the same behavior when his two older sisters and mother would constantly babble all around him until, fed up, he would exclaim, "Too many words!" As the outnumbered male, he needed silence and a video game where men tackled each other. He often got overwhelmed and needed space.

Physically near Tebow, I was overwhelmed by what I felt in the moment: love for this figure and symbol. I steeled my nerves and gave myself a break. That was enough exposure for one day. Even so, his goodness was still palpable. It blurred right in with love. That was a new lesson—there is fruit of the Spirit and not fruits of the Spirit, singular and not plural. Therefore, if we have one fruit of the Spirit like love, then we have them all: love, joy, peace, patience, kindness, goodness, gentleness, faithfulness, and self-control.

From a couple hundred feet away, Tebow exuded (at least to me) goodness that stirred love. Was it God's love, existing like the cool breeze, there for all to enjoy, or an innocent love coming from a young one in Christ brave and trusting enough to come this far? What I did know was that it was pleasant sitting on a hill, watching someone who was a stranger who could look down on me if he knew me but would not because he was a safe brother in Christ.

While Tim was entertaining one of his foundation's kids, Tom Brady and Rob Gronkowski walked in my direction. I probably made a faux pas because I up and left. I'm super awkward, but in my defense, my job was to give Tim a friggin' Bible and probably my mother's necklace cross! It wasn't to do anything else. I didn't want to be reprimanded by the God that controls the thunder and lightning. After the crowd died, I saw no way to accomplish my mission, so I handed the Bible in the box to an event staffer and said who the book was for. She said that the best she could do was give it to someone in operations. Not wanting to lose my cross for no reason, I kept it and walked away.

My mind was racing and I was self-frustrated. *When I was by the entrance asking for directions from security, they would have given me easy access to wherever I needed to go. I probably should have done something then!* I felt like I had failed the Most High God because of my idiocy. I didn't do what was needed, and I had no way to know if Tebow received the Bible. I was so humiliated at my failure, but then I also thought, *He can get his own Bible! Why doesn't he just buy one? Come on—doesn't he have people?!* All the pouting and bratty feelings from feeling worthless and weak in my exposure therapy wiped me out.

The texts I sent after thirty minutes to my family were a lot like the ones I had sent on my way down. I still had no idea what I was doing, but I no longer had any guess scenarios, only news that I might have failed because I didn't want to be rude and walk across the roped-off field. Good thing I had been alone: The friends who hadn't been able to go had advised me to hop the rope and run for it, promising to bail me out of jail after. *There's the silver lining: no jail time!*

But now I don't view this season as a failure: I received exposure therapy, fought churchianity rules to follow the Lord, and learned that, even with an anticlimactic end, journeying with God keeps you on your toes.

Chapter 31
Temptation

These things I have spoken to you so that you may be kept from stumbling.

—John 16:1 NASB1995

During the two years I spent learning from Tebow about how I should carry myself as a Christian, I often balanced learning from other godly resources. Of course, that's a given but only two of these reputable Christian resources mentioned personal accounts of supernatural encounters, specifically temptations/desires that occur after the conversion experience. Anyone who has been born again since a very young age probably forgets the big pull to sin that happens after Christian conversion.

Pastor Greg Laurie from Harvest shared a caution he received about how temptation often arrives right after becoming a Christian. Greg shared honestly and without shame how he knew that what he experienced was the temptation so many experience after being born again. Michael Ramsden from RZIM used the same formula of warning, showing how easily and naturally the Enemy's enticements arrived for new believers. *If the enemy likes using lust for tantalizing new Christians, what does this mean?* I wondered. Both were baited despite knowing in the moment that what they were tempted to do was not allowed. The brazenness of Satan and his followers astounded me! Interestingly, each older brother in Christ also explained that they realized after their provocations that they had not failed God but that the Highest simply allowed this testing.

Evil's formulaic approach to tempting and Greg's and Michael's tellings of their personal accounts stuck with me. I learned this formula for recognizing temptation via personal testimony. Personal testimonies are greatly helpful. Laughing at the men's jokes and understanding and relating to their stories drew me closer to these brave spiritual brothers. They filled in my heart a place left void by the local churches until I could find a better fit.

Kids love stories, and this Baby Gomer had undoubtedly grown into a story-loving toddler. I was so wrapped up in the stories of great Christians, but my lack of security thwarted my ability to pay attention to the world around me. Maybe I occasionally looked in the mirror to see if I looked holier. Maybe I compared my progress to other Christians to see if I mirrored them. No longer a little tyke, I had dreams of elephantine fruit, and I wasn't about to wait for someday. Maybe this same young-in-the-faith behavior had me completely focusing on the next direct encounter with the Lord instead of realizing that I had reached a milestone in my development.

When the Holiest of Spirits reminded me that I was on a Spirit-led mission and that the clock was ticking, I was one year, six months, and just a few days old. This was according to the Holy Spirit's calculations and not my own since I lost track of time . . . yet again. However, the Holy Spirit is the Great Reminder, and he let me know when the following part of my mission would benefit from careful consideration. Even without ADHD, you have to admit that it's hard to *continuously* focus on your progress or where the Lord points when his holy presence has touched your marks and made them his. My reminder proves the Holy Spirit works with us despite distractions, forgetfulness, and other weaknesses.

I got in my car on a beautiful May 2014 afternoon. It was quiet and peaceful. So was my mind. I heard that inaudible but deliberate voice of God say, *Only six months left. It's going to get harder.* God was speaking to me again.

My impression was that God was telling me to get ready and that because he was in a relationship with me, I needed to do something. Well, there is no funky mold growing on this brain of mine, so I nodded my head in innocent practicality and said, "Okay, I'm ready," out loud. Nothing happened right away. I started the car, listening to an audiobook from one of the greats, and went about the next few days, expecting and waiting.

With time to kill due to a recent layoff, I waited to hear back about a possible job at an official Christian institution. I kept going to Bible studies, trying to find my Christly path, and continued with a few more conservative group meetings. Looking for ways to contribute with my local Bible church and this conservative group, I volunteered at my church. Unfortunately, the women couldn't place me. I couldn't tell if it was disorganization or their inability to stop working so I could join in relieving their habitual burdens. They were objects in motion that stayed in motion—until I stopped showing up for Sunday morning service for weeks at a time. Then the sweet cards of "we miss you" arrived in the mail. The women in that ministry didn't realize that I still attended and very actively participated in the Sunday night services weekly. *I guess the super busy women didn't notice me, and the quiet ones around me just tuned me out. Every toddler in Christ needs a place where they are allowed to express love and be loved, receive and give.* I learned increasingly that the church was for local families. I just didn't belong. Some churches have their niche. For what they were, they had a lot going for them, but the church couldn't go beyond that wall on its own.

I was finding more inclusion with nonchurch people, and when I offered to help do little things for secular people, I chose what to do and was welcomed just as I was. Now only attending the Bible church's Sunday night small group, I wondered if this local church was worth it for me. It wasn't a place for singles, there were few people near my age range, and it still didn't fit right. Since my church was as insular as the island on which we lived, I stopped struggling to create a better place and thought maybe I'd be better not in a formal church.

Our town, still known for explosive heroin use and a teenage pregnancy pact, had been a broken culture for too long. If I was going to be in a town like this, why not just find Christians more involved in the community? The conservative group I found had passionate locals who wanted to make positive investments in the community, and a few were normal, churchgoing friends. At least I could further my Christian experience by learning how Christians should advocate for others and Christians' roles in politics and leadership.

One day, I washed a few dishes after the conservative group's lunch meeting, listening to the infighting that broke up the committee. The townie lawyers and committee head were so overdramatic and dysfunctional. Too much time in small-town politics had them threatening to sic the mafia on anyone who disagreed with them. Sigh. *Give it a shot until you start working again. The leader may have a corporate opening soon, and you're learning about how important it is for Christians to brave the political world.*

Alone in the kitchen just off the group room, I leaned toward the cupboard and stood on my tiptoes to put away a cup. The married group leader walked in and, as he held me on the back, asked me how things were going and if the arguing had scared me off. At the touch of his hand, an acute awareness to energy screamed in my brain. The energy that shot through me was so strong that I have no idea when I stepped down or how long it took me to move. The incident stunned me, as it felt like more than a casual touch. Whether the cup made it to the shelf, I had no idea. My left arm still held open the cupboard door, my right arm was at shoulder level, and my right hand was still frozen in a cup-holding position. I was staring straight ahead, but the cupboard contents were not holding my eyes at all!

The energy that had shot through the man's hand and went into and through my body was exceptionally warm, and it made me feel the most wanton form of desire I had ever felt. This is coming from someone who grew up with the sexual frustration that comes from being sexually abused as a child. The lust was so obvious that the capitalized word *Desire* popped into my brain immediately while remaining foreign. *Something outside of me made me feel Desire that was not my own at all!*

Remembering the two temptation stories from Greg and Michael, I switched from autopilot and mentally revived. The group leader left the room, and I surveyed the situation. This was it. Standing in the kitchen, this was the scheduled temptation. *I don't feel this though. Something is putting this on me. There's something outside of me that made that happen because I'm not attracted to most men . . . ever! I'm the focused one that thinks that when a friend points to a man's butt, it's because the guy's pants are awesome. I respond, "Yeah, I love men's pants and miss living with my brother so I could borrow his jeans." This feeling isn't mine just like the cloak of fear wasn't mine during the spiritual warfare. This desire is big, and it has been placed in me, just sitting there!*

The temptation blatantly confronted me in plain daylight and let me know its exact intentions. How was a person supposed to act other than shocked? I was a mess still being cleaned up, but I wasn't desperate. The more I thought about it, the more ridiculous the temptation was. Someone's married father appeared to view me as a sexual target. Odd because he seemed like a great man who possessed honor and integrity who even said he was a Christian. What a façade! Christians aren't puppets of demonic power. At thirty years older than I, why? Just why? Is nothing sacred? Sacred is profaned when Satan is involved. I assumed that just because this guy seemed good and thought of himself as a Christian who supported some church culture, he'd be fine. *Maybe Satan doesn't know that I dealt with dad issues years ago, so I'm not succumbing to this.* My prayers went straight to the Lord, and I focused on keeping my wits while finding a quick exit.

The next few days, I audited this event and thought, *How pathetic am I that my temptation wasn't someone actually good looking or flattering to me.* I had to admit, though, Freudian followers would see this seemingly perfect father figure (one who checked multiple boxes on the life-success meter) as my match. This man could potentially inveigle me into a relationship where I had my daddy needs met. The Enemy and the man would win in the resulting ultracarnal relationship. The problem with that line of thinking was that it was so beneath any respect.

I searched for strong people willing to work with me shoulder to shoulder and talk to me face-to-face when I needed it. That provides priceless community and support that strengthens my spirit. It's safe to say that I was not at all interested in being the protégé of the group leader who started showing romantic interest in me beyond that first touch. He would try to entice we with resting with him in the attached private apartment, compliment my body, or find reasons to touch me on bare skin. Anything can become perverted if you have no anchor—even this man with several advanced degrees in leadership and psychology. I would quickly learn that this married man not only lacked an anchor, but he was also tossed to and fro despite all the godly resources and individuals around him.

Through the next few weeks, I watched the temptation man while we all interacted. Everything continued normally except when I thought of the man, he would arrive at the same event or send me an email or text at the exact same time. I joked with him about this, and he called it the seventh plane of consciousness. I thought of it instead as a spiritual battle and wondered if the guy was just an innocent bystander to something sinful influencing him.

I was still naïve. I cared (inappropriately) about examining how this temptation worked. Scripture about the Enemy as a lion would pop into my head and saved digital files of devotionals just happened to be open in my browser. Everything kept protecting and warning me. After the first shock of temptation, I started to get the image of a lion at a zoo-like game preserve. That Sunday, my pastor just happened to give a sermon on temptation and brought out the illustration of a lion, of course! The pastor also included a story from when he studied outside a lion habitat. He said that the lions roaring in the African hills were loud and harrowing but locals warned him to fear the silence so much more. A silent predator is hard to keep track of. On one occasion, a lion crept to the edge of the compound where the pastor was studying. It wasn't until the pastor felt eyes on him and a shift in the energy around him that the pastor turned to face a lion just feet away and terror overtook him.

This reminded me of my childhood, learning to hide in the Georgia brush and discovering I could shift something in me so people couldn't feel whatever I was giving off. When the searcher went quiet trying to find me, I wanted to see who was looking for me. I looked at them but only with my peripheral vision so my eyes wouldn't be felt.

But that was my childhood. So much has happened to pull me away from that life and interacting like that. A grown-up doesn't use those skills; we get wrapped up in society. I'm a sitting duck, and quite frankly, I don't even have good dream interpretation anymore because I'm still wounded from the new age experiences. I can't analyze what I'm feeling and what's happening well enough to win at this.

Blessedly, I didn't have to. After the second temptation moment (similar to the first shock of desire), I used the anthropological part of my mind to study the temptation in its natural habitat. I loved watching National Geographic, so I studied actual wild lions, learning to fear them at the most primitive level. After watching a few lions standing unnoticed over their prey at night, seeing old footage of a person getting mauled just off camera, and finding a lion picture that showed an unhinged, wild lion, I could go to the events where this guy would be and feel confident that I feared what this temptation offered and the guy would immediately leave. In fact, I felt like I was (symbolically speaking) standing close to a fence where I could touch the lion of temptation. I used that daydream or vision to imagine people who would try something like this so I could reframe this behavior and get farther away from it.

I remembered a woman thinking that she could touch a polar bear through a barred fence. The bear was so strong and fast that it pulled her leg into the enclosure. Not only did I think of this, I continuously read scary descriptions of predators in the Bible. I often studied a photo of an unhinged lion (which I still have and refer to as the Hosea lion) pondering encounters with it. It was like camping in junior high with a scary book about ghosts and goblins but with a more noble purpose.

For years, I had redefined *fear of the Lord* as "reverence and deep respect." However, another level of spiritual comprehension grew when I thought on how the fear of the Lord could also mean plain old "I'm scared because you are more powerful than I am, and if I don't obey you, I can get hurt." Fear is something related to the body and how it responds, and fear of the Lord is maybe even awareness of what God tries to shield us from having to experience. Maybe even fear of what is the opposite of the Lord fits into this redefined phrase. *Maybe fear is what I need for safety.*

I struggled with my childlike compulsion to learn, learn, learn and ADHD's need for stimuli just to function as a normal person. *I'm probably safe enough, but I feel too close for comfort with this temptation man. But you know . . . I'm still on my own without kids to worry about and I've had plenty of experience in handling tough situations. I can squeeze in my learning about how the enemy uses people and maybe reach the man for the Lord. Since he said he believes Jesus isn't God, maybe I could convince him.* I would simply rely on my piss and vinegar attitude if anything got out of line. I was not going to fall for him. Not only had I completed four years of therapy and become a healthier person, but I had wandered desperately into the occult deep enough to run like crazy out of it. No way would I return. *I'm done screwing around! I can do this.* I had confronted my fear of church people and religiosity. There was still a lack of spiritual connection to the church, and healing and deliverance ministries weren't well known, but I was searching and that was a start. So I kept the temptation man at arm's length, adjusted my boundaries with the unhealthy people I encountered. and learned what I could.

Trying to do the right thing, I alerted my pastor and a Christian friend in the conservative group about the temptation person and his suggestive comments so I would have accountability and guidance. Maybe my friend could reach the inappropriate guy since my friend was male and knew him well. Unfortunately, the pastor only said, "God is doing a work in you. And this guy is doing what men do." Okay, so I checked pastoral accountability off my mental list, but there was still hope in planning a strategy with my Christian friend. Unfortunately, the perverse guy kept bringing up to my friend how conservativism and Christian living weren't nearly as good as the leadership the ancient Greeks had and how

Christianity can't be the only way for salvation. My friend wasn't able to get a word in about stopping the suggestive behavior.

Frustration pumped through me. The church told me to get out there and convert, so I prayed and tried but it's not like I could have mediated, what with being a feminine distraction and all. Being terrible at evangelism and unable to find my place felt like an awkward failure. Good intentions resulted in angry guys yelling on the very public boulevard overlooking Gloucester Harbor. I felt sorry for the Christian men in the group. They loved politics, but political organizations are based on perception and Christianity is based on truth. They wanted to spread the gospel in a multifaceted way and with my help. However, we couldn't make an impact in the quickly crumbling group.

Weren't Christians supposed to help the lost? If the men couldn't reach the temptation guy, I couldn't go further because Christians are to flee temptations, right? Not according to one of the Christian men in the group who dressed in puritanical attire including the facial hair. He accused me of "rabbit-hole Christianity." I may have let him know that I didn't ask for such an ill-equipped man such as himself to lead me.

He was one of the Christian men who recommended I join the group because "we need Christians in politics, not neglecting their leadership duties." Well, why did they recommend a younger female new to the faith join their group knowing this leader guy had issues with Christianity and an open marriage, and what about the older Jewish guy with a perverse record of assaulting women? When the Jewish guy grabbed my breast at an event of a lovely man we were helping run for office, I froze. It seemed like all that could have been avoided. Where were these older men in the faith when I walked into their group? It was the temptation man who'd warned me to avoid the Jewish man because he'd been sued for egregious behavior. I wished one of the long-time Christian men who were supposed to have my back had spoken up. I mistakenly gave grace to the temptation guy, thinking that because he expressed concern and showed me the lawsuit papers of the Jewish guy's actions, I could invite the temptation guy to church, though I should have just left the group.

This decision made my victory over the temptation delayed and messier than it needed to be.

Wanting a mature, intellectual conversation is a beautiful base for sharing passionate convictions, and often the group had this. We Christians don't always simply tell people that Jesus loved them, died for their sins, and rose again to offer humanity eternal salvation. Examining the good news and sharing our testimony is another angle that works too. Conversing intellectually is in my wheelhouse more than, say, street preaching, so sharing one-on-one insight with the temptation man was my preferred way of authentic evangelizing. *Can I make a difference in his life and set him free from being used by the demonic if I share insight that is helping me? I have to share the light that is in me!* I was naïve and ill equipped, but that didn't stop me.

As we prepared cookies for another group meeting about to start, I tried sharing. "Do you know that I had an epiphany a few days ago? I had this meditation on a father who loved his daughter from the beginning. She needed him. As she got older, she knew him and interacted with him. There were times she didn't even like him because she couldn't understand him. Despite the disrespect, he continued to love her. It was only when she realized that he loved her that she started to love him. I loved God because he first loved me."

This is why we should always flee temptation and not try to spread our passions without the Lord leading us. The temptation guy didn't hear the substance of my words, but his perception was that I wanted to convert him on the spot. In his mind, he heard a pathetic cliché trying to snag him. He immediately acted like I was lesser than he and clearly thought I misread the social situation. With his multiple advanced degrees and entrepreneurship, he didn't want my musings. The lessons God taught me from this moment were that we can't rely on the mind and intellect for saving and that pride is an enormous wall that we cannot scale on our own. When I looked at this guy, I was looking at a mirror image of my own pride. Here I was trying to reach this pathetic decoy under the influence of demons and asking God to "do a mighty work in him" when God was doing a mighty work in me, changing what I defined as intellectual and reliable.

The conversation was a bust. The temptation guy had spent so much time in relativism and being moral instead of a genuine Christian that he only claimed the faith when suitable. His ego and guard were both up, and he was trying to parry anything I said.

"I'm sharing this because I've heard about loving because we are first loved in songs, but it's ringing true now in my life."

He wanted none of this and took this conversation as an attack. I couldn't have a discussion or share the substance of what made me passionate and able to stand for our supposedly shared beliefs no matter how hard I tried. That is to say, I tried to rescue him from the temptation role he was in so that he would not be used as I had been. My bleeding heart could not change him.

When the meeting began, the leadership guy acted uncontrollably severe. He needed to be a political savant with a personal, expert agenda that flooded into the gathering. The group adjourned early with everyone wondering why on earth the guy was so erratic and kept bringing up random comments, like "There has to be more than one way to heaven. Cemeteries are empty because of reincarnation. You know what we're going to do? I have decided that this group should meet and read books together because we are all old souls from a past life." So much for a conservative group aiming to improve our town through electing people with high character and family values! It couldn't replace church, I found.

As an inexperienced Christian, I wondered what I could have done better. *If I'm supposed to win this soul for Christ as the puritan guy thinks, I'm not faring well!* I had tried to share a revelation I had. How could I not first cherish this insight, then share it? How could I not use it to introduce someone, who had spent so much of his life loving and sacrificing for his own kids, to the Trinity? This passion fell flat when offered to the temptation guy. The guy was more concerned with being right. The self must die, and good psychology can only go so far until one really stops drawing strength from within and starts drawing it from the Holy Spirit and the church as the Bible says.

While writing this with God's wisdom poured into me, I can see what I learned from this experience. Though we should all interact with the mind, we have to examine the nature and health of our relationship with it. We cannot make it a god of any sort because there is only one God despite his three forms. That means any pseudogod is no better than a demon. Zeus, Hera, Diana, and Aphrodite are all demons, not ancient mythological gods—just demons we discover in junior high and read about in Homer's epics in high school. Mind worship, fixating on modernity, and uncontrolled cravings for knowledge are gods that our mothers should warn us about. Close proximity to these entities still ensnares us via guilty by association.

If my big temptation had pride issues and everything in Christendom connects to an interactive relationship, then that temptation served as a warning for me about the effects of pride. Why didn't such ridiculous pride immediately offend me the way it does now, and why did I not run from it? Why did I analyze it and excuse it? I was guilty by association and flattered that someone accomplished in various areas had showed interest in me as a potential employee before the perversity occurred. This spoke to my pride, didn't it? If the temptation had been unsuccessful in work, finances, education, hospitality, and family, my pride wouldn't have been fed. I felt it was Jesus's authority that caused me the fear that allowed me to reject the temptation, but I understand that it was my personal and interactive relationship with God that really made my temptation rejection possible.

✧

In fairy tales, valiant princes have clear-cut victories and unblemished weapons. In reality, this princess behaved like a too tolerant woman, not a soldier of God, and my win of leading someone to Christ looked like an outhouse colliding with a windmill. Despite the pathetic nature of the temptation, my attempted victory was sloppy enough I was concerned about how my intellectual curiosity and pondering (the very saving trait that prompted me to ask to have what Enoch had with God) had allowed such obvious filth to linger in my life. Strengths becoming weaknesses are beyond perplexing. Even now, I have learned to distrust my own meditations to a certain degree because if these "Hmm, I wonder what would happen if . . ." moments are left unchallenged, this beautiful ability to wonder can still corrupt when it lives within a sin nature. Sin taints everything. Even though I am perfected through Christ, it is so easy to rely on human nature instead of God's nature. Therefore, self-protecting around the inappropriate guy involved using a picture of a rabid-looking lion (too realistic for my nerves) with a quote from the book of Hosea that warned me that the devil is on a warpath. This always worked as a warning, but sometimes this ferocious picture and the Hosea Scripture made me appreciate the Lord's story of guardianship and what that meant.

As is customary when you are in the Spirit and when God is teaching you very specific lessons, supernatural events will coincide. For example, a pastor may make a point that speaks to you, then a godly friend from an entirely different social group may bring up the same point without prompting, and three seconds later, the topic plays on the radio. These aren't mere coincidence but moments that seem orchestrated for your edification that lead to a profound sign that God's Holy Spirit is interacting with your life.

One such personal example brought me to this realization: Because God first loved me as a parent loves a baby, I could grow up and start to see how hard he loved me when I was soft on him. The more I experienced life and saw how he accepted sacrifices for my benefit and even committed himself to be the ultimate sacrifice, the more I realized how unloving I had been. I needed more healing love in my life so I could better share it with others. The deepest respect and love took root and developed.

My goal of sacrificing so that the next generation could have lesser trauma and the following generation could have healthy lives reawakened. In tandem, my spirit stirred at the type of sacrifices that I needed to make. When you love someone completely, you will do what is right even when your flesh doesn't want to. I loved the Lord now more than ever, and he deserved a deeper surrender. Because the Lord proved himself to me yet again, it was time I dedicated my children (my niece Zoe and my nephew Aaron) to him. It was also time that I explained to them that I paled in comparison to God and that they should rely on him more than me. I pressed deeper into this insight with the Lord of Lords. The result was that I dedicated—without pomp and circumstance but with sincerity and genuineness—my niece and nephew to the Lord. Though I deeply loved them, I had to admit they were better protected and served under the Lord's care.

My self, or ego, felt pain at telling the kids that someone else loved them more than I did and that the Trinity is the center of our lives.

"I love you kids a lot, don't I?" I started.

Aaron and Zoe nodded their young heads.

"Well, you know that your mom and dad love you even more than I do."

Crickets. Their silence surprised me.

"They love you a lot! Sometimes it's hard to tell since parents make mistakes, but you trust me and I know they love you. They changed your diapers when you were babies and take care of you now, so they definitely love you, right?"

"Yeah, they changed my diaper and the poop was blue," Aaron said with humor.

We chuckled.

"That's right, and I love you so much that I miss those days. You're my sweeties," I replied.

Zoe randomly added, "I peed on Nana and Auntie, and Auntie tricked Nana to clean it up. I had a lot of pee."

"Yes!" I replied. "There was so much of it. It just came out of nowhere! I tricked Nana and said, 'Oh no, Zoe wet the bed. You're better at this than I am. You know where the towels are, right?' And I rolled over like I was going back to bed!"

More laughter from the kids.

"Nana did that because she had kids and is used to taking care of them. Parents love their kids and that's how they show their love, so your mom and dad love you. They just have struggles. They must love you more than I do because they chose to have you and they take care of you."

Aaron and Zoe thought about this. I probably said the wrong thing, but it was the best I could do.

"If your mom and dad love you more than I do, God loves you even more than that!"

Poor confused kids didn't really say anything.

"Try to draw closer to your parents and God."

Simply put, I needed to make it a goal to raise the bar as high as possible for the kids to realize how loved they really are. Seems small maybe, but this felt as difficult as when the kids would ask to live with me instead of their parents and I'd have to say, "I know how your growing up is hard, but you have to keep going. I'm trying to make things better with your parents. You will get through this and it's going to be a struggle, but I love you and I will keep fighting for you!"

Biblical living isn't always easy. We've got to trust those Ten Commandments written on our hearts and minds.

Still in the sixth month before my mission's end, I had a final encounter with the first big temptation. I woke up to a lion's roar in my ears, saw a black shadow quickly receding from my bed, and found my clothes half off and twisted around my waist and arms. Sweat drenched my sports bra, but after the slowly fading nightmare and the state of my clothes and blankets, I was simply glad I still had it on.

It was so late Wednesday night that it was actually Thursday morning. I know because, after the spiritual attack, I looked at the clock, the beacon that grounded me but used to scare me when the spiritual attacks of the past showed midnight, 1 a.m. or 3 a.m. Just knowing there was a witching hour and that these attacks would happen simultaneously several nights in a row used to spook me. Now, I simply needed the grounding to wake up and get my mental bearings because something was happening and I needed alertness. Such is the change that comes to a former victim when she meets Christ!

The dream had clearly been a product of demonic attack, and it was intense. I had been up against the refrigerator in the temptation guy's office kitchen, and the story that had unfolded was like an erotic scene between a man and a woman: tearing at each other's clothes, kissing and exploring each other before consummation. It felt real and that same lust-focused desire was there, throbbing in my body. That's when the heinous lion had roared. Rousing from the nightmare, I had seen a wide, dark shadow melting away from the bed.

Immediately I felt the faith (which was easy since the lion's roar did more than wake me!), looked for a Bible, and started to rebuke in Jesus's name but didn't have time. The spirit was gone. Then, I didn't feel like a warrior, but I acted like one. After an alert, a warrior gets into position, takes a fighting stance, and reaches for her armor and sword. The Enemy intended the nightmare for evil, but God redeemed the attack. Though I didn't understand this in the moment, I would later realize that God taught me self-defense better than any martial arts teacher.

Reeling from the effects of this supernatural encounter, I thought, *Whoa, that was intense!* and felt my hot sweat in the cold night air. I got up and surveyed my little apartment, making sure the doors were all closed and locked and the stove was off. I prayed over the apartment for protection. I stayed up, pacing, wondering what this meant for my mission. Alert to the situation still, my wondering was more of being ready for the next attack and preventing as much of it as possible. I questioned if the spirits would return, as they did in my previous life, but that didn't fit. There's that point in life where you learn to fight back in an absolute way that I had done with the spirits, so I knew these demons wouldn't return.

Quite frankly, it's the truth and authority that what is about to occur is not permitted and is unacceptable at an energy level bigger than a human, so I think, at that moment, we tap into a higher power and claim our safety. I possessed that authority a few times growing up and always considered it manipulation and confidence. Perhaps, though, this is when the satanic world is trying to control God's perfectly controlled plan for our lives and the Holy Spirit, sent from Jesus Christ himself, steps in to prohibit demonic activity and the sinful hearts of humans. If that is the case, then these moments of strength and manipulation are gifts where we victims-turned-*hypernikon* (more than conquerors) are shielded by the Rock of Ages where we watch as a thousand fall at our side but nothing comes near us (Psalm 91).

After sleeping in to compensate for the night's disturbances, I didn't get up and run local errands until Thursday afternoon. I slumped in the driver's seat of my car and closed the door. The closed-in space of the car and the comfortable seats allowed me to relax and let go.

I know the driver's seat of my car is probably not the best place to unwind and lose control. This practice has borne evidence that it results in terrible driving. I get in my car, book it on out of wherever I am, and start driving until the vibrations of the rumble strip on the roadside alert me to my accidental drifting. Such is the result of a mind that always seems to exist in beta waves, but the simple solution is to roll down the windows for air. Now, in my Rip Van Winkle condition, I find that buttons replace hand cranks. Is it depression, inattentive ADHD, or the effects of trauma that fuel this state of mind? It doesn't matter in this case.

The car was my safe haven, and the sun left me with warmth that put me at ease—the best time to hear from God. Putting the key in the ignition but not turning it on, I brought up the previous night to God.

Flashing back, I shook my head at the potency of the satanic power used against me. This wasn't time for a religious prayer: I simply needed to express myself to my Lord and Savior and make a request to my adopted Father. "God, that was intense! When my grip on you starts to loosen, tighten your grip on me, Lord!" I pictured my hand clenching a bar and God's hand covering my own so when I was weak and at the mercy of the fall, the vicelike grip of another held me into place.

That's when a very prominent thought came into my head, and I realized that I had turned my head to the left, looking at something but not seeing anything. *What have you learned from Tim?* In automatic response, I pictured him working. The mental images of him going through the same yo-yo career experiences I've had fired up in my brain. I recalled seeing Tim still living life and even enjoying it despite the ups and downs. He smiled while ruffling a dog's fur, served with charities, and lived in a godly way. This was how he behaved off the clock. I thought about how he had become a better speaker and a far more mature and stronger person. My thoughts slowed and lingered on how no matter what happens, he kept going. *It's nice to have a visual of this. I always encourage people to keep going and when life is too hard just focus on maintaining. Just like Tim: "Get it right, keep it tight."* I started calling this the Tim Tebow method.

"Keep going," I said aloud, responding to the Holy Spirit's question. "No matter what happens, keep going."

Because I saw so many motivating images in what must have been only a few seconds or minutes, my confidence grew exponentially. Another image of Jesus standing before his throne pointing at me came to mind. He warned that if I acted on this temptation with the inappropriate guy, I would be turning my back on God. Maybe other people don't like to know boundaries and to receive solid instructions on what to avoid, but I felt protected and cared for, though I also felt healthy fear. So often, my fear of the Lord moments had been reverence for the Lord, but this was as if he'd said, "Hey kid, stand on the edge of this here Grand Canyon and look down. See that? If you play over here and your foot slips, you're gonna fall, slide, and roll all the way down. You. Don't. Want. That. It's. Bad. For. You."

Any sane response to God would be, "You are correct! That is not the right way to travel, and this is a terrible playing spot. I will be leaving immediately. Good day to you, Sir, and see you at the next prayer time."

I absolutely, most certainly, 100% did not want to act on the temptation! God's warning terrified me, but I simultaneously soaked up this loving discipline that only fathers who love their daughters provide. I had a smile in my heart that left no room for wanting to know the consequences. It relieved me to know this about myself. Some would want to know if God was telling me I would be permanently disowned by God for turning from him, and I doubt that's what he meant. I simply didn't and still don't care what the consequence was because my dad told me not to do something gross and stupid.

I felt relieved, so relieved. Reflecting on my sinner's prayer where I had wrestled with the Lord (pursuing him because I wanted to be with him), confessing, and asking him for what I truly wanted, I squared my shoulders and sat up in my seat. I spoke boldly and out loud now to the Lord God with a conviction to win. Again, I audaciously asked, "Lord, strengthen your grip on me. Cover my hand with yours so even if my grip weakens, your hand is on mine and I won't let go! I can't do this on my own. When my grip on you starts to loosen, tighten your grip on me, Lord!" I held up my right fist, covered it with my left hand, and gave it a solid shake. Between my godly mentor and the Trinity, I had a second wind and I meant business.

If my life were a story, this would be the part where the readers grip the book tight and think ferociously, "Yeah! Fight back!" My readers were angels and I bet their fists were in the air because they got active. But not before a still, small voice (that seemed like my own insightful thought at the time) said, "That's weird. It was just Tim, not Tim Tebow the athlete or anything about his career. Hmm . . ."

From that moment on, Tim was only Tim. In my mind, he no longer had anything to do with his chosen career, just like I wasn't defined by my job. I was even learning to have a personal identity and more self-worth, not getting it from my career or accomplishments. While the subtle changes in me occurred and because the Hosea story involves romantic love, there was a period of time where I wondered if I would meet Tim in person and a relationship would start. Thankfully, I also realized that we wouldn't be a great fit and that, because truly loving someone means you want the best for them, I could ask God to give Tim a better partner. Gratitude for Tim's modeling in my life fueled my prayers, and I prayed specific prayers for Tim on what looked to be his type: I asked God to bring him a future wife who would be a successful pageant girl, a modern woman who knew self-defense but was still a gentle lady, someone who loved God and people like Tim's sisters, etc. I loved him enough to pray for him to meet the right woman for him so he could grow that much more and help others. If my calculations are right, it's about this time when Tim met his current wife and she's exactly the woman I prayed for, although it felt deeply wounding that I couldn't fulfill that role to someone as wonderful and loving. I was at the airport when I saw Tim's engagement news, and I was so devastated at how alone I still was that I missed my flight. But God took that feeling of being a not good enough loser and put healing ointment on the wound, which did truly heal. I just had to turn to the Lord and remember who I was in Christ.

☙

Around this same time in my two-year pilgrimage, I got curious and asked God, "Where were you throughout my life?"

God directed my daydreams to reflect on various times in my childhood where I assumed that I had wisdom beyond my years. The Holy Spirit was letting me know that he had been very active in my life and was (or had angels) whispering encouragement and direction to me. It wasn't my wisdom but his. Moments of insight or intellect were put in my head, not created by myself. God was present when I didn't know it.

For a week or two, scenes from the past would come into my mind and gnaw at me until I said, "Enough is enough. What are you telling me, Lord? I'm with you." I returned to the beginning of the memories like I was a viewer watching the scene of my life before me, but I was also still in the memory.

When I was three or four, the Lord had sent angels to encourage me and give me personal attention. There were no audible voices but thoughts that were not my own. *You've grown so much! Look how tall you're getting.* I looked down at my long slender legs and tested my balance. I thought, *It's like I'm on stilts.* Though alone outside in the driveway digging in the Georgia clay, I became aware of my body. *Were those angels?* I thought about how I felt apart from my body and that something other than my physical body was my true self. As an adult, I'd call my true self a spirit, but here I didn't have the vocabulary. My body was like a machine, but something else was me, Sarah. Still pretending I was on stilts, I stiff walked to my mom and one of the aunts at Granny Herrin's trailer. Asking about this concept didn't help because the women didn't understand.

I asked further, "In AWANA and Sunday school, they say you die and go to heaven. But does it feel like how we feel now? I feel alert right now. Does this awake feeling stay in my body but then my body disappears and I get a shiny body and still feel like me?"

Perplexed, the women looked at each other and mumbled. It was a weird thought for a kid but not weird for God's angels creating this wondering in my young brain.

Another memory surfaced: When I was five years old, I would get up before everybody else and push the buttons on the television to watch "cowboys and Indians." One morning, I had walked to the middle of the living room, looking at something that was there but not something visible. "So why did I look at it?" I asked my now-adult self.

I remembered the thoughts that had come into my young brain, *They're going to try to take your goodness. Don't let them.* Still looking up, I nodded my small head yes and knew exactly what to do. Protect my goodness. Even when the sexual abuse, burnings, and playing with knives started, I had been a soldier obligated to fulfill my orders. Over three decades later, I still remembered the honor of having this mission. To Daddy John, I was something to stab at, burn, and molest, but to Father God, I was someone worth investing in so when he redeemed me, I would remember that he has always been with me and has a plan. But I couldn't help but wonder, *How did I know what this meant and what to do?*

Before the temporary memory problems hit me in 2012, my long-term memory had always been off-the-chart high. False memories were never an issue either, so it stands to reason that I was of sound mind. The modern-day revelations brought contentment to trust what the God-sent angels were telling me in my early childhood. Though I presently shake my head in awe that God gave me personal attention like this, it would make sense that God tended his own, sending angels to teach and nurture a little child. God knew what I was up against in my life, and he prepared me. In this most sacred moment, his goodness pierced me and I felt more. Sometimes love initially hurts us. However, anything of God is worth trusting because all he does results in love, and that love hurts less and less after each exposure. The Lord certainly had my attention with these revelations!

Chapter 32
The Warrior Is a Child

But everything exposed by the light becomes visible—and everything that is illuminated becomes a light. This is why it is said:
"Wake up, sleeper,
rise from the dead,
and Christ will shine on you."

—Ephesian 5:13–14 NIV

After the lesson in my car, things became more of a battlefield of the mind. Fighting boredom while waiting for a new job to start and feeling like a failure for receiving temptation, I drove to the soup kitchen café where I volunteered. God's messengers were close by, popping words of encouragement into my head. "Being tempted means you're on the right track. The Enemy doesn't like when you make progress. That's a good sign for you!" *That's right. God is in control, holding me in the palm of his mighty hand, not letting Satan go too far.* Moments like this allowed me genuine appreciation for the soldiers of the Lord who stayed close to me and followed God's plan to protect and guide me.

The charity café had meager success, but I had an opportunity to reach out to an obviously homeless and much-disfigured man sobering up. He was such a character—one of those loud drunks who walk into a situation trying to bring stimuli in the form of raucous fun. He needed someone like me, rough around the edges like him, to explain that what he thought was fun was random, loud behavior. I had learned that I did that unintentionally because my ADD brain needed excitement to not be painfully bored. I related to this man who couldn't see the disruptive, rude behavior without someone's correction.

Church leaders or corporate professionals (those who behave appropriately with ease) didn't always know how to deal with my unique behavior. Their negative reactions hurt me. Now, people who are "characters" have an ally in me to explain that I know they mean well, but their perception isn't what others are seeing. I will explain that our brains are acting up. That's all he needed.

Turns out, this guy Kevin knew my friend Doug, the genuine, friendly, and fatherly Christian who is the modern-day John the Baptizer. We exchanged funny Doug stories as if we were talking about a Jesus-loving puppy with boundless energy. Kevin was a lapsed Catholic and admitted that he loved his sins too much to turn to God, but he seemed to have some gospel seeds in the soil of his heart, thanks to the church and Doug. So for the first time, I got to learn what it was like to water seeds someone else had planted.

Ineffectually, I demonstrated a physical step down from the church landing, with my eyes closed, hoping to convey what taking a step in trust/belief/faith felt like. I looked foolish, but learning starts somewhere, doesn't it? Satan loves to see people hurt because he doesn't care that disabled, homeless people like Kevin have deep pain and weaknesses. All our pain and weaknesses can be soothed, though. It just takes a lot of work and faith.

My job here was to water seeds of faith that Doug had planted in Kevin and that certainly was a reasonable responsibility. After all, it's not like I had to go door-to-door giving out gospel tracts alone! Now that's hard, and my ego is still too big to handle that with grace. Rejection is still very painful. When the homeless man and his girlfriend pedaled off into the night, looping through the downtown traffic, I prayed silent prayers again. This time, the prayer was that the cars would see his bicycle and his dark clothes and avoid hitting him. The prayer was also that Kevin and his girlfriend would learn to hate their sins and trust the Lord our Savior before it was too late.

I wasn't naturally a front-lines person but one who wanted to evoke godly thought that elucidated someone else's efforts. That made me less of a salesperson for the faith and more of a marketer, but I was learning that wasn't okay. Driving home, I thought about these things and made sure to block emails and texts from the temptation guy and the Jewish elder who were still trying to connect with me outside the conservative group.

As I settled in for the night, the angels must have delivered some insight to me so I wouldn't feel like I was unsuccessful in helping Kevin. I was still reeling from the three supernatural temptation experiences, especially the third, but I realized something concerning my role in spiritual warfare. I had changed from being a victim and survivor to being a warrior. When the fullness of this identity change unfurled in my mind, I felt so proud of myself and felt reverence for the work God had done in me.

Since I no longer felt the need to investigate my temptation, the Lord gave me the strength to quit the conservative group. The Messiah planted seeds in my and my pastor's minds to discuss water baptism too. As it so happened, mine would take place later on August 3, 2015. Though there was very little pomp and circumstance, the humble dip and rising in a churchgoing friend's outdoor pool allowed me to focus on the moment. If I was the first born again in the family, which I was pretty sure I was, I wanted to know and experience as much as I could because I'd be leading the way for those who came after me. There was no dove-shaped spirit that said it was well pleased with me or something more realistic, but my experience was still important.

Physically the baptism was awkward despite the friendly homeowners. I still could not for the life of me feel connected with most of the people. I needed so much work still. That was okay because I trusted both of the Lord's sacraments (baptism and Communion) no matter who the audience or what the environment was. Honestly, I did hope to feel more than just the little change I felt since I made sure to keep my mouth open a tad. Aware of the silliness but not caring, I thought maybe some of that prayed-over and extra-blessed water would make me extra holy on my insides too! Yes, that's absurd, but I don't care.

My whole Christian life had been absurd! I asked the God who understands epigenetics and created shape-shifting cephalopods, the entire solar system, the Milky Way, healing, love, and even forgiveness to have not just a personal relationship with me but to be the Father and perfect parents I never had. *I won't be on my own, and you will restore me!* Subsequently, the God who created and gave us the ability to learn about the above (without imploding) agreed to engage in this relationship with me and he immediately sent me an angel that was so, so, so tall. It led me to a mentor who taught me how to live with more hope and motivation.

Maybe swallowing some pool water makes me dumb as a wood post, but it was a wood post that closely held the Savior of humanity while he sacrificed his spotless life for mine. I haven't given up my intelligence, but when it comes to the Lord, I simply have nothing to offer him that he can't provide for himself. I may as well do what pea-brained sheep do to get closer to the Shepherd in any and every way possible because if the act itself doesn't get me closer, it will at least make God laugh, and I'm pretty sure I'll get points for that!

※

The next month, God kept putting it on my heart to address my health. He wanted me to care for myself again and to start moving with the current of life. I started scheduling appointments with doctors, happy to be moving again. There's nothing more depressing than atrophy of the body and spirit. I invited into my life a plethora of doctors, including a Christian psychologist to see if I needed a second round of therapy. Whatever it took to make an appointment with a neuropsychologist to get an official diagnosis of my brain issues, I did. It took finagling to determine which doctors were necessary and how long I should see each, which is normal, but doors and medical coverage opened up for me like never before. Everyone (including retired neurosurgeons!) was concerned for me. I would start to self-deprecate and apologize for not discovering a cure for my sorry state because I didn't know how to react to such personal kindness.

Contrary to my previous experience, people were nurturing. I would get a stern reprobation when I displayed self-frustration. I had figured that back disc and neck issues were so common and so complex that these professionals understood why I was coming to see them even after a two-year absence of seeing any doctor. Both humorously and unfortunately, I found that medical staff took me and my chronic pain much more seriously when I was in my thirties and when I didn't give two royal craps about what happened with any doctor. As a hopeful but scared nineteen-year-old, I was just a number despite being eager to learn what each doctor had to offer. Clearly, the Holy Spirit was still directing me to have more hope and direction while he worked with my apathy.

Because I had invested four years in cognitive behavioral therapy in the past and tried various medications and modalities, I received the green light for a full neurological exam that was normally impossible to get approved. Well, praise God! I'm glad all that trial-and-error testing that left me feeling like a heavily medicated lab rat paid off. The downside to the comprehensive exam was laying out my detailed story for a normal person who would by dazed by the unique dysfunction and confusion in my family. It had been so long since I had to talk to someone about the stories that made up my whole story. I gave the intake nurse some tips, prepared her for what she would encounter, and told her only the main issues in chronological order and based on topic. She also had two assessment surveys from my brother and my mom pertaining to my past and present behavior. Getting current behavior observations from two family members who I only saw during the holidays was somewhat pointless and Mom's memory had tanked, but Ecclesiastes 9:10 rang in my head: "Whatever you find to do, do it well because where you are going—the grave—there will be no working or thinking or knowing or wisdom (VOICE).

The neuropsych group struggled with piecing my families' responses and prior records together, but I helped translate who meant what and how to classify medical notes and common themes that needed to be diagnosed. All relationships are best when they involve genuine interaction. Engaging with doctors as if you're equal partners makes a big difference. Because I had meditated on the concept of being in relationship, the wisdom trickled down to how I functioned daily. Thus, biblical living and a relationship with God enhanced my interactions with this medical group so we could partner in my diagnosis. We prevented confusion by tag teaming through evaluation stumbling blocks like when Mom noted to the doctors about the time she "gave [me] to the Mexicans." Medical professionals had no idea what on earth that meant. I explained the reference to being cared for by Mexicans as a baby, working with the staff so they could invest better care in me. And wasn't investing in my own health what the Lord was leading me to do?

The oral exam started, and I gave a rundown of the usual things medical people want to know including the childhood playground accident where I found a chain pulley wrapped around my neck. Chronic pain infused into my life that day, and it left a crippling mark. After the physical ailments, they needed some details on the child abuse that brought us to Maine.

"We were whipped on our bare behinds with belts and switches as well as the actual sexual abuse I've described. You may want to make note of the ways we tried to ask for help but didn't receive it. I remember telling my mom more than once, 'I don't want him to watch us. He's mean!' Sometimes Daddy John heard our rushed whispers to Mom, and sometimes she repeated what we said to him offhandedly. I'm not sure why doctors like you guys write that down, but it's what you do."

The intake nurse said, "Thank you, yes. I'll pass this along to Dr. Laurie. What else?"

"I still wrestle with guilt and self-esteem issues. At about age twelve, I had to ground myself to my room because I did something wrong like swearing, but no one thought about it enough to ground me. 'Don't do it again' was the only response. That had to leave an unconscious message that I wasn't loved enough to be disciplined or something. I don't know. I guess I also struggled with the move to Litchfield, Maine. It was so remote compared to Augusta. I remember sassing Mom once and calling her fat. She got upset like a kid and exclaimed, 'You kids have changed! You're so spiteful!'

"She went to her room, and I stood in the living room feeling guilty, as I should. Walking into the master bedroom to apologize, I saw her under her comforter crying loud sobs. 'I'm sorry, Mom. Don't cry.'

"She sobbed back, 'You're so mean! Ever since we came to New England, you kids have become so bratty. You were so sweet and polite in Georgia. I don't know what happened!'

"Daddy John and Gramma Peggy happened plus a life of turmoil. But I didn't have those thoughts then. I knew Mom was right, and I didn't know what to say. I reacted the way I saw other kids and took it out on my own mother. She was the same mom who gave me at-home traction when my neck hurt so bad that I would cry. She'd gently pull my skull from my neck to alleviate the pain and schedule appointments with the chiropractor." I looked down in shame. The intake nurse kept typing.

A few hours later, the physical testing began. The only hiccup was the expected ask, "Would you mind spending some extra time, like an hour or so? Could we call you to learn more over the next few weeks?" *Yep, they've gotten a little turned around. My life is confusing no matter how linear and easy I try to explain it.*

I prayed hard before and after but had little capacity to silently pray during the six hours. *Why is my working memory no longer than fifteen seconds? Do I have inattentive AD[H]D, and will medication work even though nothing has yet? Do I have depression that requires meds forever, or is there still hope that "love covers a multitude of sins"? Could the Lord's blood rinse away the two layers of depression that I felt set on me at age twelve? Should I tell the neuropsych people about Jesus and give them my testimony? How'd this thought get in here? I'm supposed to be getting a secular evaluation. I'll just define* repentance *and* faith *so the ladies know how to meet the Lord. Maybe I shouldn't have eased up on the elimination diet after all. I'm so ADHD. Well, I did warn them.*

At the six-hour mark of testing, I finished exhausted but to the best of my ability. Focusing on my weak areas so we could explore them was frustrating but needed. My self-observations were eye opening. It's sad to struggle with tasks that are simple for others. It's sadder still knowing that your struggles are because you are still hurting. Again, I gave the test my all and alerted the group to problems like lapses in time and the working and short-term memory loss. This emotional poking and prodding on the sorest of spots made so much more sense than what the small Congregational assemblage had offered me. This group of neuropsychologists was warmer, more professional while casual, respectful with their questioning, knew why they were there and what role to play, and more helpful overall. I'm still grateful for the church assemblage for helping the way they knew how. Some put their hearts on their sleeves. It's just that working with people at the neuropsych place was an environment full of knowledge, experience, and kindness and devoid of fear, which allowed us to get to the heart of the matter. With the Lord backing this, I was able to grieve.

The evaluation simply said what we already knew—ADHD, post-traumatic stress, and depression—but I finally had clear direction! Off I went to scheduling a speech and language pathologist for executive function training, physical and occupational therapies, a pain management doctor, and a chiropractor. I saw them all and gave them my all and it pleased the Lord, but I'm glad I've moved past having to use all of these therapies.

To cheer me up, my friend Doug told me, "Yes, you do sound like a real mess, but there's good news and bad news. The bad news is that you have a lot of problems. The good news is that the doctors are probably going to name a new disorder after you!"

With time, a large chunk of the trauma healed quite nicely and I learned to remove dairy, artificial colors, and artificial preservatives from my diet to lessen ADHD symptoms. I moved from bewailing ADHD and depression to simply disliking them and the same went for my chronic pain. This meant that I had one less stronghold in my life. Seeing the physical and occupational therapists, I started feeling like I had direction again when in a gym. Because of this godly guidance to get medical help, I have found people with shared issues and I've been able to make a difference in their lives—even to some of these very doctors. Praise God for that!

The next month, God had a new assignment. The doctors had noticed that I was so down on myself and my pathetic life and that I desperately needed medication. We started searching and found new options that actually worked for long periods, and I also searched for a better fitting workplace than the college where I worked only to feel drained. To help, I "put on the Christ" every morning, marinated in Scripture and theology in the afternoon, and took anything God Almighty had to offer. But there I go slipping into Christianese. Let me explain "putting on the Christ."

Picture yourself before the most powerful judge in existence, wearing a yellowed cover-up. This cover-up is normal for you to wear, and it identifies who you are. In fact, it's like a second skin. Now, the judge is convicting you of whatever law you broke. You're a regular person who makes mistakes, but you did the crime so now you're about to serve the time. You are not acquitted; you are guilty, and you have to compensate for the damage you caused. Christians call this indemnification of a situation or deed *expiation*. While it's important to make amends, expiation only makes amends. It covers the crime and focuses on the criminal's reparation.

Because the judge is no ordinary judge but *the* Judge, his wrath has to be appeased. He is so holy that he provides true and complete justice. Not only do you need to pay for the wrongs you did, you need to pay for all the suffering. So if you gossiped and slandered someone, your words probably traveled from person to person like feathers in the wind. There is no earthly way you can take that back, can you? No matter what your punishment, you cannot erase the hurt felt nor can you restore relationships that were severed. Expiation isn't enough. You need propitiation because it is powerful enough to heal and restore everything. However, it can only come from complete purity and perfection, one without blemish.

So one minute you're condemned a criminal, the next minute, Jesus walks into the courtroom with a crimson cover-up. Jesus is without sin, a completely perfect person. When he tells the judge that he will take your place by paying the penalty for your sin, propitiation is starting because Jesus can satisfy the Judge's righteous wrath, and he is the only one who can.

We know that Jesus was sacrificed for our sins on the cross. He died and his crimson blood was shed. So picture Jesus in that courtroom knowing that he is the propitiation for your sins, and he does the most merciful things ever done to anyone in humanity. He imputes your sin onto himself and his righteousness, holiness, and justification onto you. This looks like Jesus's crimson cover-up coming off Him and being replaced with your yellowed, sin encrusted cover-up. You now have his crimson cover-up, and if you put it on, you are no longer identified by your sin or as your former self (the apostle Paul refers to this as the *old man*). So you are "in Christ" and a "new creation" (2 Corinthians 5:17).

When a Christian talks about "putting on the Christ," this is a visual of what that means. It's important enough that Paul wrote about it also in Romans 13:14 and Galatians 3:27. "Dying to self" and "putting off the old [sin] nature" are pointing at the same concept. All that to say, the goal is to have a Christ-covered life, one that isn't cheap or secondhand. But I say that Christians must *live* a Christ-covered life so they are not afraid to step outside of religion and explore God's kingdom and people.

Now back to facing those doctors. I showed up for my appointments and impressed the doctors with my dedication. Who wouldn't show appreciation? I didn't just do my work with them but made sure I got my six hours in the gym each week and some biking or elliptical work. I started having fun and decided to get huge. Well, lady huge, not man huge. I wanted to be healthy and have muscle definition so I could be like a normal person. For me to get to that level, I would have to work out for months. However, I did get there, bathed in sweat and reading Bible verses about the fruit of the Spirit and Romans 6.

Amidst all sorts of "funny coincidences" of frustrating moments interrupted by pleasant surprises and godly validation, the Lord used the church to inspire me. Carefully jogging near my apartment in the feeble, no impact way I've learned to "run" one afternoon, God-given sapience came to mind: *You are more than a conqueror!* This unexpected surprise was a tender note from the Lord who sacrificed himself for me and patiently waited for me to notice what he had and was doing for me. It was soothing to hear, and I treasured those moments. God is so considerate of someone so small she's not even a speck in the universe.

Finally, I got into Christian counseling so I could get some accountability and healthy Christian guidance. While learning to self-advocate within the Christian sphere, it helped to get permission to change churches. Churches preach that you should serve and serve a lot. "You shouldn't ever be one of those people that abandon a church just because major internal upset like a divorce or scandal breaks out, because the church is a family." How true!

The Pentecostal church of my youth, Shepherd of Faith, disbanded over one divorce. That's all it took. As an adult, I realized that I internalized church splits and upheavals as I did all my parents' divorces. *This is just how things are*, I thought. But a side effect of divorce is that people don't stay with one another and love is seen as conditional. So my siblings and I had learned that church groups are no different than town baseball leagues that peter out when the dads stop volunteering to coach. The dads only volunteer when their kids are on the team. The kids get older, so the coaches move on. So you either get a new coach or you have to find a new sport with someone willing to invest in you.

With church, I didn't see the loyalty I saw in TV gangs, that once you're in, you are part of a family and it's for life: That's what I wanted! I saw some Christians on fire for God and bleeding for those around them. Critics said that Christians should be role models and have their lives together, and I believed that, never really questioning this. I inadvertently demanded my suffering to end out of ignorance, pride, entitlement, and a deep fear that I had to control others or they would control me.

However, I now encounter many people functioning as parts of a body, pulsating with life that arrests and awes. The stories I've heard and been a part of don't even have to be about missionaries on jungle adventures who reached out to cannibals and taught them how to hunger for Christ. Well, maybe not *hunger*, but you know what I mean. People take up offerings for someone laid off and create local foster-care programs. The impression of missionaries being alone on their journeys with Indigenous people is just as real and important in my life as the daily good things happening here in the US.

The Christian psychologist advised me to find a church where I could serve *and* be served. Since I was in an out-of-touch and disorganized church where I wouldn't even get contacted for the ministries that I volunteered for, going elsewhere was fine especially since I had tried hard for two years, not bouncing to a new church each month. I needed that validation. I also developed less fear in dealing with the Christians who juggle similar struggles as I do. Those with debilitating pain have every excuse to close people out of their lives, but they're trying to keep going. It's hard to help others amidst your own life's trials. These wounded warriors don't scare you when God heals you enough to love them, but I needed counseling on boundaries so I could learn how to help others without taking on their baggage.

I found a new church family that actually met in a public school auditorium, and it felt like the early church! All the churchgoers even knew what "movement" (aka denomination) we were a part of and could answer my church and Bible questions. When a creepy, disheveled man wandered into the elementary school doors one Sunday afternoon, he loitered in a way that alerted some of the women's intuition. Instead of pretending the world is without sin, the women looked out for one another. Someone subtly gave the heads-up, "Ladies, don't go to the lobby alone." One of the men found the shifty guy wandering intoxicated and handled the situation, inviting him to respectfully join or leave since the school couldn't have loitering. I had never seen that in a church. It felt like a safe community. And because so many of us had Jesus on our side and the Holy Spirit living within us, the community was engaged with one another.

Missionaries were always stopping in, and most of us went on mission trips and prayer outreach events regularly. When there's an event, people know where it will be and what time, something that I had not always experienced at churches. Dialogues about important topics like how to handle sexual trauma and healing happened. People came together to offer personal support. We genuinely got to know each other. There were even a few connectors extending welcomes into their homes for fellowship groups and birthday parties for those who didn't have family in the area. Ministry leaders were able to lead and stepped down when breaks were needed. I saw a new side to church that started healing previous church hurt. No one cared that I'm neurodivergent or single because many of them were too. It felt like we were the Lord's flock, serving *and* being served.

Chapter 33
Planting Seeds and Growing Fruit

For you were once darkness, but now you are light in the Lord. Live as children of light.

—Ephesians 5:8 NIV

SURPRISINGLY, FOR A month, God put it on my heart that some people aren't genuine Christians and just say they are. This lead to me sporadically planting seeds of faith, growing fruit, and learning why "narrow is the gate" was being revealed to me. I spent the entire next month reading, hearing, seeing, and feeling examples and concepts that drilled home to me what Jesus meant by that statement. There were black-and-white lessons like how Jesus is a door we walk through and not a deceivable Lord that we can diminish and walk all over like a welcome mat. God was not teaching me blanket judgments on others' experiences but how to recognize how few actual Christians there are. Many call themselves Christians but say that they are not born again despite Jesus specifically saying, "You must be born again." I would walk over a doormat and through a door still fiddling with a loose doorknob when something would stir in my heart a further comparison of how people try to manipulate the Lord.

Long after the end of this lesson and the two-year mission, I have continued to learn more how we can be Christians and backslide to a certain degree. I've realized that there are people who I wouldn't label as falsely converted but view them more as someone who hasn't finished putting their salvation on tight. However, when I'm with someone who is clearly not a Christian in the least bit who insists that he or she is, I let them know how to encounter the Lord more. Sometimes they make these comments about my testimony, "No, you were really protected always. You were Christian. God is love, and you were really a good person. Good things happen to good people."

This is where I firmly stand. "I was a broken mess and needed the Holy Spirit. I was on a two-year mission, and thirty-one days of that mission's end focused solely on learning that 'narrow is the gate.' We must be born again, and everyone who has been born again knows it because there's that supernatural change that happens, whether sudden like mine or gradual. That's why so many people remember the exact date of their conversion. It's that big of a deal. You can disagree and I won't think less of you, but you will still be biblically and spiritually wrong." I never want to assume that anyone is a Christian just because they say they are. Their lives matter too much to me.

That lesson was such a big deal that I had these reverse witch trial thoughts. You know, when you're looking around and no one acts like a holy person but just regular, decent people. However, there's nothing in their life that points to faith. Therefore, I started to wonder, *Is the pastor right that this area is more unreached for Christianity than India? Are so few people Christians?* I even had to ask some people—who knew I was simply trying to learn if they were of the faith and not being rude—questions like, "But if you're a Christian, how come . . . And wouldn't you have . . . ?" Christianity was so confusing to me, and I knew nothing. The faith was contrary to so much of what I knew and lived.

Trading helpfulness for legalism, I decided that everyone needed the Lord until the Lord sought fit to tell me I was being too much of a legalist. Eye roll moment. New Christians fall into legalism so easily though; we are blushing brides desiring to do our best, but I fell into a bit of being a yahoo too. It's hard to know how to react to the presence

A Tatterdemalion's Testimony

of the Lord. Christians have prayed so much for me and gone the extra mile countless times and with such compassion. I existed in confusion and doubted myself. *Maybe everything I knew about Christianity is wrong?* Uncertain, I just kept following the Lord, cluelessness and all.

⁂

The pilgrimage countdown was still in motion, and it was a time of accelerated learning, housekeeping, and tying up loose ends. Knowing how badly I wanted some spiritual fruit in my life, the Holy Spirit let his light shine through me. My goal since regularly attending church had been to marinate in the Word, which included the Word taught from godly people as well. I figured if I spent sufficient time studying the Lord that I would imitate Him better and hopefully have some of his glory rub off on me too. This required relentless work and very little stepping back, checking to see if I was glowing in the Spirit, if you will. Imagine, then, my surprise when my mother started regarding me oddly and then had a follow-up conversation with me later where she beamed at me with proud mama eyes.

Standing in the front of my sister's apartment, I could feel my mom looking up at me while I spoke to my sister. Mom had wandered out of our conversation until something caught her eye. That something was me. Well, my sister and I continued talking because our casual chat had evolved into a conversation of substance and discovery.

A plastic lighter had caused an insignificant fire on the stovetop at my place. As I had been unsuspectingly stretched out on the floor, an air current had blown micropieces a few feet over to me. I rose and snuffed out the tiny nuisance and wiped the soot off the stove when the plastic cooled. Soot and tiny bits of ash were across the stove, on the floor, and on and inside the cupboards and the mixing bowls within, which was a complete surprise. *How did it get in there?* Soot was even clinging to the grooves in the refrigerator door gasket.

"The fire was so small that it must have gone for at least two minutes before it dawned on me that there was a problem. The fire was so tiny

I blew most of it out and covered it with a towel that wasn't even damaged," I further illustrated to my sister.

When I made my point, gesticulating in the air, my attention was slightly diverted to Mom now examining me with her eyes. Something was different, and she wasn't quite sure how it was different, but I was on a mission full of ADHD's gifts of passion and hyperfocusing.

"The ash was everywhere, Becky, and at that moment, I knew I had a fuller understanding of unmerited sin. Praise God! I wanted something more than my previous visual example of people swimming in a pond with algae clinging to them even if the swimmers were innocent of attracting the algae [sin] in any way. Well, this was it! It doesn't matter if you earn a sin or are born into it. It gets into everything and that's the problem."

Like a dog finally getting the peanut butter inside a dog toy, Mom figured out what she was seeing in me. Becky shared about needing to draw closer to God because she felt she was changing when she trusted him more.

"Me too!" I replied. "We can feel when we have that born-again experience, but it probably looks to the world like we Christians are not very different. After we go off to college, for example, we feel changed, but we often look the same to everybody else."

"Yes, I can see that!" Mom interrupted with a bubble of excitement.

I stopped talking and saw her light up with happiness. Her eyes were darting back and forth over my face.

"You are reading me! Look at you, Mom. You are reading me and seeing things."

"Yep," she said with a big head bob, and she chewed on her bottom lip like she had a secret.

Later on, we were talking about ways to explain spiritual questions to my mom's fourth husband, Dave. Dropping out of high school and slumming through life had deprived him of the skills that would make biblical comprehension and spiritual reasoning easier. Mom's comparisons were simple enough to him, but her lessons to Dave didn't take root. I didn't see him often, but at least I could take Mom's answers and attempt at reaching Dave's soul to the next level. Nonetheless, he was still struggling, and we were brainstorming how we could take what we knew and minister to his needs while showing him how to help himself. Honestly, I thought the best testimony would be my mom's and that if she put her salvation on tight, that would speak volumes.

"I think you're absolutely right, and that's what I see in you," she said. "It's amazing how you are growing, and I don't just mean what you normally do. You are just . . ." She went on remarking how she saw the Holy Spirit influencing my life.

Though I didn't have the ability to see fruit-bearing potential in myself, I had a mother who could, and those mama eyes reflected the best mile marker. If I was growing fruit, could that influence my mom? I had no doubt, but Mom still thought she was saved like I had been, so I kept working on her since I knew her lifestyle. She needed to ensure that she wasn't yet another false convert but someone who saw the narrow gate and would pass through it.

What I also learned at this time was that my "joke" to God about not forgetting the Holy Spirit's importance just before encountering the eight-foot-tall angel was such a worldly joke. God's name is so sacred the ancient Jews wouldn't write or speak it. But the sons of Zebedee, James and John, had made a similar mistake. They wanted to be at Jesus's left and right sides, places of honor at Jesus's throne. They were acting so worldly and not of God, and I had acted the same. No wonder God sent me an angel to immediately correct my "humor" and base living. I behaved clueless like two men who knew the Christ for a few years and acted so ignorantly. My superficiality needed correcting.

Chapter 34

The Finish Line

I have fought the good fight, I have finished the race, I have kept the faith.

—2 Timothy 4:7 NIV

October 2014 was an interesting month. It felt like the final stretch, which any athlete knows brings excitement and anxiety but also a focus that almost feels like peace (I said almost!). I didn't turn from Tim's teachings or the Lord's, but I didn't understand why finishing strong mattered. One of the godsends of escaping perfectionism and the insecurities and injuries that come from that practice is learning that you simply have to get through life. It's like life is a pass or fail class, not one where you are graded. There's less of a legalistic focus on the grade and rules and more freedom to learn what the instructor and the class environment are teaching. It's hard to cap this skewed thinking with the finish strong lesson because they seem so contrary. However, that was my end cap. I listened to one of Tim's talks on finishing strong and rewatched the documentary, which still had a special blessing over it so I still connected to it and got the motivation I needed.

At work, so many in the community at the college were so sheltered and soft that grown adults had trouble functioning individually because everything had always been done for them. Working in that environment felt like I was a street fighter who had somehow gotten roped into learning how to fence and was challenged to a preppy duel where all her skills were not only against the rules but were archaic and shocking. Outside of that environment, real life persisted. Being forced into a gentleman's fight against easily injured, spoiled people is challenging. Maintaining a focused endurance when, outside of this struggle, there are dark, heavy issues (like needing to help my sister's neglected neighbor kids) is overwhelming.

During this period, my sister's husband invited a male neighbor to live in my elementary-school niece's walk-in closet. The neighbor made the rest of the family uncomfortable, but my sister said she was too afraid and didn't know how to ask him to leave. The junky man radiated anger and dysfunction.

His girlfriend's twin daughters, Zoe's classmates, came over to visit when I was there. We loved spending time together, and the girls opened up to us and explained that the man kicked their pregnant mom in the belly. That's why he was living in my little girl's closet for a few weeks. They touched on some physical abuse and yelling. The junky guy's toddler son almost fell down the steep stairs and got his fingers in a fan since no one was supervising, so I corralled the underfed kids with snacks and whisked them away to a playground where I called Child Protective Service. The mom received a lot of government care and had mentioned CPS involvement before, so I called and relayed the information I heard, but I didn't have the exact address or know last names since I just visited the area twice a month. Did my statement make a difference? I don't know, but the crippling emotions I felt went straight to my neck where the chain had caused so much damage.

My own experience with neglect came back and throbbed in my neck like a migraine. I had to keep fighting and do something for these children too. That was my job just as much as making sure Daddy John's location and not just his name were filed on the Georgia Sex Offender Registry. No one else pushed for this, and it was the right thing to do, even at the risk of looking like I hadn't "gotten over" the abuse. I learned that we aren't entitled to have other people, like the government or a social services group, handle these things. We all need to get involved to make a difference. It hurt to be close to trauma, but I could help by acting and praying to the God I now knew.

What early on in my pilgrimage involved learning Christian living from Tim became developing better character and not just motivation. I used this lesson as the biggest friggin' stick this desperate toddler in Christ could find to smack the tar out of desperation and sadness, clearing obstacles out of her path so she could finish her God-given mission. I wouldn't let disillusionment over the twins' situation keep me down.

Not even six hours after dealing with this delicate matter, I awoke and left my apartment to find that someone had smashed into my car, leaving black streaks along the driver side and glass all over the street. In my quiet neighborhood, someone just so happened to do thousands of dollars' worth of damage without one of the retirees or families seeing or hearing anything? There was no note left, of course, just thick black tread marks showing that a huge vehicle like a bus or construction truck had backed up in a three-way residential intersection. My thoughts beyond *You have got to be kidding!* returned to how defeated and sore necked I had been the night before. The neck pain had been so bad, my muscles still hurt and that was rare. *Maybe things do come in threes. Ugh, superstition! I can't have this car mess and examine what God is teaching me through the mess with the neglected twins while trying to finish the two-year pilgrimage.*

I knew all this wasn't coincidental, and I wanted to fight back. The damage was so absurd that I've never seen one vehicle cause that kind of damage to another, not even when I worked in automobile claims just after college. The taillights and rear bumper were busted, the driver-side front mirror was knocked off, and the door was caved in. All the other cars on the crowded street remained untouched. I wanted to finish strong no matter how cliché it sounded. I was in fighting mode for days and made good progress with both work and family. I showed up to every church and charity event and Bible study group expected of me. I read through church history articles and seminars during lunch and while at the gym. Even exercising like planking was free time to get through a couple more paragraphs of Judeo-Christian relations in the Renaissance or whatever reading would bring this soldier up to speed on how to survive in a gentleman's kingdom. I had read the New Testament and made sure to continue through the Old Testament. I circled back again with my family doing my best to be their voice of reason whether they hated it or not, and they absolutely hated it. "You have to live right. Follow God. Trust Him!"

When you run across a finish line, there's so much happening at once. Because I was competing for my own benefit but also learning to die further to self, I was my own competition in this two-year mission. Regardless, I was not sure how I placed. Every race has a winner if not first, second, and third, right? After a few more days, I wasn't even sure if I had placed. The second week of November 2014 came and went, and I tried not to look at the dates or think about the mission results. It was high school track all over again. I had no problem waiting for results in school because the coach would tell me what I needed to know before too long. When God is a coach, he does things contrary to what is normal and expected. When I started frothing at the mouth, my mom had to tell me, "You keep telling me about these things that are incredible. You have been on this spiritual journey. Think about all the things that you have seen and done! Would your God bring you this far and leave you wandering? He will give you what you need."

She was right. She's often not reliable for counsel, but every now and then she provides gems like the above. Soaking in those words gave me relief. To be able to relax finally after the two-year race because I knew God would tell me if I had finished strong or not almost put me in a state of rest. However, I couldn't get my mom's words out of my head. Doesn't the born again in you notice immediately that this self-proclaimed Christian had said, "Would your God . . ."?

I thanked Mom and got off the phone with her. You know, after a tough workout, you have to do a little more exercise to break up the lactic acid buildup, and I had just received confirmation that my Mom was my cooldown. Out loud with no thought of spiritual warfare and not caring where I was, I made a declaration.

"God, I want my mom. I want her called to Christ! Use me however you will. The family belongs together, and may I be a part of it." My cooldown never officially ended, and I did laps, stretched, and massaged while praying. I swear I prayed to keep from self-injury because I repeated those steps with every phone call, email, and in-person conversation with my mother and her husband, and I prayed before and after each event with silent prayers of *Help, God! I'm fumbling!*

Mom learned to step aside so I could work with Dave on learning more about the Christian way, but what she didn't know is how much I prayed, for both of them. I think all my born-again prayers for Mom rang loud and clear. Mom had me talk with her husband so I could minister to his spiritual and biblical questions and concerns. However, she was nearby listening and/or getting a recap on what I discussed with Dave. Why I took my path instead of the one she would have chosen made another impression on her.

That teaching and all the loving discipline I laid on that little round mother of mine finally came to fruition within the next year when—after much prayer, a diagnosis that led to getting treatment for bipolar, and churchgoing—my mom received the Lord's "Shekinah Glory." She became a born-again Christian, feeling God pouring anointing oil over her head. I felt like I had a small part in that, so it counted as actually having spiritual fruit.

Now I'm the older sibling in Christ and have an infant to tend. She requires a tight grip sometimes, but this new woman in Christ has made great strides. I'm crazy impressed with her ability to adapt to biblical living so quickly and her zeal is infectious! If I am to her what Tim was to me, I'll have to learn far more self-discipline and tenderness.

This disciple-making stuff is hard! I wish I could run next door to Tim's place and say, "What did you do when you had to clear this path for me? How do I handle patience with others? My little sister in Christ doesn't hesitate at all! She runs up and down the paths I've cleared out and sometimes makes her own, but they end up leading right back to mine. Oh, and you are not going to believe this: For some reason, she keeps peeing on the decorative flowers that I've placed along her path! What am I supposed to do with that?" Mom is as zany a Christian as I am!

Following Tim will be a tough act. At this point, I'm more likely to bypass giving Mom a spiritual diaper rash and go straight to chafing her hind end until it looks like it belongs on a feral baboon. Nevertheless, what can I expect? Justifying, sanctifying, and salvation are instant, but they also never stop, so we're always growing and getting better.

As I am no longer a toddler in Christ, my young Christianity blooms along with the growing pains that come with physical growth. My relationship with the Lord is not ideal but waxes and wanes. Many pains are still present, and only some are challenges that I can tackle alone. Sometimes little things like seeing my dad's military jackets at my sister's house cuts into me. Even they were given to my sister. Everyone forgot that they were promised to me. However, my sister's family appreciates them, so that's where they belong.

It's just a bit sad that the only thing Dad left me were some of his physical features. Reflecting in a mirror are my father's eyes, the language of his life expressed behind mine. The beautiful eye color is often commented on by others. The lenses through which I see life preoccupy my time far more than these natural passages to my identity do. I share some crooked attitudes with my dad, but there's hope to break this chain, isn't there? My Father in heaven has clothed me in righteousness; I simply need to be aware of it and keep wearing it.

Through personal encounters with God, my sister's family and Mom have grown into Christians and made significant strides in life. Living with trauma and mental illness are life-altering, but it's helped us understand each other better. After seeing my niece frozen in place for over a minute because she was envisioning herself as a horse playing on a farm with happy sunshine around her and freedom in her mane, I'd say it's pretty obvious to see ADD. It was easy to point out, "She's got to be tested for a mental disorder. It's sad if we don't help her now." Zoe was tested and put in a special program and didn't have to wait until she turned thirty like I did.

Though Becky and Mom say I "let us off the hook" in this memoir, I'm okay leaving out incriminating behavior because we've all screwed up. It's how we change and move forward that matters. Some guilt and shame are still embedded in my work-in-progress life, but forgiveness remains long after relationships break and bodies fail. Forgiveness for ourselves and others is something we all must keep practicing. Just because someone doesn't love you how they should doesn't have to stop you from loving them the way they need. Love covers a multitude of sins (1 Peter 4:8), and it leaves the giver and receiver changed.

Once my two-year journey of refinement was over, I looked back on my progress and how much I learned from Tim, despite the distance and other barriers between us. It's been years since my mission ended, and I am happy with the great strides I have made since and look forward to how much God will continue to move in my life. After the mission's end, I missed God's "deep magic" in my life and learned to trust God at a whole new level. God became even more real. Yep, that's possible! We can trust Him like a husband in the flesh. It's almost like he's off running errands, but the bathroom mirror still has steam on it and he left the kitchen light on. I can't see him, but I can see that he was around. How do you get your mind around that? This same God controls the biggest booming thunder. And he wants this kind of relationship with us.

I took a hike to this ice cave near Baxter State Park in Maine after learning to trust God deeper, and I felt more restored than I have in more than a decade. It was like going home. God made that possible by unexpected checks arriving in the mail. I am one of *those* people now. But I'm still learning at a more complete level that people don't have to earn God's love. I want to ensure I know that with every fiber of my being and doing. This way, I can actualize that if God's love isn't earned, it can't stray either. If that is the case, then how much more boldly and completely can I live knowing God won't give up on me? I have question after question. *Can I unlearn the two layers of depression that have been with me since age twelve? Should I work in orphan care?*

Despite my questions, God brings people in my life who need discipling and I find that not only can I help them, I love them. Even though I'm still in New Testament theology class each week learning to be a disciple, God's willing to use me to help others. I still need a lot of work and have spent quite a bit of time in Christian healing services and in counseling. There's just this push still to grow beyond where other people stop and to live who we are in Christ, forgetting whom we thought we were and that we had to carry our burdens and yokes on our own. No doubt, Tim's sphere of influence acted as my stepping stone for this work.

Being able to see a masculine and strong leader loving the weak and broken as Jesus loved, my imagination could create a scene where someone cared about me, a stranger, enough to fight for me by being a living model. This filled a void in my life. The first step in filling this void was to know that it existed and to feel it. Then I could go beyond living what I knew as a hurt middle child raised by a dysfunctional mother and damaging father figures.

Tim's Christian world had expectations and consequences. The rules of biblical living needed to point back to those expectations and consequences. Rather than reading yet another something on biblical living, I watched Tim and saw his rules for godly behavior and saw the short- and long-term results. I'm so genuinely happy that he learned this from his own mentors and family members, passing it down to people like me. The feelings of being left behind and neglected had been with me for as long as I can remember, even back when my brother and I were young enough to eat dirt because we thought it was food. I feel it far less now. There's a famous quote that says, "It's never too late in life to revise," and God, though he had already performed signs and wonders in my life, used Tim to help me revise mine. I didn't expect to get more out of God, but I did! He makes everything better, even my attitude toward Him.

Though I have outgrown learning from Tim, as the two-year mission is over, it took so long to get used to not having his influence in my life.

The "magic" is gone. I can watch the documentary about him, and it's not illuminated anymore. The luxury of having him as a visual is not replaced by anyone else, but I've made a point to stay the course by learning from Henri Nouwen, Lisa Bevere, Francis and Judith MacNutt, and other born-again and biblically anchored people more advanced than I.

While the year after the mission end taught me so much, I grappled with what came next. It's scary thinking that the relationship and all we shared was over. *Dad was good looking and fun, but after marriage, he stopped trying and everything went fallow. This could be it. It's over. Maybe I'll give up and fail like Dad?* In between this sad worrying, I had a hard time understanding why I was waiting for another event. Logically, God doesn't let people down, so why wasn't he prepping me for another assignment? *The longer you wait, the later I get started. I'm just sitting around, Lord. I'm ready!*

God's ways are mysterious, but the lesson to garner from waiting on the Lord is this: Followers of Christ live in eternity. When we grow anxious that the sands of time are trickling away, watching the grains slip past isn't doing nothing. It's preparation to open the follower so she can hear from the Holy Spirit, resting and learning the next step. I learned that God wouldn't leave me. I simply needed to mark time before the next march. Learning to wait with active trust takes some getting used to, but the outcome is worth it, especially when you realize that the Lord hasn't finished with you yet. Some steps in our lives don't leave footprints, and that's okay.

With the sobriety of salvation comes a clear view of the free will all around us once we are Christians. There are no limits to living and interacting with our world. Something else I have learned is that evil has a face, and the Enemy knows Scripture and theology expertly despite his youthful visage. Nevertheless, he is not perfect, and he leaves the ravished alive so he can watch them live in torment. This is where the body of the church finds and cares for us despite our ailments. Once we are safe and wrapped in the rock of the Holy Spirit, a caring friend invites us to return to the crime scenes in an attempt to restore our memories. No doubt, the pain that comes from seeing all that blood stained on the concrete reopens a wound so deep in us that we cannot know its end without the eyes of Christ, but that is what we use. We face our past, feelings, and fears to overcome them all as Christ overcame all sin.

That is not where the story ends because the Holy Spirit points to Christ, and he didn't die so that we—his most cherished, beloved, and redeemed—would stay in agony. We're just at that point in the order of our salvation where we fight back! I know from other fights that the Lord will be present, but how cathartic to have members of the body of Christ—the church—all around, joining in the fight. Evil has knocked down and out several families and generations, but God is strong and good. We must rely on the Lord every day as if for the first time. Maybe we like this, maybe we don't, but it's how things are. When my dependence on God frustrates my fiercely independent spirit, I remember the Lord's angels surrounding me throughout my life, fighting for me, and serving me in secret while the Lord, the divine Son of God himself, prayed for me. The truth is that those of us who were lost but are now found stand in Christianity (faith) and not churchianity (religion). God is our new normal. His holiness deeply penetrates every born-again believer and is whispered to children by the Lord's mighty angels.

Works Cited

1. Strong, James. 1890. *The Exhaustive Concordance of the Bible.* Abingdon Press. "1922. epignōsis."
2. Henry, Matthew. *Matthew Henry's Commentary on the Whole Bible.* "Genesis 5" (concise/online edition), BibleHub / Bible Gateway. Accessed August 11, 2025.

About the Author

Sarah Vigue is an American author and has been an authentic Christian since the end of 2012 involved in several ministries. A reformed overachiever, Sarah ran with the Olympic torch and graduated from UMASS Amherst with bachelor degrees in Comparative Literature and English. She received her first real payment for writing twenty years ago and continues to write. Sarah has over fifteen years' experience in various marketing and writing related business endeavors.

She authored and received awards for multiple writing projects including the Norton Women's Society Award for excellence in memoir Essay, the cover story "No Fish" in *Shortcuts*, and the long-form colloquium, "The Rape of Grace." She loves examining literature, which serves her well during theological studies.

Sarah came to Jesus just as she was, surrendering to Him with her very own version of the sinner's prayer and passionate candor. The funny and awkward, born again talks fast and thinks even faster. She loves traipsing through nature and currently lives on the North Shore of Massachusetts.

Outside of work, you can catch Sarah in a theology class or fundraising marketing for charities. She is intensely passionate about showing people how to align their daily lives with biblically anchored and Spirit-led living despite being a little "twitchy." To learn more about her, visit https://sarahvigue.com.

I HAVE A FREE EBOOK FOR YOU!

Break free from doubt and share your testimony with courage! Do you know how much your story matters? Whether you struggle with not knowing if you should share what God has put on your heart or have this empty feeling like you might not even have a Christian testimony, you have a calling to share what God has done for you and how he has influenced your life.

Download my free ebook *Sharing Your Testimony: 32 New Testament Scriptures on Spreading Your Story (And Why It's Essential)* to push fear aside and start taking charge of your faith story today.

Thank you so much for reading :-)

It means the world to me that you spent time with my story. If anything in these pages stuck with you—made you laugh, cry, reflect, or just feel a little less alone—I'd be grateful if you'd take a moment to <u>leave a review on **Goodreads** and **Amazon**</u>. This helps other readers find this book and will let me know my testimony left a mark in your life.

Thanks again for being part of this journey with me!

www.ingramcontent.com/pod-product-compliance
Lightning Source LLC
Chambersburg PA
CBHW030818090426
42737CB00009B/778